Preaching Racial Justice

Preaching Racial Justice

Edited by
Gregory Heille,
Maurice J. Nutt,
and Deborah L. Wilhelm

ORBIS BOOKS
Maryknoll, New York

Founded in 1970, Orbis Books endeavors to publish works that enlighten the mind, nourish the spirit, and challenge the conscience. The publishing arm of the Maryknoll Fathers and Brothers, Orbis seeks to explore the global dimensions of the Christian faith and mission, to invite dialogue with diverse cultures and religious traditions, and to serve the cause of reconciliation and peace. The books published reflect the views of their authors and do not represent the official position of the Maryknoll Society. To learn more about Orbis Books, please visit our website at www.orbisbooks.com.

Library of Congress Cataloging-in-Publication Data

Names: Heille, Gregory, 1947- editor. | Nutt, Maurice J., editor. | Wilhelm, Deborah Lynn, editor.
Title: Preaching racial justice / edited by Gregory Heille, Maurice J. Nutt, and Deborah L. Wilhelm.
Description: Maryknoll, NY : Orbis Books, [2023]
Identifiers: LCCN 2023007267 (print) | LCCN 2023007268 (ebook) | ISBN 9781626985438 (print) | ISBN 9798888660027 (ebook)
Subjects: LCSH: Social justice—Religious aspects—Christianity. | Anti-racism—Religious aspects—Christianity.
Classification: LCC BR115.J8 P73 2023 (print) | LCC BR115.J8 (ebook) | DDC 261.8—dc23/eng/20230629
LC record available at https://lccn.loc.gov/2023007267
LC ebook record available at https://lccn.loc.gov/2023007268

Contents

Part III
Ancestors and Stories
Introduction by *Deborah L. Wilhelm*

Preface

Gregory Heille

> "Maybe it really is like it says in the Bible," I offered. "God is a shepherd and we're his flock and he watches over us." . . .
>
> Finally Albert whispered, "Listen, Odie, what does a shepherd eat?"
>
> I didn't know where he was going with that, so I didn't reply.
>
> "His flock," Albert told me. "One by one."[1]

In the novel *This Tender Land,* as quoted above, two teenagers in a non-Catholic residential Indian school in 1930s southwest Minnesota talk about God. Their view of God aligns with the same sort of personal and culturally wounded experiences that, for many, still put the credibility of the church (and God) in an untenable position today. In the institutional Petri dish of this fictional residential school, racial prejudice and sexual abuse are all mixed together—and in the eyes of many, nothing much has changed to this day.

The authors of this book are preachers, teachers, catechists, and pastoral ministers who have worked to make a Catholic response to racism that is intelligent, pastoral, and prophetic. Though we can hardly be surprised to hear when our colleagues in church ministry find themselves in a reluctant, anxiety-producing, or seemingly untenable position regarding preaching or teaching about Christian responses to racism, we say: Do not give up! Our

---

1. William Kent Krueger, *This Tender Land* (New York: Atria, 2019), 53–54.

vocation to God's mission challenges us as disciples and ministers of the Good News of Jesus to learn how to hold in creative tension the competing values at play in society, our lives, and the church—for the sake of the gospel. Together we can make a difference.

Our listeners have different expectations about our teaching or preaching or even talking together about such hot-button social issues as racial justice. While many preachers and teachers want to address complex social problems, they understandably are concerned about appearing too political or polarizing or losing listeners.[2] Young adult and adult formation about the church's social teaching is thin, and many listeners are adamantly opposed to hearing social issues mentioned from the pulpit. Other listeners, especially the historically and culturally oppressed among us, consider it our Christian responsibility to confront these social issues.

Like our listeners, we preachers and teachers also diverge, differ, and argue about the politics of today's racism, why the church would involve itself, and whether we can meaningfully respond. We might do well to listen to Martin Luther King Jr.'s teacher at Boston University, Howard Thurman, who, in his iconic *Jesus and the Disinherited,* writes: "Many and varied are the interpretations dealing with the teachings and the life of Jesus of Nazareth. But few of these interpretations deal with what the teachings and the life of Jesus have to say to those who stand, at a moment in human history, with their backs against the wall."[3]

After the 2014 death of Michael Brown, the Ferguson Commission in St. Louis called upon civic and church leaders to serve as catalysts for the uncomfortable conversations, alignment, and empathy needed to effect positive change. The report, "Forward through Ferguson: A Path toward Racial Equality," also calls for applying a racial equity lens, asking who is disproportionally impacted or left out. These questions and these conversations are

2. See Leah Schade, *Preaching in the Purple Zone: Ministry in the Red-Blue Divide* (New York: Rowman & Littlefield, 2019), Chapter 2, "Preaching about Controversial Justice Issues."

3. Howard Thurman, *Jesus and the Disinherited* (Nashville: Abingdon Press, 1949; Boston: Beacon Press, 1976), 1.

acts of leadership. They can and should happen in the church—in local congregations and neighborhoods and on a diocesan and national scale.

In this book, we authors believe this dialogue can be a source of tremendous creativity for mission in the church. This challenging work of gospel reconciliation can measure how we participate in God's mission, a reign-of-God mission that, in the words of Martin Luther King Jr., has to do with person-to-person transformation into *beloved community*. We preachers and our communities can become "a living sermon."

Can we, the church, say *presente* and find a way forward?

The Church's (and God's) Credibility Is at Stake

How can we pastoral ministers, church theologians, and the entire baptized community courageously talk about the anti-gospel values that feed the institutional racism, sexism, and elitism that so pervasively infect our popular culture, our churches, and our homeland? Can we effectively represent an experience of God and religious institutions in which, to use Pope Francis's image, the church is a field hospital? As the authors of this book think and talk about Christian responses to racism, we aspire to truth and reconciliation. We believe that God has sent a *good* shepherd. In Jesus's name, our goal is to help heal the trauma by charting some paths toward preaching and teaching in the beloved community.

To achieve the goals of truth and reconciliation, we believe it will help if church ministers and academic theologians consult together to bring the tentative insights of dialogue to the problem of the church's response to racism. One voice from the theological side of this conversation is Katie M. Grimes from Villanova University. In "Breaking the Body of Christ: The Sacraments of Initiation in a Habitat of White Supremacy,"[4] Grimes makes a disturbing assertion about the abuse of baptism in the practice of

---

4. Katie M. Grimes, "Breaking the Body of Christ: The Sacraments of Initiation in a Habitat of White Supremacy," *Political Theology* 18, no. 1 (February 2017): 22–43.

slavery: "Baptism served slavery in the following ways: it severed the kinship ties of the women and men it helped to enslave, it re-branded their bodies with marks of white ownership, it coerced slaves into Christian community, it served to infantilize enslaved adult women and men, it aggrandized white women and men as masters of both heaven and earth, and it helped to make and maintain race."[5] Katie Grimes writes that "black slaves were incorporated into Christ's body not so much by eating the body of Christ, but by being eaten by it."[6]

In this view, if white-bodied church folk unknowingly or unintentionally engage in segregationist practices that effectively bless white bodies over and against all others, then the church's sacramental signs are corrupted. In all probability, the gospel is no longer preached or heard. Grimes argues that the church cannot save itself if it takes white flight from the otherness in its midst. Grimes correctly argues that there can be no social redemption for a segregationist church with white supremacist ritual practices without a more porous understanding of the wall of apartness separating the church from the larger culture. The church is part and parcel of the larger culture and remains deeply influenced by America's original sin of racism.

Theologian M. Shawn Copeland from Boston College also has looked at racism through the lens of baptism, though she has done so differently. In a lecture on "Memory, Emancipation, and Hope: Political Theology in the Land of the Free," twenty years before Katie Grimes's article, Copeland responds to the original sin of five hundred years of slavery, racism, and white-body supremacy in the Americas with a theologically direct invocation of the core message of the Christian gospel (the kerygma):

> What sort of Church are we? What sort of Church must we become? We cannot live authentically—that is, attentively, intelligently, reasonably, responsibly—under the aegis of the

---

5. Grimes, "Breaking the Body of Christ," 24.
6. Grimes, "Breaking the Body of Christ," 31.

reign of God and sleep through the distortion and deformation of the whole people of God.

In rethinking ways of being Christian or ways of being Church, we must begin by taking up a place before the cross of Jesus of Nazareth. It is here that we grasp the enormity of the human suffering and oppression of the Indians, Africans, and mestizos. It is here that we grasp the meaning of a triumphal church's collusion (intentional or not) in that suffering and oppression.[7]

Shawn Copeland acknowledges the political and theological challenge of claiming hope and agency for change in the face of the cooption of our sacred practices by impersonal systemic sin:

Thus, the incarnation, that is to say, the concrete, powerful, paradoxical, even scandalous engagement of God in history, changes forever our perception and reception of one another. Jesus of Nazareth forever changes our perception and reception of the human other, of humanity. For humanity is his concern, neither merely, nor incidentally; rather, humanity is his concern comprehensively, fully. It is for the full and complete realization of humanity, for our full and complete realization, that he gave his life.[8]

As church people, we invoke the power of the Holy Spirit to guide our efforts to disempower and heal the effects of slavery, institutional racism, and privilege corrupting our communal and sacramental experience. Shawn Copeland reminds us of the iconic stumbling block of the cross. How, in Word and Sacrament, can we authentically invert this "experience of contrast" that is racism?[9]

---

7. M. Shawn Copeland, "Memory, Emancipation, and Hope: Political Theology in the 'Land of the Free,'" *The Santa Clara Lectures* 18 (Public lecture, Santa Clara University, Santa Clara, CA, November 9, 1997), 10.

8. Copeland, "Memory, Emancipation, and Hope," 15.

9. "Experience of contrast" is an expression of theologian Edward Schillebeeckx, OP.

A past president of the Catholic Theological Society of America and author of the much-acclaimed *Racial Justice and the Catholic Church*, Father Bryan Massingale is a priest of the Archdiocese of Milwaukee and Professor of Theological and Social Ethics at Fordham University. In his book, Massingale correctly asserts, "Racial solidarity is a *paschal* experience, one that entails a dying of a false self and a renunciation of racial privilege to rise to a new identity and a status that is God-given."[10] He then speaks to the "radical equality conferred in baptism" and the "social egalitarianism at the heart of the Lord's Supper."[11]

We, the authors in this book, aspire to believe as Massingale believes: "The faith community thus serves as a kind of incubator for new life. Through its rites and sacred story it offers the assurance of new life and identity on the other side of loss and transition. In this way, it can sustain the journey undertaken to a fuller and more authentic racial identity, once purged from the set of meanings and values that justify racial supremacy and white privilege."[12]

The challenge for preachers and teachers is to put pastoral flesh on these theological bones. The church's pastoral-theological conversation can be difficult when competing interests come into play. Just as stepping from one foot to another makes possible the controlled falling that we call walking, it is okay and even necessary—however awkwardly—for practitioners and academics to engage the topic of racial justice and the church. This thoughtful, tentative, and heartfelt articulation and dialogue can be halting, scary, upsetting, and, at times, exciting, inspiring, and transformative. We are resurrection people who believe that Christ is alive in us individually and corporately, calling us to be about God's mission in the world. This mission bridges the racial divide and announces salvation and healing for all of God's people.

---

10. Bryan N. Massingale, *Racial Justice and the Catholic Church* (Maryknoll, NY: Orbis Books, 2010), 121.

11. Massingale, *Racial Justice*, 123, 124.

12. Massingale, *Racial Justice*, 122.

Christ Calls Us to Be Prophets,
Pastors, and Practical Theologians

This book contributes a Catholic voice to the literature of preaching about race. In vetting contributors, each of whom participated in a community of practice over nine months of online dialogue and during a one-week writing retreat in St. Louis, the editors sought multiple voices and perspectives to model the core values of dialogue and inclusion constituting authentic values of catholicity. The editors have kept in mind three voices traditionally understood to contribute to theological conversation and reflective practice—the scriptural and liturgical tradition and teaching of the church, the traditions and voices of culture, and the *sensus fidelium* or thoughtful understanding of the believing community.

The book includes three sections of five diverse authors each: The Preacher's Journey, Black Lives Matter, and Ancestors and Stories. Please search for evidence of the tradition, culture, and believing community in the book's interplay of chapters and sections.

To consider how the voices of tradition, culture, and the believing community contribute to preaching or teaching about racial justice, we can do well to consider the possibilities presented by the insights of Kenyatta R. Gilbert, who teaches preaching at Howard University School of Divinity. In *The Journey and Promise of African American Preaching,* Gilbert speaks of African American preaching in ways that also apply to preaching racial justice. He says preaching "is truly catalytic, holistic and most completely actualized only when marked by three consecutive orientations—the scriptural voices of *prophet, priest,* and *sage,* which, theologically, follow a trinitarian pattern," and he describes this as "*trivocal preaching.*"[13]

We encourage our readers to consider Gilbert's following definitions of these voices. When preaching and teaching about racism or other hot-button social issues, we encourage our readers to draw upon and employ all three voices.

---

13. Kenyatta R. Gilbert, *The Journey and Promise of African American Preaching* (Minneapolis: Fortress Press, 2011), 11.

The prophetic voice is a mediating voice of God's activity to transform Church and society in a present-future sense based on the principle of justice. The prophetic voice speaks of divine intentionality—what God demands and expects of God's own human creation. The basic biblical feature of this discourse is that it opposes idolatry, particularly self-serving and self-deceiving ideologies. It refuses the temptation to absolutize the present; it drives toward a new, unsettling, unsettled future. It is a word that speaks to the predicament of human suffering from the perspective of God's justice. This speech, at all times, assumes a critical posture over and against established power. Last, the prophetic Word is a word of relentless hope.[14]

The priestly voice is a sacramental mediating voice of Christian spiritual formation that encourages listeners to enhance themselves morally and ethically by integrating elements of personal piety . . . and abstention from cardinal sins. . . .
The priestly voice of Black preaching emphasizes the importance of congregational worship, . . . intercessory prayer . . . [and] the "ministry of presence."[15]

The sagely voice is a wisdom-focused, dialectical, communal voice of both preacher and hearer. Sages interpret the common life of a particular community of worshippers.[16]

We recommend these ministerial voices of the prophet, pastor, and practicing theologian as indispensable to preaching a social gospel. However, consider Kenyatta Gilbert's caution that a long-term preaching strategy that privileges any of these voices at the

---

14. Gilbert, *The Journey and Promise*, 12.
15. Gilbert, *The Journey and Promise*, 12–13.
16. Gilbert, *The Journey and Promise*, 14.

expense of the others is impractical and may lead unnecessarily to polarization.[17]

What Is a Holy Saturday Spirituality for Witnessing to the Trauma of Racism?

Two vocabulary words proving helpful to those who read widely to learn about the history and effects of racism are *trauma* and *caste*. As behavioral counselor Resmaa Menakem points out in his discussion of white bodies, Black bodies, and police bodies in *My Grandmother's Hands: Racialized Trauma and the Pathway to Mending Our Hearts and Minds*,[18] racialized trauma touches each of us. To understand this, we can systematically explore the trauma of racism, as done so well by Isabel Wilkerson, the author of *Caste*.[19] In a *New York Times* article a month after the killing of George Floyd by police officer Derek Chauvin in Minneapolis, Wilkerson described America as an old house. She writes: "Like other old houses, America has an unseen skeleton: its caste system, which is as central to its operation as are the studs and joists that we cannot see in the physical buildings we call home. Caste is the infrastructure of our divisions. It is the architecture of human hierarchy, the subconscious code of instructions for maintaining, in our case, a 400-year-old social order. Looking at caste is like holding the country's X-ray up to the light."[20] Later in the same article, she writes: "Caste is the bones, race the skin. Race is what we can see, the physical traits that have been given arbitrary meaning and become shorthand for who a person is. Caste is the powerful infrastructure

---

17. Gilbert, *The Journey and Promise*, 61.

18. Resmaa Menakem, *My Grandmother's Hands: Racialized Trauma and the Pathway to Mending Our Hearts and Bodies* (Las Vegas: Central Recovery Press, 2017).

19. Isabel Wilkerson, *Caste: The Origins of Our Discontents* (New York: Random House, 2020).

20. Isabel Wilkerson, "America's Enduring Caste System," *New York Times,* July 1, 2020; updated online, January 21, 2021.

that holds each group in its place. Its very invisibility is what gives it power and longevity."

Resmaa Menakem's insights about the trauma of racism also can be considered theologically, both in the academy and by preachers and teachers in the field. Shelly Rambo, a theologian at Boston University School of Theology, has been strongly influenced by the writing of Resmaa Menakem. In her *Spirit and Trauma: A Theology of Remaining*, Rambo refers to a question posed by Swiss theologian and priest Hans Urs von Balthasar in a radio broadcast on Easter Saturday, 1956:

> He asks them to take a step back and to think about the day between the account of the passion and the resurrection: Holy Saturday. Positioned between Good Friday and Easter Sunday in the Christian liturgical calendar, Holy Saturday is often overshadowed by the two days and remains, in many traditions, a day that merely marks a turn between the events of Jesus' death and resurrection. . . . Holy Saturday, if attended to theologically, provides the key to interpreting Christian redemption.[21]

As you read, we invite you to meet Jesus in the tomb, in the "already and not yet" in-between place from which we struggle to understand and negotiate our Christian life. What is a Holy Saturday spirituality for preachers and teachers giving witness to the trauma of racism?

The authors of this book are not looking for a naive and easy fix to racism. Instead, we wish for our readers to witness the trauma of systemic racism, to testify to the relevance of the gospel in teaching and preaching about a Christian response to racism, and together to find ways forward to beloved community.

The authors wish to express a word of gratitude for the support of the Lilly Endowment Initiative to Strengthen Christian Preach-

---

21. Shelly Rambo, *Spirit and Trauma: A Theology of Remaining* (Louisville, KY: Westminster John Knox Press, 2010), 45–46.

ing. With this book, we also reach out to the extended ministerial community of Aquinas Institute of Theology and give thanks for Aquinas Institute's mission: "Impelled by the Catholic faith and the Dominican mission, Aquinas Institute of Theology educates men and women to preach, to teach, to minister, and to lead."

Part I
The Preacher's Journey

Introduction by Gregory Heille

In 2016, when Pope Francis elevated the church's liturgical commemoration of Mary Magdalene from a memorial to a feast, a new preface for the eucharistic prayer was promulgated. In the Preface for the Feast of Saint Mary Magdalene, found readily online, the church calls Mary Magdalene "The Apostle to the Apostles" and prays:

> He appeared in the garden
> and revealed himself to Mary Magdalene,
> who had loved him in life,
> witnessed him dying on the Cross,
> sought him as he lay in the tomb,
> and was the first to adore him, newly risen from the dead.
> He honored her with the office of being an apostle to
> the Apostles,
> so that the good news of new life
> might reach the ends of the earth.

The lectionary for this feast of the first preacher of resurrection juxtaposes Mary Magdalene weeping at the empty tomb (John 20:1–2, 11–18) with a passage from the Song of Solomon (3:1–4b). The fountainhead of our Christian faith is an empty tomb where, in our most profound impulse to love, we are each called by name and sent to testify to what we have heard, seen, and touched (1 John 1:1).

1

Preaching racial justice is a lamenting and loving journey of discipleship for each of us. Like the disciple Magdalene, we find ourselves weeping at the empty tomb of our world's pain and injustice. Where has our world laid Jesus? We keep vigil, and in new and unexpected ways, God, incarnate in Jesus, calls our name. In this eternal return to a personal encounter with the Risen One, we are lifted up and sent as apostles to see and call others by their truest name. Preaching racial justice is a deeply personal journey of lamenting, hearing, seeing, naming, and touching. In discipleship, like Mary Magdalene, we do unto others as Jesus has done to us. When God privileges us to preach racial justice, the Holy Spirit instantiates Jesus in our graced living into and from the Golden Rule.

As we learn to preach justice, we will have a personal story or several stories to tell. A story takes its listener on a narrative journey, and a good story takes its listener on a journey of narrative tension and release. In a good Christian story, whatever the narrative complication of sin, in the end, the Good News must predominate. This news of resurrection is our hope in the Body of Christ. This Good News is the goal of any preaching that confronts the sin of racism to preach justice. In preaching racial justice, we most certainly will lament, but in some graced way, we count on Jesus showing up in our circle of discipleship to call God's people by name, lift them, and send them by turns to renew the face of the earth. What God is doing in us, we hope to do for others.

The opening and closing essays in this section on "The Preacher's Journey" tell the stories of a Black Disciples of Christ minister and a white Roman Catholic priest in St. Louis, Missouri. Dietra Wise Baker tells the story of the transformation of her preaching life in the shadow of the Michael Brown shooting in Ferguson in 2014. I tell the story of my civil rights pilgrimage to Alabama and its claim on my discipleship and ministry.

The remaining three authors in this section are white voices speaking from a world of diverse pastoral experiences. Episcopal priest Stewart Clem writes about original sin. He makes the ethical claim that our national story about racial justice in the United

States requires so much more than a Puritan claim to personal responsibility. Preaching racial justice, he argues, is a communal journey into social responsibility. Educator Lynne Lang brings a wealth of diocesan, parish, and nonprofit experience to discuss virtue-based restorative practices for discussing racial justice in our communities. She demonstrates how we can help the members of our communities to tell their stories and to engage the complex topic of racial justice in a way that builds community rather than degenerates into polarization. Catechist Louis J. Milone takes us on a journey into apophatic mystical theology to challenge the preconceptions of language we bring to the pulpit. Preaching racial justice is, in his thinking, a journey into the cloud of unknowing where we can be tentative in our language and find God at home in darkness.

In her book *Undoing the Knots: Five Generations of American Catholic Anti-Blackness*, ethicist Maureen O'Connell tells five generations of her Irish Catholic family's Philadelphia story.[1] She courageously does the meticulous research necessary to spark insight into her family's complicity with racial injustice, as Irish immigrants and Catholic hierarchy built their increasingly white identity at the expense of Black coworkers, neighbors, and coreligionists.

Perhaps we can emulate Maureen O'Connell in working hard to surface and challenge our assumptions about race in America, particularly in our personal and communal lives. O'Connell calls this "undoing the knots," a reference to Mary, Untier of Knots, a Baroque painting in Augsburg, Germany, in which Mary undoes a knotted ribbon, all the while with her foot on a coiled snake.[2] Can we dare to place a foot on the satanic evil of racism and dispose ourselves to undo the knots of racism in our personal, family, and national stories? This endeavor for justice will take research

---

1. Maureen H. O'Connell, *Undoing the Knots: Five Generations of American Anti-Blackness* (Boston: Beacon Press, 2021).

2. *Maria Knotenlöserin* (1687), painted by Johann Georg Melchior Schmitner (1625–1707), St. Peter am Perlach Church, Augsburg, Germany.

and study, the courage to have been wrong in some of our most cherished beliefs, and the freedom of person-to-person transforming encounters. Call it a story, call it a journey, call it a pilgrimage. Mary Magdalene, pray for us preachers. Mary, Untier of Knots, pray for us sinners.

1 How Racial Justice Can Change Our Preaching Life

Dietra Wise Baker

I did not want to be there. I thought it was a waste of time. I hesitated to go to the Ferguson streets. This hesitancy is the part of the story I rarely tell—that, to be honest, I was afraid. I saw the pictures of my close colleagues, classmates, and kids I had served in front of tanks and with milk in their eyes. The chaos frightened me, but a week after Mike Brown was murdered, I made my way to the streets.

The day Mike Brown was murdered, I was in the opening session of the Gamaliel Networks National Leadership Training for community organizers at the National Shrine of Our Lady of the Snows in Belleville, Illinois. Belleville is part of the St. Louis metropolitan area, and we were less than thirty minutes from Ferguson. My strong, well-known colleague, Rev. Traci Blackmon, was enrolled in the training for that week. Traci lasted until Tuesday, but the streets and community were heating up, and she could not stay.

The first session started Sunday late afternoon, and before and during the session, Facebook Live feeds from Ferguson began surfacing. We could see Mike Brown for a while uncovered in a puddle of blood, then later with yellow tape and a growing crowd in front of the Canfield apartments. The feed showed family members arriving and wanting to get to the body. We began to hear his mother's wailing. Now that I have become a mother, I understand how we knew those screams and sounds were his mother's, even through Facebook Live. I am not sure this is true, but rumor had it that the coroner's wife showed up to talk to her husband and ask why Mike Brown Jr. was still lying in the hot August sun. He lay there for four and a half hours in the August St. Louis heat. It was not that we are not used to seeing dead bodies in St. Louis streets; it is an unfortunately regular occurrence. It was how long his body lay there. It was how long we listened to his mother's cries. It was how we watched a community be traumatized and how clear it was that Black lives don't matter. It was how much power we realized we did not have; the injustice was in our faces.

When I left training the following Saturday, I went straight to a protest. I was the co-leader of the Metropolitan Congregations United Clergy Caucus with Samuel Vothshrag, a Mennonite. In St. Louis, we are the ecumenical clergy group, and we started organizing clergy and congregations to respond to the requests from the frontline protesters for organized and coordinated clergy to show up and contribute their leadership. I was asked to do an opening prayer in front of the St. Louis County jail, a place I had walked into many times as a chaplain, accompanying kids who were certified to stand trials as adults. The protest this day targeted infamous prosecuting attorney Bob McCullough. The crowd shouted to the beat of a famous hip-hop song, "Move Bob, get out the way, get out the way, Bob, get out the way." One of the concrete wins from Ferguson was that the community later built enough power to remove McCullough and replace him with Wesley Bell, a young African American lawyer with a progressive agenda.

The protest against Bob McCullough was in the middle of the day in Clayton, a wealthy white suburb. Other demonstrations were mostly at night in front of the Ferguson police station, where the police would line up in rows outside in riot gear. When I finally arrived later that night in Ferguson, one of the kids from my church youth group grabbed me, threw me in the air, and gave me a big hug. He was one of the front-liners leading the protests. That evening I ran from the police, got pepper-sprayed (it burns bad), learned there was a practical reason for scarves (other than fashion or rebellion), and brought my own milk (the medics run out pretty fast). My baptism was complete: police, youth, pepper spray, and milk. I did not believe it would make a difference. I thought it was a waste of time. I resisted, but I ended up there anyway.

The following year with colleagues and community on the streets of Ferguson and St. Louis changed my life, our church, and my ministry—and, for purposes of this book, that year changed my preaching.

The Preaching Life

It is still hard to believe that we protested for a year. Protest leaders in our community were out there every night, multiple daily protests for a year. Some of my colleagues tried to share their street baptisms with their congregations. They started preaching their baptism while they were in transformation. I did not hear many of the sermons, but you know how fresh converts sound excited, naive, and often judgmental. Looking back, it was not the time for preaching; it was time for the preaching life.

Our church had an inverted preaching life. We often expect action to follow preaching, but action preceded preaching during Ferguson in our community. Preaching about Ferguson in our congregation stopped; there was nothing to preach about, only to live. Our church stopped regular worship for over six months because key leaders and I were often on the streets or coordinating work and relief related to supporting the ongoing protests. Our acceptable sacrifice, we believed, was being made in the street, where the Holy Spirit was beckoning us, and we were worshiping, and we were preaching, though not with our words. We sang chants instead of hymns; we walked streets instead of pews.

The inverted preaching life comes from our encounter with God in community instead of preaching to encounter. Some of my colleagues paid the price, costing them their ministries as they attempted to evoke congregations who had not experienced the inverted preaching life. It became clear that with racism, one could not preach people into right action and that the work of confronting racism is not something that can be done in a sermon. To ethically preach about racism, the congregation and the preachers must be in formation and have experienced some level of transformation.

The Spirit took the long way to get our church to the streets. It was not an episodic reaction to the gruesome murders and lynching of Brown and Black bodies. It grew out of who we were. I am here to warn you that a sermon will not change your congregation. A sermon on racism might get you fired.

This is not to say that we were not formed by all the preaching before Ferguson. I am simply saying that, at times, the Spirit will invert the preaching life. My argument is that this is the foundation of preaching on racism. Racism is best not preached as a topic, an experience, or an educational exercise, but after a period of formation. Sacred conversation on racism is best suited as an entrée to begin the inverted preaching life, not the pulpit, at least not first.

My simple introduction to the preaching life goes to the components of preaching: sermon, preacher, and community. These elements are not static but dynamic and evolve from our shared life in the world. In the case of Ferguson, it was not just the life of the preacher but the shared life of the community. It was the notion that preaching is not just what we say but how we live. This chapter asserts that you cannot preach radical justice unless you have lived radical justice. There must be a recognition that we have been formed and shaped by white supremacy and that the gospel of Jesus Christ calls us to be reformed in the image and likeness of God. Our misshapenness is a formation, and we must be reformed. Preaching on racism is best when this formation is planned, intentional, and informed.

Unless your community of preachers is acting in the racial justice movement, committed to the racial justice movement, and risking, learning, and being formed by the racial justice movement, preaching on racism will be topical, not formational. Preaching might check a box instead of growing out of a more significant commitment from the congregation to enter and stay in the movement of work for racial justice. Formation happens because of sustained local and theological practices in the church and the community.

The Inverted Preaching Life as Local

Preachers preparing to preach on racism must ask about their proximity and quality of relationship with people of color in their communities. Montgomery is different from Savannah in terms of historical trauma and current practice. Has your relationship journey been long and deep enough in your community to understand how racism has functioned locally? Many people came to St. Louis during Ferguson, and I understood wanting to be at the touch point, but I often wondered if these people were inspired to do the same work in their hometowns. Local movements inform what is good news in that place. A movement for racial justice looks different in a border city, a gentrified area, a sprawling suburb, or on a reservation.

Is the preacher aware of their church and denominational history around racism? Can the preacher discern or directly survey the level of education, exposure, and experiences of the congregation? Can the preaching and work be engaged through collaboration and partnership, where a group of clergy and other leaders organize a weekend of action and preaching? Are partnerships built with local and state organizations that center racial justice and movement building in their missions? Is there a plan to do something other than preach about racism?

Finally, preachers must reflect on how racism impacts their lives and relationships. Who is allowed in your home, church, or organization, and who is in your space? What patterns of life must change to form a fuller antiracist practice? Recently I observed in my work a deep need to learn the histories of other people of color and build intentional relationships with Indigenous communities. The call is to a life, to a practice, not to a moment. Our formation in the antiracist inverted preaching life must be ongoing, reflective, and deliberate.

The Inverted Preaching Life as Theological

What we believe about God shapes our behavior and actions on behalf of God. What is at the heart of the gospel for the congregation? Can they see how the church departed from that witness and what it would take to repent and be redeemed? Where there has been progress, someone has made intentional choices. What can we learn and imitate from those choices? Where are we stuck, and why are we stuck? If the preacher can proclaim a gospel through that stuckness, the congregation will move toward formation.

The history books are full of pro-slavery sermons. Like a country that has whitewashed history with civil rights allusions to equality, so has the church and the preacher. In response to the Black Lives Matter movement, preachers again called for a moderate response to contemporary racism, with sermons named "All lives matter"—once again providing a sacred canopy under which antiracism sentiments can thrive.

How have preachers' operative theologies of preaching constructed a scaffold for racist practice in our country that disassociates preaching from the preaching life? Kelly Brown Douglas in *The Black Christ* talks about "slaveholding Christianity and slave Christianity."[1] Slaveholding Christianity enabled messages and theology to be preached that concentrated on eternal life and heaven. Slaveholders very tightly controlled the preaching and access to the Bible. This preaching enabled slaveholders to escape the ethical consequences of their oppressive actions. Preaching on racism must close the gap, resisting purely ideological sermons. If our theology demands no here-and-now ethic, our preaching will not make a difference.

Recall the horrors of the Jim Crow South, with white terror under the banner of a cross and congregants attending a lynching after church on Sunday. What kind of theology makes that disconnection possible? How did preachers sermonize on Sunday and not serve communion to Black parishioners in their congregations while requiring them to sit in segregated places? How did preachers hold slaves? The ability to do any of that is the separation of preaching from the preaching life. Perhaps the most radical call

1. Kelly Brown Douglas, *The Black Christ* (Maryknoll, NY: Orbis Books, 2004), 10–27.

of this book to those preaching on racism is to remember that we must first live the gospel—and then preach it if we must.

Preaching Life for BIPOC (Black, Indigenous, and People of Color)

In my role as a seminary professor of contextual education, our senior graduate students engage in a capstone project inviting them to interrupt the structures of racism in their context. Students receive supervision as they go into the community, but what a challenge these projects offer. One challenge is the extent to which many of our conversations, work, and training around antiracism are white centered. This challenge is also true for preaching on racism. When you are not part of the dominant group, and the conversation of antiracism does not apply in the same way, what are you to make of preaching on racism?

Are we BIPOC preachers able to recognize the patterns of internalized racism in our preaching? Can we activate brave space and invite our communities to deal with their internalized oppression and how it impacts our ministries? By actively learning about the history of oppression of other social groups, such as women or LGBTQ people, we can learn not to become the oppressors ourselves. Tell the stories.

To have an unbroken liberating hermeneutic in our preaching, some of us preach a liberating gospel for our subgroup and then stop short with groups we have deemed as other. Respectability preaching attempts to order Black life according to white, middle-class norms of morality. For example, some Black churches have opted out of the Black Lives Matter movement because clergy leaders disagree with the tactics or strategies employed by movement leaders. In Ferguson, for example, Black clergy leaders wanted protest leaders to have meetings with public officials that were brokered and controlled by the established Black clergy. One day, the protest leaders began a chant in front of a Black church where a clergy leader was preaching respectability. They chanted, "Out of the church and into the streets."

Another example is how some Black churches and communities confuse class with caste. As author and journalist Isabel Wilkerson says,

> It is the fixed nature of *caste* that distinguishes it from class, a term to which it is often compared. Class is an altogether separate measure of one's standing in a society, marked by level of education, income, and occupation, as well as the attendant characteristics, such as accent, taste, and manners, that flow from socioeconomic status. These can be acquired through hard work and ingenuity or lost through poor decisions or calamity. If you can act your way out of it, then it is class, not caste. Through the years, wealth and class may have insulated some people born to the subordinate caste in America but not protected them from humiliating attempts to put them in their place or to remind them of their caste position.[2]

In this kind of "confusing caste with class" sermon, you will hear the problems of poverty and violence as the personal responsibility of Black families or Black people with no reference to the contributions of historical or contemporary structures of racism as factors of these problems. Recently, Ryan Coogler, the film director of *Black Panther*, attempted to withdraw money from his bank account using all proper credentials. Yet, he was still deemed suspicious, and police were called to the bank for an attempted armed robbery.[3] In the pulpit, preachers believe that accepting white, middle-class cultural norms will protect them from caste and race, but it will not.

The call to BIPOC preachers is to attend to how we have internalized racism and attend in our preaching to the systemic and

---

2. Isabel Wilkerson, *Caste: The Origins of Our Discontents* (New York: Random House, 2020), 106.

3. Johnny Diaz and Michael Levenson, "'Black Panther' Director Ryan Coogler Mistaken for Bank Robber in Atlanta," *New York Times,* March 9, 2022, www.nytimes.com.

structural impacts of racism on our communities. We can do this by sharing the history and drawing implications in our sermons for mission and ministry. Are BIPOC preachers repeating in our practice of preaching what was done to us? Does our preaching ignore the plight of people right outside the church doorstep? Do we assuage white supremacy of its structural implications and take the blame on ourselves? Do we promote a broken hermeneutic of liberation? BIPOC preachers must consider this examination in our antiracist practice of preaching life.

Preaching on Racism for Whites

White preachers must locate themselves and be in a formation process before daring to accompany the white congregation. Unfortunately, white guilt and shame about historical oppression can create fragility in white preaching on race. Whites must show willingness, insight, and confession of complicity with white supremacy. White preachers must figure out how to preach the truth in love.

God blesses whites willing to do their work and initiate relationships with different people of color. The work involves a willingness to be in Black or Brown space without being catered to and not knowing or understanding the language or culture. The work consists of getting used to being in decentered white space and inviting one's faith community to intentionally put themselves as a minority in that space. Intentionality is critical since many white people do not live in communities with people of color.

White people also need their circles and spaces to surface the narratives, stories, and histories they have inherited that conflict with their current values and how those embedded narratives unconsciously may work in their lives and the community. I remember being at a conference when a colleague shared that their family had a Black maid growing up, and how she, her family, and especially her grandparents saw the maid. My colleague could see vestiges of white supremacy in how the maid was forced through economic necessity to stay during the week at the white house and to care for the white family more than her own children.

Most importantly, white people must come to terms with the disparities created not by inherent inferiority but by the misuse of power and privilege in human history. Join the public demonstrations and confront white supremacy. Be ready to embody risk for the sake of the gospel and to be the change in the arena of oppressive racism.

Definitions

We need a common language and a collective understanding of terms related to racial justice. We share the following definitions and their relevance for those preaching about racism as an agreed taxonomy of authorial assumptions underlying this book in the following chapters.[4]

- *Oppression* is a social process that unequally and unjustly affords *privilege* to one person or group at the expense of another. Oppression manifests in three forms: *interpersonal, internalized,* and *institutional.*
- *Racism* is oppression based on race, in which *power* and *privilege* are misused to unjustly deny equity to historically oppressed social groups, often based on skin color. Racism is a form of oppression related to other oppressions because the mechanisms of oppression are the same, even if deployed differently depending on the social group.[5]
- *Power* is the ability to act by organizing money and people to get what is wanted in the public arena.[6]
- *Privilege* is unearned power available because of social group membership.

---

4. The following definitions align with definitions given by E. J. R. David and Annie O. Derthick, "Oppression 101: An Overview," *The Psychology of Oppression* (New York: Springer, 2018), 1–20.

5. See David and Derthick, *Psychology of Oppression,* 23.

6. Drawing on the Gamaliel Network National Leadership Training definition.

- *Prejudice* refers to a positive or negative affect or feeling one consciously or unconsciously experiences toward a specific person or group.
- *Stereotypes* are general beliefs about a specific social group.
- *Discrimination* is immoral or unethical behavior that results from or acts upon an individual's prejudices or stereotypes.
- *Interpersonal Racism* is racial oppression applied between individuals through prejudice, stereotypes, or discrimination.
- *Internalized Oppression* is a type of oppression existing between or among members of the same social group, usually inherited from a dominant group.
- *Institutional Racism*, also known as *Systemic Racism*, is a form of racial oppression in which prejudice, stereotypes, and discrimination are enfolded into the statutes, norms, or practices of a society or organization.
- *Antiracism Work* is the long-term ongoing work of the white social group and higher caste people of color to eliminate discrimination and inequalities and to dismantle interpersonal and institutional anti-Blackness.
- *Racial Justice Work*, as a Black-led movement, seeks to dismantle institutional anti-Blackness and systemic racism while healing from internalized racial oppression.

Isabel Wilkerson's *Caste: The Origins of Our Discontents* also has contributed to the taxonomy of language used about racism. The caste system in America is built on anti-Blackness. When enslaved people converted to Christianity and religion could no longer be used to support social ranking, skin color became the basis of a new social order. According to Wilkerson:

> A caste system is an artificial construction, a fixed and embedded ranking of human value that sets the presumed supremacy of one group against the presumed inferiority of other groups on the basis of ancestry and often immutable traits, traits that would be neutral in the abstract but

are ascribed life-and-death meaning in a hierarchy favoring the dominant caste whose forebears designed it. A caste system uses rigid, often arbitrary boundaries to keep the ranked groupings apart, distinct from another and in their assigned places.
. . . A caste system endures because it is often justified as divine will, originating from sacred text or the presumed laws of nature, reinforced throughout the culture and passed down through the generations.[7]

Based on these definitions, we must address one more critical issue. American culture tends to individualize everything, but racism is not understood well if seen as an individuated concept. Contemporary racism has social and historical roots passing from generation to generation, and social groups in each social context must address it. Racism is the most misunderstood term because people ignore its structural and systemic impacts and zero in on the self-interest of being individually guilty. This assertion has nothing to do with individual moral convictions or moral choices. Instead, this systemic understanding of racism speaks to the white power and privilege accumulated in the United States and elsewhere across generations and decades. White people as a social group are implicated in American racism and must address it.

So here lies my final caution to those preaching on racism: Preach past interpersonal aspects of racialized oppression. Lead your congregation to the transformative understanding of that systemic dimension of white supremacy that devastates Black life and the lives of people of color worldwide. People likely will assume you are preaching about the interpersonal dimension of racial oppression. White people must take due care to marry interpersonal and institutional racism. If you are BIPOC, you have the work of internalized and institutional racism to dissect with people. Antiracism work is not only an individual spiritual journey; it requires community and context.

---

7. Wilkerson, *Caste*, 17.

All social groups have stereotypes and prejudices that can be discriminatory. Still, only one social group has accumulated enough power and privilege to enact its assumptions and feelings in every dimension of the public sphere, with disparate impact, according to a far-reaching anti-Blackness/caste scale. As institutional systems weaken, we see an insurgence movement wanting to reestablish and ensure the white social groups that would place themselves at the top of the caste system and the social order.

In response to Martin Luther King Jr.'s "Letter from Birmingham Jail," white and Black preachers pleaded for a moderate stance and response to racism. The questions remain. Where will history place us, and how will we preach? Will our sermons resound with a bold and explicit affirmation of the gospel of Jesus Christ? All people live in the image of God; all are welcome, and all are worthy. Undoubtedly living up to this creed has been not only America's problem but also the church's, and surely the preacher's, problem.

2 Sin, Solidarity, and the Human Condition

As widely reported in the news, on March 17, 2021, a young man armed with a gun drove to three Atlanta-area massage parlors and killed eight people—six employees, all Asian women, and two others who were simply in the wrong place at the wrong time. The sheriff posed a question of possible sex addiction, and other reports had it that the shooter had spent time in a halfway house to battle sexual urges that he understood to be at odds with his evangelical Christian faith. Some public figures framed the incident in terms of structural racism and sexism. For example, U.S. Representative Bee Nguyen from Georgia publicly stated that the shootings appeared to have been at the "intersection of gender-based violence, misogyny and xenophobia."[1] Some analyses suggested that the attacker's failure to acknowledge the significance of his victims' race was evidence of systemic racism.[2] As the media churned out commentaries, perspectives became sharply polarized. Was this young man battling inner demons and perhaps mental illness, or were his actions an effect of the systemic racism and misogyny in American society? No one excused or exonerated the killer. No one went as far as to say that he was a passive agent, a mere victim of the system. But

---

1. Kate Brumback and Anglie Wang, "Man Charged with Killing Eight People at Atlanta Massage Parlors," *AP News*, March 17, 2021, www.apnews.com.

2. Bess Levin, "Why Are We Taking Robert Aaron Long's Word for It that the Georgia Killings Weren't about Race?" *Vanity Fair*, March 17, 2021, www.vanityfair.com.

the American public was essentially asked to choose between two options: (1) Systemic racism and misogyny are real and relevant. Therefore, the killer's account of his motivation—that he was trying to root out the source of his sexual temptation—was either duplicitous or indicative of false consciousness. (2) The killer's actions were not motivated by gender or race. Therefore, claims about systemic racism and misogyny reflect an increasingly vapid wokeism promoted by liberal progressives.

Of course, I am describing popular discourse about an event that was widely covered by American news media. We shouldn't expect a high degree of nuance. Indeed, with a bit of effort, a case can be made for more sophisticated analyses of the Atlanta shootings.[3] I draw attention to this case because, in many ways, it mirrors a bifurcation that we find in our pews every Sunday morning. Christians in the United States seem to have two different modes of talking about sin, with few discernible attempts to connect these different modes. In one mode, *sin* is meant to identify unjust social structures that prevent individuals and groups from achieving their full humanity. In the other mode, *sin* identifies an action committed by an individual, primarily against God but potentially against other human beings. The latter mode refers to the things that can be confessed to a priest in the sacrament of reconciliation. The former refers, by definition, to things for which responsibility cannot be placed on the shoulders of any one individual. No matter how zealous I may be about combatting systemic racism, I cannot confess the sin of systemic racism in the confessional.

Almost every Christian in America would affirm that racism is a sin, but ask how to define the sin of racism, and you'll receive a host of competing definitions. These differences are reflected in

---

3. See David French's essay, which delves into the intricacies of modern evangelical sexual ethics while also acknowledging that Long's actions reflect disturbing cultural patterns that sexualize and exploit Asian women: "Why the Atlanta Massacre Triggered a Conversation about Purity Culture," *The Dispatch*, March 21, 2021, www.thedispatch.com.

and undoubtedly influenced by the sermons these Christians hear from their pulpits. While American Catholics, mainline Protestants, and white evangelicals seldom hear entire sermons on racism, the vocabulary preachers use even to make passing references to racism can be revealing. A recent Pew study found that in historically Black Protestant churches, preachers especially tend to use terms like "Black community" and "white supremacist" when addressing racism. In contrast, evangelical Protestant preachers use terms like "racial tension."[4] The same survey found that Catholics were far less likely than their Protestant counterparts to hear about racism in a sermon. While there is widespread agreement among Christians that racism is a sin, our preaching reflects profound discrepancies about the nature of this sin and how it should be addressed from the pulpit.

As a moral theologian, I have wrestled with the problem of racism for many years. Reading the work of authors working in Black-church contexts and listening to the stories of those whose lives are affected by racism daily, I have been deeply challenged intellectually and spiritually. But as I've grown in this area, I've also become more keenly aware of how difficult it can be to preach to predominately white congregations on racism in a manner that doesn't alienate or collapse into platitudes. My context for ordained ministry is the Episcopal Church, an overwhelmingly white, affluent denomination with mixed political affiliation. Like Catholic homilies, Episcopal homilies are usually no longer than fifteen minutes, and most parishioners would be put off by anything resembling a theology lecture or a Bible study. The homily is nonetheless an opportunity to convict hearts and change minds— it is the Holy Spirit who does the real work, anyway—but how can we preachers make the most of this opportunity? What can we do with God's help to equip our people to confront the sin of racism in their hearts and lives?

---

4. Dennis Quinn and Aaron Smith, "Pastors Often Discussed Election, Pandemic and Racism in Fall of 2020," Pew Research Center, July 8, 2021, www.pewresearch.org.

Am I My Brother's Keeper?
The Importance of Solidarity

On a rather ordinary morning in 1958, the Trappist monk, renowned mystic, and best-selling author Thomas Merton was standing outside an old hotel in Louisville, Kentucky. Nothing about this scene would have stood out to the average bystander, but in the crowded street, on the corner of Fourth and Walnut, Merton had a religious experience. Sometimes referenced as a "vision," he didn't so much *see* but instead came to *realize* something. In his own words:

> [I] suddenly realized that I loved all the people and that none of them were, or could be, totally alien to me. As if waking from a dream—the dream of my separateness, of the "special" vocation to be different. . . . I am still a member of the human race—and what more glorious destiny is there for man, since the Word was made flesh and became, too, a member of the Human Race! Thank God! Thank God! I am only another member of the human race like all the rest of them. I have the immense joy of being a man![5]

This moment reflects a turning point in Merton's life and his sense of vocation. Today, at the intersection of Fourth and Walnut, a plaque explains how this moment "led him to redefine his monastic identity with greater involvement with social justice issues."[6] But even more fundamentally, this realization shaped Merton's understanding of what it means to be a human being. To be a human being is to belong to a group: the human race.

The idea that there is a human race to which each of us belongs is not a uniquely Christian doctrine; this idea is affirmed in many other religious and philosophical traditions. It is an idea that is so

---

5. Thomas Merton, *A Search for Solitude: Pursuing the Monk's True Life, The Journals of Thomas Merton. Volume 3, 1952–1960,* ed. Lawrence S. Cunningham (New York: HarperCollins, 1996), 181–82.

6. For an image of this plaque, see http://merton.org/TMSQ/DSCN0004a.jpg.

often taken for granted that it's rarely an object of critical reflection. Yet, philosophical libertarianism rejects this claim, especially in the form popularized by Ayn Rand and her followers.
In the moral universe spawned by philosophical libertarianism,
new generations of young people can think of themselves as self-
defining individuals with no ultimate obligations to anyone else,
much less to the group.[7] In this account, you are the hero of your
own story. It offers an alternative to commonplace notions and
proclaims that you are not a member of the human race—you are
an *individual*.

The Christian tradition tells a different story. While its affirmation of human connectedness is not unique, it does reframe this
affirmation by proclaiming that there is, in fact, a hero in the story
of the human race. That hero is not you or me. The hero is God's
Son, who became human to conquer sin and death by dying on a
cross and rising again three days later (1 Cor 15:3–7). While there
are several different atonement theologies within the Christian tradition, virtually all presuppose that Jesus's death and resurrection
have significance for all humanity. By becoming incarnate, Jesus,
the Son of God, represents the whole human race before God.

This representation is the mirror image of another representative of the human race: Adam. In the traditional Christian account,
Adam's fall into sin afflicted the whole human race. "Therefore just
as one man's trespass led to condemnation for all," the Apostle Paul
writes, "so one man's act of righteousness leads to justification and
life for all" (Rom 5:18). Elsewhere the Apostle writes, "For since
death came through a human being, the resurrection of the dead
has also come through a human being; for as all die in Adam,
so all will be made alive in Christ" (1 Cor 15:21–22). The idea
that all humanity dies together through one human being and is
made alive together in another human being presupposes the fundamental interconnectedness of humankind. This interconnected-

---

7. Ayn Rand's philosophy is expressed in her novels *The Fountainhead* (Indianapolis: Bobbs-Merrill, 1943) and *Atlas Shrugged* (New York:
Random House, 1957), as well as in her numerous essays.

ness is an essential feature of the biblical drama and its pattern of creation, fall, and redemption. It would not be an exaggeration to say that Christianity is unintelligible unless it presupposes the connectedness of the human race.

The connection between human beings—the basis for speaking of *humanity* as an integral whole—has a theological name. That name is *solidarity*. The *Catechism of the Catholic Church* explains, "The principle of solidarity, also articulated in terms of 'friendship' or 'social charity,' is a direct demand of human and Christian brotherhood."[8] While couched in normative terms, solidarity is grounded in a claim about the nature of reality, namely, that the human race constitutes a family. Solidarity is often described as a state we should strive to achieve, but it is equally intelligible as a statement of fact. Human beings are not merely individuals; certain properties can be appropriately ascribed to humanity as a whole, and some actions can affect humanity as a whole. As Pope Francis writes in his encyclical *Laudato si'*, "Once the human being declares independence from reality and behaves with absolute dominion, the very foundations of our life begin to crumble."[9] We can try to ignore this reality, but it will ultimately be to our detriment.

On the one hand, the doctrine of solidarity is basic and intuitive. We also find it affirmed in many places throughout the biblical texts. In the book of Genesis, when God asks Cain, "Where is your brother Abel?" Cain responds with the question, "Am I my brother's keeper?" (4:9). God does not directly answer this question, but the implied response is, "Yes, you are." Elsewhere, we encounter challenges to the assumption that our moral obligations extend only to those within our families or local communities. For example, Jesus's parable of the Good Samaritan (Luke 10:25–37)

---

8. *Catechism of the Catholic Church: Revised in Accordance with the Official Latin Text Promulgated by Pope John Paul II*, 2nd ed. (Washington, DC: United States Conference of Catholic Bishops, 2019), no. 1939.

9. Pope Francis, Encyclical Letter *Laudato si'* (May 24, 2015), no. 117, www.vatican.va.

contains the clear message that the commandment to love one's neighbor as oneself (Lev 19:18; Matt 22:37–39) is expansive and meant to include all human beings.

On the other hand, the doctrine of solidarity raises complex questions about the nature of moral agency and responsibility. The *Catechism* states, "The equal dignity of human persons requires the effort to reduce excessive social and economic inequalities. It gives urgency to the elimination of sinful inequalities."[10] But how much responsibility do we bear? If I was not involved in establishing the structures that led to "sinful inequalities," am I still obligated to remediate them? Am I still participating in sinful social structures even if I'm not knowingly or willingly engaging them?

Some readers might expect me to suggest that preachers should draw upon biblical themes and theological implications of solidarity to address the problem of racism. I wish it were that simple. I wish we could say, "As white Christians, we cannot stand by while our brothers and sisters suffer daily injustices because of the color of their skin. We must do more to make sure that the world is an equitable place for the entire human family!" But that's not an adequate strategy. For one, it veers in the direction of Pelagianism. Racism is not a problem that will be solved by mobilizing Christians to work harder for racial justice.[11] More importantly, it does not dig deeply enough into the hearts and minds of those who will hear our sermons. It does not confront the *sin* of racism, and by the same token, it does not proclaim the power of the gospel to overcome that sin. If we want to see the gospel do its work—and if we are going to participate in that work through faithful preaching—we need to revitalize how we think and talk about sin.

---

10. *Catechism of the Catholic Church*, no. 1947.

11. One of the many problems with this mindset is that it ignores the empirical fact of Christianity's role in the development of racism as we know it today. For a detailed account of this relationship, see Willie James Jennings, *The Christian Imagination: Theology and the Origins of Race* (New Haven, CT: Yale University Press, 2011).

Saved from What? The Reality of Sin

Most American Christians have a heterodox view of sin. I realize this is a bold claim, and I cannot provide empirical data to support it. My data is anecdotal, but it is drawn from a lifetime of church attendance across multiple denominations, more than a decade of ordained ministry, and a steady diet of popular media written by American Christians of all theological stripes. What I mean by a heterodox view of sin is an implicit rejection of the notion that biblical revelation "gives us the certainty of faith that the whole of human history is marked by the original fault freely committed by our first parents."[12] Generally speaking, I have found it true that theologically conservative Christians are more comfortable with the language of personal sin. In contrast, theologically progressive Christians are more comfortable with the language of social or structural sin. But in my experience, both conservative and progressive Christians tend to replace the language of sin with the language of moral wrongdoing, developmental flaws, psychological weaknesses, mistakes, or the necessary consequences of inadequate social structures.[13]

While there is no canonical list of American values, I think it is safe to say that personal responsibility would be near the top if there were such a list. As an American, I was taught early on that I am ultimately responsible for my actions. I cannot blame my flaws or faults on anyone else. Perhaps less emphasized yet equally important, the converse of this idea is that I cannot be held responsible for anyone else's actions. Such thinking sits in tension with the Christian doctrine of original sin—a doctrine that proclaims that Adam's sin is our sin (Rom 5:12). This tension runs deep in the soil of the American imagination, articulated quite clearly in Europe during the so-called Enlightenment of the eighteenth century. The philosopher Immanuel Kant, in *Religion within the Boundaries of*

---

12. *Catechism of the Catholic Church*, no. 390.

13. Here I am paraphrasing the *Catechism of the Catholic Church*, no. 387.

Mere Reason, scrutinized the core doctrines of Christianity and compared them to his "rational system of religion" (which does not depend on any appeal to divine revelation). He concluded that the doctrine of original sin must be abandoned. He developed his account of "radical evil" to explain the human propensity toward moral wrongdoing. Still, he rejected on philosophical grounds the notion that Adam's guilt could be imputed to other human beings or that the corruption of our wills is an inheritance from our first parents.[14] Most American Christians are not as bold as Kant in their rejection of Christian doctrine, but many harbor the same doubts.

I suspect that many American Christians are skeptical about the possibility of systemic racism precisely because they have a heterodox understanding of sin. The doctrine of original sin—and the very idea of living in a fallen world—grounds the logic of structural sin.[15] Of course, this doctrine does not mean that any particular claim about systemic racism in the United States must be true. Still, Christians have generally been too quick to dismiss such claims. Plenty of serious, thoughtful accounts of systemic racism cannot simply be dismissed as propaganda or products of ideology. My current home, St. Louis, Missouri, was the subject of a recent study by Walter Johnson. In *The Broken Heart of America: St. Louis and the Violent History of the United States*, Johnson describes in

---

14. Immanuel Kant, *Religion within the Boundaries of Mere Reason and Other Writings*, trans. George Di Giovanni and Allen Wood (New York: Cambridge University Press, 1998), 55–66.

15. While the theological bases for the concept of structural sin arguably extend over several centuries, the earliest explicit papal references to structural sin can be found in the encyclical letters of John Paul II, *Reconciliatio et paenitentia* (December 2, 1984) and *Sollicitudo rei socialis* (December 30, 1987). For some helpful contemporary analyses of structural sin, see Daniel J. Daly, *The Structures of Virtue and Vice* (Washington, DC: Georgetown University Press, 2021); and Daniel K. Finn, ed., *Moral Agency within Social Structures and Culture: A Primer on Critical Realism for Christian Ethics* (Washington, DC: Georgetown University Press, 2020).

painstaking detail the methods used by those in power to ensure that white people would benefit at the expense of the city's minorities and people of color.[16] Even if we were to quibble with this or that detail, we could not deny that the harmful effects of these laws, policies, and tax codes can still be observed today, even if many of them have since been overturned or are no longer in force. Racism in St. Louis is not limited to discrete acts of discrimination or the individual residents who harbor prejudices against people of color—although there is still plenty of that to go around, too.

While I have focused my analysis on American Christianity (this is a book about preaching, after all), sometimes it takes someone outside the church to capture a theological idea in an especially poignant way. The recent work of John McWhorter, a Columbia linguistics professor and *New York Times* opinion columnist (and an atheist), displays a startling, unreflective, unnuanced analysis of religion and racism. However, McWhorter's analysis is illuminating because it articulates a popular strain of thought rarely stated so clearly. In his book *Woke Racism*, McWhorter describes contemporary Third Wave Antiracism as a religion. To be clear, he does not argue that it is *like* a religion, but that it *is* a religion.[17] He refers to the believers in this religion as "the Elect" who "have magic, clergy, and also a conception of original sin. Under Elect creed, the sin is 'white privilege.'"[18] He explains, "Nominally, one acknowledges original sin as a preparation for admittance to living in the grace of Jesus after death. . . . In the same way, this acknowledgment of white privilege is framed as a prelude to activism, but in practice, the acknowledgment itself is the main meal."[19] In McWhorter's

---

16. Walter Johnson, *The Broken Heart of America: St. Louis and the Violent History of the United States* (New York: Basic Books, 2020). Another important study that is both historically and analytically rigorous is Richard Rothstein's *The Color of Law: A Forgotten History of How Our Government Segregated America* (New York: Liveright, 2017).

17. John McWhorter, *Woke Racism: How a New Religion Has Betrayed Black America* (New York: Penguin, 2021), 23.

18. McWhorter, *Woke Racism,* 30.

19. McWhorter, *Woke Racism,* 32.

view, belief in white privilege, like the doctrine of original sin and religion in general, is ultimately grounded in blind faith.

I concede that many of McWhorter's specific criticisms of contemporary antiracist rhetoric, which I do not have the space to engage in this chapter, are valid. But his outright rejection of the concept of white privilege mirrors his rejection of the Christian doctrine of original sin. He is right to see a connection between the two. Still, McWhorter's woefully uninformed analysis of Christianity should lead Christians to question his rejection of concepts like white privilege and systemic racism. If human solidarity truly reflects the order of God's creation, and if the doctrine of original sin is true, then Christians should find the reality of systemic racism unsurprising. Tragic, indeed, but unsurprising.

Antiracist Preaching and the Logic of the Gospel

Where does this leave us as preachers? What can we say in the space of fifteen (or ten, or forty) minutes that will stir the hearts and minds of our congregations to pursue love and justice? What I suggest here is not a comprehensive program for antiracist preaching. Instead, I wish to articulate three important yet neglected principles that will lead to more effective antiracist preaching and help us avoid common pitfalls in the pulpit. These principles are most relevant to those who, like me, find themselves preaching to predominately white congregations in the United States. Finally, I should note that all these principles do not (indeed, they cannot) apply to any single sermon or homily. But instead, they are meant to shape the practice of preaching over an extended period.

Antiracist preaching begins before we start talking about race. We tend to think of antiracist preaching as topical preaching, but in fact it is the very heart of the Christian gospel. The good news of Jesus Christ and the liberation from sin and bondage that has been won for us should be at the heart of every sermon. Racism is not an issue that the preacher may or may not choose to address. Whether they realize it or not, preachers are helping to shape the way their congregations think about race and racism. Christians who have been formed by preaching that addresses them as individuals and their private spiritual lives will inevitably think about racism as one issue among several contentious issues. Similarly, Christians who have been formed by preaching that reduces Christianity to a basis for social transformation will never find themselves challenged by the proclamation of the gospel. Antiracist preaching begins with human solidarity and ends with the proclamation that "all will be made alive in Christ" (1 Cor 15:22).

Antiracist preaching should not uncritically adopt the jargon of contemporary discourse. Anyone who has attempted to preach about racism in an American context knows the monumental task set before the preacher. Sometimes it feels impossible to navigate the strong opinions (or at least strong feelings) of those in the pews and to speak a word that will challenge and inspire. But we work against ourselves when we rely on secular jargon and buzzwords to do the work of preaching. It is simply the wrong tool for the task. I am not arguing that preachers should never borrow vocabulary from secular discourse; I merely suggest that we never do so uncritically. For example, despite the controversy around the phrase "Black Lives Matter," I believe preachers can use it to significant effect when discussing contemporary racism. But preachers who use this phrase should avoid using it as a mere slogan, a verbal sledgehammer to beat our listeners into intellectual submission. Instead, the meaning of the words should be explained, with prudence and an awareness of one's context, so Christians can boldly affirm with one voice that Black lives indeed matter.[20] Equally important is that our preaching on racism is informed not only by the work of public intellectuals but by the words and experiences of our brothers and sisters in Christ. One of the greatest gifts we can give our congregations is introducing them to the theological fruits of Black ecclesial traditions and other underrepresented voices in the church—voices that can convict and awaken us spiritually.[21]

---

20. Part Two of the present volume, "Black Lives Matter," explores this very theme.

21. There are too many resources to list in a footnote, but good

Antiracist preaching should embrace the language of sin. One of the preacher's greatest assets, especially when compared to secular orators, is the rich lexicon of the biblical drama and the Christian theological tradition, including terms like *sin*. The language of sin is crucial for antiracist preaching, not only because we have the opportunity to name racism as a sin. At a more general level, the language of sin and solidarity can help people more clearly see the relationship between their actions and the actions of others and between their lives and the problems confronting today's world. Consider the Atlanta shootings that I described at the beginning of this chapter. I can ask myself: do I share the guilt of the murders in Atlanta? No, not if we mean that I am responsible for another person's actions. But I can also ask: Do I live in the same society as the killer? Is my way of life sustained by the same structures as his? Are these structures the loci of vices that shape and influence my behavior, whether I like it or not? Do my actions (perhaps far less heinous) perpetuate and reinforce these structural vices? The answer to these questions is yes. And this means that events like the Atlanta shootings are an occasion not merely for lament but also repentance. Helping our congregations think this way is a lifelong task and can only be done with a robust vocabulary of sin and solidarity.

Sin does not, thankfully, have the final word. The purpose of talking about sin is not to dwell on our wretchedness but better to grasp the hope we have been given. Herbert McCabe, OP, once referred to original sin as a "cheerful doctrine" for precisely this reason. It allows us to reframe our perception of the world's problems—even huge, complex problems like systemic racism—as "leftover effects" of original sin.[22] Talking about sin means we

---

starting points include Esau McCaulley, *Reading While Black: African American Biblical Interpretation as an Exercise in Hope* (Downers Grove, IL: IVP Academic, 2020); and James Cone, *The Cross and the Lynching Tree* (Maryknoll, NY: Orbis Books, 2011).

22. Herbert McCabe, *Faith within Reason* (New York: Continuum, 2007), 161.

should neither deny systemic racism nor fear it as an insurmountable enemy. Preached rightly, the gospel will never lead us to despair or complacency. Instead, it awakens us. It reveals to us who we truly are. It tells us that we are our neighbor's keeper. But it also tells us that we are not the liberator; that title belongs to the one who declared that God "has sent me to proclaim release to the captives and recovery of sight to the blind, to let the oppressed go free, to proclaim the year of the Lord's favor" (Luke 4:18b–19).

3 Restorative Compassion in Homes, Congregations, and Schools

Lynne Lang

> I'm not concerned with your liking or disliking me. . . . All
> I ask is that you respect me as a human being.
> —Jackie Robinson, major league baseball player[1]

The historical accounts of unimaginable cruelty inflicted on Blacks took root in the outrageous and false belief in their inhumanity by a significant percentage of our United States population.[2] The day I learned this was as though the air had been vacuumed out of the room, and I was too stunned to retrieve it. Treating human beings as animals or objects without feelings or the capacity to emote defies reason. How could white families picnic on lawns drenched with the blood of lynching, laughing and talking while eating their sandwiches and cakes? The fact that whites could act with barbaric cruelty toward people perceived as objects rather than persons simply does not align with my fundamental belief that all human beings have inviolable dignity as sons and daughters of God. Living in my Midwestern, white suburban bubble as a young mother of five, I saw that the padlocked door protecting my happy Catholic world was no longer secured. I had discovered the shattering reality of suffocating oppression for generations of

---

1. See Lonnie G. Bunch III, "Jackie Robinson's Legacy in Changing America," *Washington Post,* April 13, 2013.

2. See Phillip Atiba Goff et al., "The Essence of Innocence: Consequences of Dehumanizing Black Children," *Journal of Personality and Social Psychology* 106, no. 4 (2014): 527.

people longing to breathe in the deep, righteous justice as God's children.

Since that day, for decades, I have walked with courageous humility (what I call a "compound virtue") to continue discovering what else I've missed in my life. Courage is the willingness to stand for what is just, even when standing alone. Humility is recognizing our lowly position in order to be teachable, trusting in God's omnipotence. Through the practice of virtue, my journey has brought me here to the pages of this chapter. I am offering companionship for your journey as well. I'll address what it means to uphold human dignity, practice holy habits of excellence found in the virtues, and integrate restorative practices. This journey of healing and restoration is for anyone affected by the sin of racism. The chapter concludes with a practical guide to restorative dialog using facilitated listening circles. This guide offers a structured process, which I've named Restorative Compassion, for sharing experiences with racism.

The common expression "We're all in the same boat" may be somewhat true, but another expression seems more accurate: "We are all in the same *storm* with very different boats." Some of us live extravagant, self-absorbed lives in luxurious yachts, experiencing privilege with little turbulence. Others are terrified in tattered rafts, wondering whether they will survive the storm as they are tossed about, unprotected from inevitable destruction. Racism has woven itself into the fabric of our American life. It began as transported enslaved people were pressed into service when the earliest settlers first stepped foot onto this soil. Enslaved people were perceived as beasts of burden, used for lifting, hauling, and building, as a limitless labor source for colonial advancement.

The astonishing speed with which society has advanced and evolved in technology and innovation in our lifetime is a shocking contrast to the slow, painful pace of our efforts to create a harmonious and diverse world where everyone is accepted as a child of God. One powerful bridge to achieving such a deep, enriching state of acceptance and belonging is to train our minds to stand still and listen deeply. Each word of our shared stories must be absorbed into our hearts, releasing the healing balm of compassion within our shared humanity. Only through such engagement can we rouse solidarity to restore relationships and repair the collective harm we have inflicted on one another. We owe it to ourselves and to one another to share the experiences of being in our "boats." We can then fully acknowledge the past, create equity, and look ahead to a more just future. Until we fully recognize the truth about our history with racism, it will be impossible to "move on" and "get over it."

Human Dignity: Agency, Voice, and Belonging

> We believe in the sacred, inviolable dignity of every human being as created in the image of God, full stop, no small print, no exceptions. —Bryan N. Massingale[3]

The *Catechism of the Catholic Church* states, "Being in the image of God, the human individual possesses the dignity of a person, who is not just something, but someone."[4] Article 1 of the United Nations Declaration of Human Rights reads, "All human beings are born free and equal in dignity and rights. They are endowed with reason and conscience and should act towards one another in a spirit of brotherhood."[5]

Yet the American Psychological Association published a study proving that society is more likely to condone violence against Black criminal suspects due to its broader inability to accept African Americans as fully human.[6]

John Bailie, PhD, a colleague in the field of restorative practices, grounds human dignity on the belief that all humans must possess

---

3. "Fr. Bryan Massingale: How the Church Can Combat Racism and White Privilege," *Behind the Story* (streamed live by America Media on June 5, 2020).

4. *Catechism of the Catholic Church: Revised in Accordance with the Official Latin Text Promulgated by Pope John Paul II*, 2nd ed. (Washington, DC: United States Conference of Catholic Bishops, 2019), no. 356.

5. www.un.org.

6. Goff et al., "The Essence of Innocence," 527.

a sense of belonging, voice, and agency in the matters that affect them.[7] Bailie asked people, "How do you wish to be treated?" The answers were the same throughout the world: "With respect" or "Like I matter."

We belong to God. We are made in the image of God, created out of a deep desire for companionship (Gen 1:26). We belong to neighborhoods, families, communities, churches, workplaces, and sports teams because they anchor our "boats." In the second creation account of Genesis, God creates Adam and all that lives in the Garden of Eden (Gen 2:18–24). Adam was given authority over all these creatures, naming the animals and plants when God gave him voice. God shaped Eve out of Adam's rib, a sign of their interconnectedness to each other: God, Adam, and Eve. God instructed them to avoid the tree in the garden, yet God created them with agency in giving these first humans the free will to make decisions. God created us to belong to and care for all creation by giving us a voice. Decisions and actions that originate from free will are evidence of our belonging and the fullest expression of our dignity.

The Holy Trinity also exemplifies the perfect model of belonging, voice, and agency. As Creator, God brought us into existence to belong, both with the Divine and with one another. Inspired by our companion Jesus and the wisdom of the Holy Spirit, we journey together toward our heavenly home. The clover leaf's simplicity as a metaphor reminds us that we belong, even as we are unique.

I once lost my husband when we were leaving an event in which hundreds were moving toward the exit. Confident that he was not far away, I scanned the crowd pressing toward the stairway and caught only a glimpse of his jacket just ahead. I knew it was him without seeing his face, then quickened my pace to grab his arm.

The familiarity and intimacy we have with one another are comforting when we are reunited, lonely, or ill. God, who made

---

7. John Bailie, "A Science of Human Dignity: Belonging, Voice and Agency as Universal Human Needs," paper from the International Institute for Restorative Practices World Conference, Detroit, MI (2018).

us for such intimacy, has counted the hairs on our heads (Luke 12:7). Imagine you could be closely connected with others, even those you dislike or disagree with or choose to avoid altogether. If you had to invite these prickly individuals to your holiday dinners and maintain close contact, what would be different about your interactions? Perhaps you'd be so intimately interconnected that you would barely recognize those relationships as you otherwise know them. Such is the belief of Kay Pranis, renowned author and trainer in peacemaking circles. She challenges groups to imagine a world where everyone belongs without eliminating anyone.

The drive to belong is so strong that we often see painful situations in which young people steal, damage property, or hurt others as a way to prove themselves worthy of belonging to a group. Gang initiations involve violent acts or hazing, which can have deadly consequences. Such examples strip away voice and agency and diminish human dignity.

Racist thinking and actions might include segregated neighborhoods and churches that communicate a club mentality that insulates people from what lies beyond their comfort zones. Their set social lives define a system of belonging. These familiar habits bring comfort and a sense of security. Extreme examples include witnessing or participating in hateful or criminal behavior ranging from racial slurs to killing or actively supporting false beliefs that Blacks are less intelligent, more dangerous, should live in segregated communities, and have fewer opportunities than whites. Seeing Blacks as "other" prevents the fullest expression of inviolable human dignity because our humanity is rooted in all elements of belonging, voice, and agency as children of God.

Africans understand this concept of human dignity as *Ubuntu*, which means "humanness." *Ubuntu* is expressed through their solidarity, believing that the essence of a person is complete when there is unity with others. Interdependence and moral ideals are fulfilled and celebrated. Archbishop Emeritus Desmond Tutu, who led the Truth and Reconciliation Commission in 1996, recognized that *Ubuntu* defines Africa as a society, saying in an interview, "We are all connected. What unites us is our common humanity. . . . We think of ourselves far too frequently as just individuals, separated from one another, whereas what you do, what I do, affects the whole world. Taking that a step further, when you do good, it spreads that goodness; it is for the whole of humanity."[8] *Ubuntu* reminds us that no one is an island. There is no "me," only "we." Whatever we do, good or bad, affects those close to us and society as a whole. Our boats are unique, but we are weathering the same storm.

The Virtues

The goal of a virtuous life is to become like God.
Catechism of the Catholic Church[9]

We are called to walk the thorny path that may cause discomfort, pain, or uncertainty. The intentional practice of virtue offers a gentle challenge to address the sin of racism within our congregations and communities because virtues are best practiced in relationship with God. Start by discerning one virtue to practice as a congregation or in your community each year. Bring it to life from the pulpit, church activities, and beyond. Note where it is seen in Scripture, and document how one virtue can change us and our circumstances.

There are many tools available for the study of virtue, but you can begin with the *Catechism of the Catholic Church,* Part III, Life in Christ: The Virtues. Here you can take a practical first step in learning about the cardinal and theological virtues. Studying all virtue is essential, so continue growing a vocabulary and include those found in Col 3:12–15:

As God's chosen ones, holy and beloved, clothe yourselves with compassion, kindness, humility, meekness, and patience.

---

8. Desmund Tutu, interview reported by Marianne Schnall on the day of Tutu's death, "Wisdom Shared with Me by Desmond Tutu: 'We Are All Connected. What Unites Us Is Our Common Humanity,'" *Forbes,* December 26, 2021, www.forbes.com.

9. *Catechism of the Catholic Church*, no. 1803.

Bear with one another and, if anyone has a complaint against another, forgive each other; just as the Lord has forgiven you, so you also must forgive. Above all, clothe yourselves with love, which binds everything together in perfect harmony. And let the peace of Christ rule in your hearts, to which indeed you were called in the one body. And be thankful.

To set your work in motion, pray with this Scripture and discern a virtue to be practiced for the year ahead. Write a prayer about your virtue. Learn about and share this virtue in the community, and the fruit of virtue will inspire action steps to address racism. Be open to surprises, and keep a virtue journal.

For example, choosing kindness when you would rather do otherwise can inspire someone to offer a needed apology, leading to a moment of shared grace and harmony. A smile can transform a bad mood or an angry moment, because virtues have natural and supernatural qualities. By prayerfully putting the virtue of kindness into an ordinary circumstance in the natural world, you point to the divine love that surrounds you.

"Kindness in God is the act of creation and the constant preservation of the world in existence. From divine kindness flows, as from a fountain, the powers and the blessings of all created kindness."[10] Our acts of virtue are a response to God, who first extended kindness to us in giving us all of creation and in the resurrected life of Jesus. All kind acts are intentional rather than random when we understand God's plan. Virtue always directs us toward the good, requiring a firm disposition to do the good without room for prejudice, judgment, hatred, or "otherness." If your community can set a strong foundation of virtue for your antiracist activities, hearts will open and receive our Black brothers and sisters. "A new heart I will give you, and a new spirit I will put within you; and I will remove from your body the heart of stone and give you a heart of flesh" (Ezek 36:26).

---

10. Lawrence G. Lovasik, *The Hidden Power of Kindness: A Practical Handbook for Souls Who Dare to Transform the World One Deed at a Time* (Manchester, NH: Sophia Institute Press, 1999), 5.

Restorative Practices

> For whoever is of Christ, belongs to one body, and in him we cannot be indifferent to one another. . . . I greatly desire that our communities may become islands of mercy in the midst of the sea of indifference! —Pope Francis[11]

The field of restorative practices is an emerging social science of relationships and ways to improve them within communities. This field intersects with education, psychology, criminal justice, and social work. These practices were rooted in ancient traditions within Indigenous communities before there were systems of standardized education.

People in restorative communities are driven by the deep desire to improve relationships continuously. Quality relationships are more valuable than property and possessions. When harm and destruction occur, repairing relationships precedes repairing or replacing damaged property. This priority may seem countercultural because society values upward mobility, equating success with money and possessions. But life is unpredictable, and people can be unreliable. Disasters and violence are more commonplace. Scripture instructs us first to seek relationship with God and one another, then all our material needs will follow.[12]

According to the Navajo tradition, "The moral force of the group was used to persuade people to put the group's good above the individual welfare. It is said of a wrongdoer that, 'he acts as if he had no relations.'"[13] The wrongdoer had become so disconnected from the community that they had no idea about the impact of their actions. The notion of offending relatives or

---

11. Message of His Holiness Pope Francis for Lent 2015, "'Make Your Hearts Firm' (James 5:8)," October 4, 2014, www.vatican.va.

12. "But strive first for the kingdom of God and [God's] righteousness, and all these things will be given to you as well" (Matt 6:33).

13. Robert Yazzi and James W. Zion, "Navajo Restorative Justice: The Law of Equality and Justice," *Restorative Justice: International Perspectives*, ed. Burt Galaway and Joe Hudson (Monsey, NY: Criminal Justice Press, 1996), 157–74.

dishonoring the family name was a deterrent to committing any harmful acts that would affect the Navajo tribe. The solution to these types of occurrences was to sit in a circle with the tribe and talk about what needed doing to make things right, and every tribe member was present. This notion is unfathomable to us today in such a disconnected world. Our busy schedules would stand still, and we would abandon other responsibilities to affirm the value of relationships as an essential business. This reconnecting, or peacemaking, requires that we listen and reach mutual understanding.

Restorative practices aim to develop community and manage conflict and tensions by repairing harm and building relationships. These practices are proactive (building relationships and growing community) and reactive (repairing harm and restoring relationships). Organizations and services that react to harm without building social capital beforehand are less successful than those that also employ proactive practices.[14] Success involves increasing the time spent building community in families, schools, and organizations.

Establishing a "trust fund" can support relationship building to buffer the inevitable conflicts that will arise. Using the Indigenous tradition of talking circles in an open space is one example of a community-building practice. Holding these circles as a container for hearing stories in a structured format builds trust.

Two foundational concepts of restorative practices are the social discipline window and fair process.

Concept #1: The Social Discipline Window
To illustrate the restorative approach, imagine four panes in a "social discipline window."

- Restorative WITH: *high* support and nurture with *high* expectations and structure (collaborative, win-win, respect)

---

14. Les Davey, "Restorative Practices in Workplaces," paper from the 10th International Institute for Restorative Practices World Conference on "Improving Citizenship and Restoring Community," Budapest, Hungary (November 7–9, 2007).

- Paternalistic FOR: *high* support and nurture with *low* expectations and structure (protective, rescuing, learned helplessness)
- Punitive TO: *low* support and nurture with *high* expectations and structure (power and control, win-lose)
- Neglectful NOT: *low* support and nurture with *low* expectations and structure (passive, indifferent, inactive)

We are more productive, open to improving our behavior, and collaborative with authority figures when we are *not* ignored. Decisions that directly affect us are made *with* us rather than *to* or *for* us.[15] The punitive and authoritarian *To* mode and the permissive and paternalistic *For* mode are not as effective as the restorative, participatory, engaging *With* mode. To effectively address the sin of racism, we must commit to investing *with* all stakeholders in changing the culture.

Concept #2: Fair Process

Three essential practices support the *With* pane of the Social Discipline Window:

1. *Engagement*—Actively pursue relationships in community life. Make every effort to be supportive of communication that builds up the Body of Christ and establishes compassion, kindness, peace, and love.
2. *Explanation*—Be transparent in explaining the "why" of decisions directly affecting people. Explanation establishes trust, even if people disagree with the decision. If you have engaged people in the process, allowing every voice to be heard and explaining the reasons for the decision, people feel a sense of justice.
3. *Clarity of Expectation*—Take time to explain what is expected with absolute clarity, whether it affects people in your community in big or small ways. Explain what you expect and give examples to be sure people understand the expectation.

---

15. International Institute for Restorative Practices, "What Is Restorative Practices?," www.iirp.edu.

Consistent with fair process, the more we study our faith, the more we understand and appreciate the clarity of God's laws. Vices exist to trip us up. For every vice, there is a counterbalance of grace in the virtues. A restorative faith community has a moral responsibility to activate virtue to nurture healthy relationships. We model Christ-like behavior when we love, forgive, and inspire others to do better, especially when they fail. Jesus is restorative. When he was questioned or challenged, his response was always a great question:

- "Do you want to be healed?" (John 5:6)
- "May I have a drink from the well?" (John 4:7)
- "Who do you say that I am?" (Luke 9:20)
- "For which is easier, to say, 'Your sins are forgiven,' or to say, 'Stand up and walk'?" (Matt 9:5)
- "Won't you stay an hour with me?" (Matt 26:40)

When the woman caught in adultery was brought before Jesus, he invited the one among the crowd without sin to cast the first stone. When the accusers left, Jesus asked, "Woman, where are they? Has no one condemned you?" (John 8:10). He affirmed her dignity, advising her to go and sin no more. The crowd took accountability for their sins.

Gospel accounts are consistent with restorative practices in illustrating the transforming power of love, mercy, and redemption. Our congregations can be places of healing and restoration. When we commit to holy habits of virtue and quality relationships, we show solidarity with Jesus and one another. Imagine eradicating racist thinking by affirming the dignity of all our brothers and sisters. This kind of imagination calls us to Christian action.

Practical Ways to Illustrate
What It Means to Be Restorative
- You sit in an open circle without desks or tables, seeing one another's eyes.
- You set group norms that eliminate distractions.

- Each person has an uninterrupted turn to speak honestly with kindness without feeling judged, criticized, or given unsolicited advice.
- Decisions are collaborative whenever possible, and fair process is used, even when decisions may not be popular.
- You choose to listen more and talk or lecture less.
- You use open-ended questions that offer space for explanation rather than yes or no answers.
- Ask restorative questions when there is harm:
  - What happened?
  - What harm has been done, and who will repair it?
  - What is the hardest thing about this for you and the community?
  - What do we need to do to make things right?
  - Is there a place to grow virtue in this situation?

Here Are Great Engaging Questions to Use Anywhere, Anytime

- Share the story of why you are here and why you came.
- What do you hope for your identity here?
- What do you need from this community?
- What are we doing to welcome you?
- What can we learn to do better?
- What is one thing you wish we knew about you?
- What is one thing you would like to know about me or us?
- How can we begin to discover the gifts and possibilities you bring?[16]

As a constant backdrop to our United States history, disturbing trends of violence against Blacks continue, and whites have allowed this, with little protest. This silence on the part of the white community places a heavy burden on society. Today, whites have more ways to communicate and connect than ever before but are more

---

16. See www.restorationmatters.org for more information and resources on implementing virtue-based restorative practices.

disconnected than at any other time in our history. Research studies reveal the disturbing trends of loneliness and social isolation among youth, young mothers, and senior adults.[17] It's no wonder that whites have fallen silent. One antidote for loneliness is cultivating quality relationships through restorative dialog. The goals of restorative practices are to increase social capital and achieve social discipline through collaborative decision-making as a way to

- strengthen civil society
- address wrongdoing
- reduce crime, violence, and bullying
- provide effective leadership
- restore relationships
- repair harm.[18]

Restorative Compassion: Practical Steps for Parishes

> Racism is a moral problem that requires a moral remedy,
> the transformation of the human heart that impels us to act.
> —United States Conference of Catholic Bishops[19]

Here are preliminary steps to move from the pulpit and pews into the greater community that result in the process that I have named Restorative Compassion: (1) Have your congregation discern a virtue for the year. Challenge individuals to discern a personal virtue, too. This step will accelerate your efforts at racial harmony. In my journey, the fruit of courageous humility has been increased intimacy with God and better relationships with others.

---

17. Mark É. Czeisler et al., "Mental Health, Substance Use, and Suicidal Ideation during the COVID-19 Pandemic—United States," *Morbidity and Mortality Weekly Report* 69 (June 24–30, 2020): 1049–57.

18. International Institute for Restorative Practices, "What Is Restorative Practices?," www.iirp.edu.

19. United States Conference of Catholic Bishops, "Open Wide Our Hearts: The Enduring Call to Love—A Pastoral Letter against Racism," PDF at www.usccb.org (November, 2018), 20.

(2) Gather the stories of changes in and around you and your community. These adventures in virtue reveal the story of divine love. (3) Teach listening skills so people of diverse backgrounds, life experiences, and opinions can express themselves. Create spaces for listening to flourish.

Over time, using restorative circle processes inspires groups to action using new strategies for addressing the sin of racism. Stories shared in listening circles promote self-discovery and reflection, resulting in action-planning steps for a restorative, antiracist journey.

1. Gather an enthusiastic leadership team for a book study using this resource.
2. Host a four-hour training session for listening circle facilitators (training materials available upon request at info@restoration matters.org). Emphasize the benefits of listening, and establish mutual agreements or norms. The trained facilitator asks a specific set of questions using a formal circle process.
3. Divide the group evenly into circles with up to seven people. Every person in the group will have two minutes to answer each question (assign a timekeeper in each group). Have each person record a theme or thought to share with the larger group.
4. Debrief as a large group while enjoying refreshments.
5. Expand your listening circles to include various groups, organizations, and the general congregation. Invite other diverse groups to explore the topic of racism and modify the topics over time. Within the structured circle process, ask these questions:
   • What brought you to this circle today (include name, where you are from)?
   • What has been your experience with racism?
   • What has been the most challenging thing about this?
   • What is one thing you can do to take care of yourself when this session ends? (Don't plan action steps. The purpose of this session is to listen and reflect.)
6. Continue follow-up circles to advance in awareness and understanding.

Over time, repeated listening can lead to actions that might include:

- visits to neighboring congregations
- celebrations of diverse groups
- intergenerational circles on Sunday afternoons
- beginning a movement toward Truth and Reconciliation talks.

Some of my loved ones have left the Catholic Church to find more accepting and diverse spiritual communities elsewhere, and they ask what keeps me here. My answer remains the same: The Eucharist expands my capacity to evangelize through holy habits for human excellence. Virtue is a way to change the church from within and inspire love and service.

Restorative Compassion has been the catalyst for creating sacred, brave spaces to hold difficult conversations. I have used this process with congregations to address racism, the political divide in America, clergy sexual abuse, and the closing and opening of parishes. When we stay present to the inviolable dignity and humanity in one another, we can hear the voices of those longing to be heard. Racism must first be acknowledged, freeing us to see the world from someone else's point of view with Restorative Compassion, one story at a time.

4 Apophatic Approaches to Uprooting White Supremacy

Louis J. Milone

Growing up in the eighties and nineties on Long Island, I felt drawn to the margins, to what society considers unpopular, different, and even unappealing. Then I discovered God, and with God, the stories of the saints—Francis of Assisi in particular. Fascinated by their lives, I knew what I wanted: holiness. But how does one become holy? Through that question, I discovered the writings of some Trappist monks: Thomas Merton, Basil Pennington, and Thomas Keating. I started to practice sinking into contemplative silence. And with that, I stumbled upon a marginal tradition in Catholicism: the apophatic tradition—recognizing God as a transcendent mystery and keeping that central to how one talks about and connects to God.

I practiced contemplation. I would sink into the *nothingness* deeper than all self-consciousness, fear, despair, ego, and imprisoning mental habits. My prayer was the null state: gracious yet mindless oblivion within, God as God beyond God. Blessed nothingness! Disappearing into the Nothing, I discovered everyone. I experienced genuine love.

Because of my sinking into the divine nothing, I have come to see that my thoughts and life assumptions are not as important as I thought; I have come to know that I am one with humanity, indeed, the whole world, and must therefore work for justice. The space God created in me through interior silence allowed me to listen to the stories and tragedies of the Black community. I began

47

to see my white privilege and how being Black in America makes one marginal. And so, two margins unite in this chapter: the radically disruptive mystical tradition of apophasis and the oppressed community of Black and Brown people. The gospel imperative flowing from these two margins is clear: subvert institutionalized white supremacy.

These margins unite in preaching. The preaching event hinges on the preacher's and the assembly's relationship with God. As a preacher, I use language to describe and deepen this relationship. The language I use for God matters because it shapes the people assembled for worship. The images, ideas, and names I use for God can reflect egocentricity or unity with the divine.

Whom Do We Worship?

A spiritual question is at the root of all injustice: Whom do we worship? Is it God or a culturally authorized image of God? A conventional idea of God propagates myths like redemptive violence, uninhibited greed, crass patriarchy, and institutionalized white supremacy—the oppression of Black and Brown communities enshrined in and sanctioned by the institutions of societal life in America. James Cone says it clearly: "Oppressed and oppressors cannot possibly mean the same thing when they speak of God. The God of the oppressed is a God of revolution who breaks the chains of slavery. The oppressors' God is a God of slavery and must be destroyed along with the oppressors. The question then, as black theology sees it, is not whether blacks believe in God, but whose God?"[1]

God language is crucial for how any community understands and acts out faith. Jesus Crucified shows me a different way of worship and reveals a God wholly different from the one presented by conventional American culture, which is, at its root, institutionalized white supremacy. In opposition to this disease at the heart of

---

1. James H. Cone, *A Black Theology of Liberation* (Maryknoll, NY: Orbis Books, 2010), 61.

American culture, the Christian apophatic mystics throw caution to the wind and embrace a dangerous language for the worship of God revealed in Christ Crucified.

I propose a way of preaching shaped by the unique metaphors and subversive message of apophatic mysticism. Metaphors and messages matter. Indeed, the images about God that a preacher chooses to use matter powerfully. For example, if congregations hear only metaphors of light as descriptive of goodness while metaphors of darkness and blackness describe evil, preaching will validate institutionalized white supremacy. If preachers are not careful in their choice of language, any liberating action on behalf of Black lives and against white supremacy can falter at the level of non-liberative imagination. Congregations can easily fall prey to crude notions of light versus darkness and a hierarchical master-slave understanding of our relationship with God. An apophatic way of preaching seeks to undermine these atrocious homiletic tropes in the service of uprooting racial injustice.

In Christianity, light opposes darkness: light and associated metaphors stand for the good, and metaphors of darkness stand for evil. While there is a rich, transformative tradition of light imagery in the Bible, white supremacists coopted this tradition to justify their oppressing, enslaving, and killing Black people.

Apophatic mystical theology recognizes the same problem regarding God and goes to the root: the divine transcends all names, ideas, categories, experiences, and even being itself. Human reason can never capture the reality of God. When anyone holds that ideas or images of God are identical to the divine, idolatry flourishes. Oppressors forget this and use a god drawn from the measure of their greed and monstrosity to impose their injustices.

I read a rich vocabulary in the Christian apophatic mystics. Some words they use most include darkness, silence, incomprehensibility, unknowing, emptiness, stillness, desert, void, oblivion, solitude, beyond, and nothingness. Often, the mystics use the same or similar words to describe God, the soul, their encounter, and the way to encounter God. For example, for Pseudo-Dionysius the

Areopagite, God is the Divine Darkness experienced in the darkness of unknowing.

I have found that the apophatic mystics used and even played with negative terms, metaphors, and images to communicate divine truth. Apophatic vocabulary appears to be a ripe resource for preaching. Familiarity with the vocabulary, a willingness to use this vocabulary, and a desire to play with this vocabulary to create new expressions of divine mystery could serve antiracist preaching. If I use words like *darkness* and *blackness* for God and the encounter with God, I could subvert the religious metaphors that sanctify institutionalized white supremacy. Simultaneously, I could affirm the goodness of Black and Brown bodies. This possible approach is one half of an apophatic way of preaching for uprooting racism.

The other half of this way of preaching comes from the message of the apophatic mystics. Suppose I understand and experience my relationship with God as lord-servant or master-slave. Then I am less likely to challenge the racist power dynamics that shape society at a critical level. Indeed, this can be the default model of pastors relating to their people, deriving from an encompassing hierarchical model of power in the Catholic Church. While the word "Lord," like "light," has a venerable tradition in Scripture, in actual practice, Jesus does not relate to us as a lord. Contrary to hierarchical power dynamics, Jesus says: "I do not call you servants any longer . . . but I have called you friends" (John 15:15).

I preach from a particular vision of God and a particular vision of the relationship between God and the soul. Inevitably, I carry this over into my behaviors and attitudes. These attitudes carry over into social institutions. Suppose I preach using only "light" imagery, with the idea of a master-servant image of the soul's relationship with God. In that case, even an excellent antiracist homily could reinforce white supremacy.

Light language is not the only language for God. The master-servant model of relating to God is but one model. The Christian tradition has other ways of understanding God and the soul's relationship with God that can uproot racism rather than bless it.

John Scotus Eriugena and Meister Eckhart

Simply using a new vocabulary could go a long way toward a preaching revolution. Indeed, changing primary metaphors from light to darkness can challenge a congregation to a more nuanced and inclusive Christian imagination. For preaching to have a real revolution toward racial justice, the content of preaching also needs to change. The apophatic mystical tradition provides a theme you and I could repeatedly proclaim: the soul's oneness with God. The Christian apophatic mystics describe this oneness with negative vocabulary.

John Scotus Eriugena and Meister Eckhart appear as wonderful resources for taking an apophatic rather than a white-supremacist approach to preaching. John Scotus Eriugena was a ninth-century Irish mystic, theologian, and holy scholar at the imperial court of Charles the Bald. Through his position, he received the opportunity to translate the works of several Greek fathers of the church. His reading of Pseudo-Dionysius the Areopagite, most of all, deepened his spirit and theology. His best-known work is the *Periphyseon*, a massive theological-philosophical dialogue between two characters, the "alumnus" and the "nutritor," which covers the whole of reality.

In the theology of John Scotus Eriugena, God is Nothing. When the alumnus asks about the theological understanding of "nothing," the nutritor explains: "By that name is signified the ineffable and incomprehensible and inaccessible brilliance of the Divine Goodness which is unknown to all intellects. . . . [S]o long as it is understood to be incomprehensible by reason of its transcendence it is . . . called 'Nothing.'"[2] With apophatic glee, he says creation is from the Nothing that is God. Hence all things are the theophany of the infinite nothingness. Every creature is, in its most profound reality, the Nothing. This assertion allows for

---

2. John Scotus Eriugena, *Periphyseon (The Division of Nature)*, ed. I.P. Sheldon-Williams; rev. John O'Meara (Washington, DC: Dumbarton Oaks, 1987), 307–8.

radical equality between God and creature as both emerge from the Nothing. Eriugena challenges hierarchies, even those between God and creature.

The Nothing includes and holds all because everything arises from and returns to the Nothing. Astonishing in cosmic scope, the Nothing appears in the panoply of the created universe. Every existing thing, from an atom of helium to a Bengal tiger, is a theophany: "Everything that is understood and sensed is nothing else but the apparition of what is not apparent, the manifestation of the hidden, the affirmation of the negated, the comprehension of the incomprehensible."[3] God is Nothing, and God is everything. Creation is still itself, distinct from God, but, paradoxically, remains divine. John Scotus Eriugena elaborates, "We ought not to understand God and the creature as two things distinct from one another, but as one."[4] The Nothing is All.

One realizes the unity of the divine nothing and all things by transcending all things. Eriugena's way "is a spiritual means of transcending the temporal and created condition and gaining a timeless participation in the oneness of God's infinite nothingness."[5] John Scotus Eriugena seeks the soul's spiritual freedom. His way "liberates the mind from attachment to the *being* of creatures" and propels the soul into unity with the Nothing.[6]

Eriugena advises us to "abandon all the senses and the operations of the intellect," and then, in "a state of not-knowing," we are "restored to the unity . . . of Him Who is above every essence and understanding."[7] In unknowing, the soul stops thinking and rests in God. The soul's consciousness expands to embrace the Truth: the divine nothing is the essence of all things!

Meister Eckhart was a Dominican friar, a popular mystical

3. Eriugena, *Periphyseon,* 250.

4. Eriugena, *Periphyseon,* 305.

5. Dermot Moran, *The Philosophy of John Scotus Eriugena* (New York: Cambridge University Press, 1989), 240.

6. Moran, *Philosophy of John Scotus Eriugena,* 240.

7. Eriugena, *Periphyseon,* 107.

preacher, an able administrator, and a highly esteemed theologian in the late-thirteenth to early-fourteenth century. Today, people know him best for his sermons, through which we meet a man who embodies the best sense of "master": a top-notch scholar and deep thinker, a profoundly advanced contemplative, and a spiritual guide who can show us the way into the mystery of God.

Meister Eckhart evokes the numinous in his preaching. He does not rely on staid orthodoxies but breathes mystical power into his readers, as I imagine he did while preaching to the people of Cologne or Erfurt in medieval Germany. Puzzlement and surprise erupt in the soul upon venturing into his sermons. But they also refresh and awaken the soul.

In one sermon, Eckhart describes justice as equality between God and humanity. He bases this on an understanding of life: "God's being is my life. If my life is God's being, then God's existence must be my existence and God's is-ness is my is-ness."[8] The reality of God is the soul's life. This language is not mere rhetoric. Eckhart means, "God's self-identity [is] my self-identity."[9]

To live is to be equal with God. But what does it mean for the soul and God to be equal? Eckhart gets specific: "Those who are equal to nothing, they alone are equal to God. The divine being is equal to nothing, and in it there is neither image nor form."[10] As equal to nothing, the just one is equal to God. God is nothing, formless and imageless. Neither a thing, nor a form, nor an image, God transcends all. The just person, transcending thinking through detachment, reduces to nothing. And, those who are nothing are God, for God is nothing.

Daniel Barber highlights nothingness as "what the soul and

---

8. *Meister Eckhart: Essential Sermons, Commentaries, Treatises, and Defense*, trans. Edmund Colledge and Bernard McGinn (New York: Paulist Press, 1981), 187.

9. *The Complete Mystical Works of Meister Eckhart*, trans. Maurice O'Connell Walshe, ed. Bernard McGinn (New York: Crossroad Publishing, 2009), 330.

10. *Meister Eckhart: Essential Sermons*, 187.

God already have *in common*."[11] Barber clarifies, "Nothingness, as Eckhart articulates it, is not what separates us from God, it is what identifies us with God."[12] Typically, religion assumes that God and soul are separate, rigidly held at a distance from each other. God reigns in some empyrean heaven; humanity resides in the lowly earth-bound realm. Eckhart wipes away this assumption by prioritizing nothingness over any distinction between the soul and God.

If one is equal to Nothing, then one is equal to God. We are nothing when we stop thinking and rest in faith. In this nothingness lies equality. Eckhart then draws out a significant implication for the soul, namely, the abolishment of any servant-master dynamic in the relationship: "If I were accepting anything from God, I should be subject to him as a servant, and he in giving would be as a master. We shall not be so in life everlasting."[13]

We are friends of God because of our equality with God. It is not a master-servant relationship. In petitioning God, the soul acts as a servant does to a master. However, that is not how it is in eternity. Eckhart challenges the asymmetrical relationship between God and the soul. He counsels us to stop treating God as someone outside of the self. Instead, he encourages us to relate to God within the self and even as one's deepest self.

John Scotus Eriugena and Meister Eckhart testify to the oneness of God and the creature resting on the divine nothing and not a Supreme Being. They celebrate the incomprehensibility of the soul's relationship with God. For apophatic mystics, union with God does "not amount to union of one thing or one substance or one entity with another. . . . [Rather] union in the ground of superessential nothingness, what one might call *unio in nihilo*, is quite the opposite."[14] Here is the message of the apophatic mystics:

11. Daniel Barber, "Commentarial Nothingness," in *Glossator: Practice and Theory of the Commentary, Volume 7: The Mystical Text*, ed. Nicola Masciandaro and Eugene Thacker (New York: City University of New York, 2013), 51.

12. Barber, "Commentarial Nothingness," 51.

13. *Meister Eckhart: Essential Sermons*, 188.

14. Michael Sells, "Comments," *Mystical Union and Monotheistic*

we are always already one with the divine nothing, and we realize this oneness and equality by letting go of the self.

Two Spiritualities with Consequences

For Eriugena and Eckhart, prayer means more than reciting words. Prayer is the silence of pure nothingness. And in this nothingness, we realize divine equality and divine unity.

Still, a conventional and oppressive spirituality grips the church. It facilitates the silence around the suffering of Black and Brown bodies while sanctifying their exclusion and violence toward them. This spirituality relates to God as a Supreme Being who lords over us as a hierarchical, patriarchal, white-race-dominating master. This spirituality continues to feed white supremacy. We have projected our notions of lordly and racist authority onto the Supreme Being. In America, the white holders of power have used that constellation of ideas and images to validate a system of racialized violence to their benefit.

Supreme Being spirituality sees God as a master being. This language, appearing in the creed and doctrinal formulas, pairs light-being language with male metaphors. Practically, Jesus's God becomes Zeus: a male, white entity above us who is looking for a reason to smite us. Now we have a Master God who blesses slavery and racial subjugation as the holy way.

By using and policing exclusive images of God—male, being, light—God appears outside and apart from us. Christianity becomes a moral contest: If one is moral long enough, one might experience union with God. But it is reserved for a privileged few, like monks. This approach leads to a codependence on the clergy to access God. Devotees of the Supreme Being consider working for justice in this world a waste of time, and they addictively crave the afterlife. Of course, the worshiper of the Supreme Being would never think to seek oneness with God, assuming it to be the unit-

---

Faith: An Ecumenical Dialogue, ed. Moshe Idel and Bernard McGinn (New York: Macmillan, 1989), 172.

ing of two separate substances. Relationship with God is understood in stuffy terms: God stuff and person stuff would never mix.

John Scotus Eriugena and Meister Eckhart offer an alternative spirituality from ancient and medieval sources: apophatic spirituality. God is Nothing: no-thing, beyond being, and even the nothingness beyond God. This spirituality affirms inclusive images: we can image God as anything! Since we are one with God, we can enjoy this oneness anytime. Then religion is a joyful life with God and others here and now. There are no spiritual elites. Instead, the Spirit has given everyone equal access to God. Finally, oneness with God does not mean the union of two distinct substances but enjoying our original equality with the Nothing.

Now, these spiritualities do not simply reside in neutral hearts. They are bound to historical contexts. Americans in the twenty-first century have ideas about God from European slavers of the seventeenth century. These colonial Europeans kidnapped, abused, and enslaved Black bodies to benefit their white settlements in America. These very actions shaped the developing theology of New World colonies to the extent that enslavers edited out all references to freedom in the Bibles they gave to their slaves.[15] Through violence condoned and protected by the United States government, enslavers had the power to do whatever they wanted. They were power players. How could their actions not have affected the way all people in America understood God?

This contextual racist theology mixed with the Catholic picture of God as Supreme Being led to a hierarchical, patriarchal, white-centered power structure based on a lord-servant relationship. The Supreme Being spirituality I describe above is the benign version of oppressor religion, which still oppresses. It is still with us. Therefore, will we worship and preach the Supreme Being who blesses and proselytizes racism, or the God revealed in Jesus Crucified, whom the mystics call the divine nothing?

John Scotus Eriugena and Meister Eckhart communicate the dangerous and liberating experience of Jesus's unity with God.

---

15. See Slave Bible exhibit at www.museumofthebible.org.

How do their vocabulary and message help preach against white supremacy and for racial justice? I believe they present us with three clear homiletic imperatives involving the vocabulary, the message, and the goal of preaching.

The Vocabulary, Message, and Goal of Transformational Preaching

Use the words. Preaching with the apophatic vocabulary is straightforward. We choose words like "silence" or "darkness" to name God. We can be creative with this vocabulary, using, for instance, phrases like "the dark mystery of God's mercy" or "cruciform silence."

Bring depth to the message. Can we preach *unio in nihilo*? The content of our preaching requires drastic change. The people crave preaching that guides them into living faith, into living in the presence of the mystery of God. Can we communicate this gospel experience of God's mystery at the heart of our being?

Be one with the Nothing! The way to being a good preacher is to realize *unio in nihilo*, unity with the Nothing resulting from contemplation and letting go. The bliss and freedom of knowing the mystery of God is a transformative experience that can propel the preacher to act with nonviolent love for racial justice.

Homiletician James Henry Harris affirms, "Liberation preaching is preaching that is transformational. This means that it is intended to effect change in the nature and structure of persons and society."[16] Preaching can change things. Using apophatic language and giving depth to our preaching through the message of *unio in nihilo* is a significant step toward preaching racial justice and effecting transformation. Harris states, "The process of transformation begins with a new understanding of consciousness which requires a mental and spiritual transformation."[17] We need to realize our equality

---

16. James Henry Harris, *Preaching Liberation* (Minneapolis, MN: Fortress Press, 1995), 8.

17. Harris, *Preaching Liberation*, 8.

with the divine nothing that overflows into the experience of equality with all people. Preaching can play a pivotal role.

In 2015, director CJ Hunt began filming the city council hearings in New Orleans, Louisiana, which met to resolve the removal of four Confederate statues in the city. This initial set of footage became a transformative documentary: *The Neutral Ground.* The documentary captures the unbelievable yet believable racist reaction to removing monuments to white supremacy. Early twentieth-century supporters erected these statues and plaques across the country to celebrate the Confederacy, the seceding movement in mid-nineteenth-century America that wanted to maintain slavery at all costs.

Christian apophatic mysticism subverts idolatry in all its forms and, as such, remains fiercely loyal to Jesus, a radical committed to non-idolatry. Mystics like Eriugena and Eckhart seek to topple the false gods in our hearts, as well as the idolatrous statues that dot our country's landscape and oppressively lash the soul with the evil message that whites are superior. To be one with the Nothing is to oppose such sin and, even more, to join Black and Brown sisters and brothers in the work of justice.

Preaching with the vocabulary, message, and experience of apophatic mysticism can open the preacher and the congregation to the solidarity-inducing nature of the Nothing. Everything comes from and returns to the Nothing. Our vocation is to realize blissful equality with the Nothing. In the mind-blowing mystery of God, one discovers everyone else. The experience of *unio in nihilo*, of unity with the Nothing, engenders compassion and solidarity, that incredibly active virtue of seeking the good of all people, especially the most marginal, because I know we are all in this together. In other words, my experience of the Nothing demands a commitment to the common good of all by paying particular attention to marginal peoples. Black and Brown communities are the most marginal in America. Hence, any experience of the mystery of God propels one into solidarity with Black and Brown people.

Still, the rantings of white residents in the city council meetings in New Orleans suggest that people need good formation. I may have an experience of the Nothing, but I still need to connect the experience to action and my biases. I need to hear the stories and cries for justice from Black and Brown voices. I need to envision goodness and mercy. In short, we all need formation. And the preeminent place of formation for Catholics is the homily.

When the pro-Confederate forces erected statues and plaques to celebrate the slaveholding South and its military heroes, they were engaging in practices of cultural formation. Bryan Massingale reflects on how racism in America is cultural:

> In the United States (and Western societies in general), racism functions as a culture, that is, a set of shared beliefs and assumptions that undergirds the economic, social, and political disparities experienced by different racial groups. This set of meanings and values provides the ideological foundation for a racialized society, where society's benefits and burdens are inequitably allotted among the various racial groups.[18]

Massingale describes this culture of racism as something internal, shaping mass and individual consciousness. The culture is a white supremacist culture. White people, in general, are "malformed, conformed, and deformed—by a value-laden web of racial significance and meaning that it is largely invisible and outside of their conscious awareness."[19]

The preaching I advocate is the type that counter-forms, that uses the vocabulary and message of the apophatic mystics and contemporary prophets to expose white supremacy and positively form congregations in the transcendent love of God revealed in Jesus. And this formation, done in preaching, should aim to topple idols and form people for unity with the Nothing and solidarity with marginalized Black and Brown communities.

---

18. Bryan N. Massingale, *Racial Justice and the Catholic Church* (Maryknoll, NY: Orbis Books, 2010), 24.

19. Massingale, *Racial Justice*, 33.

5 Preaching Racial Justice as a Civil Rights Pilgrim

Gregory Heille

When I went away to college in 1965, the first book assigned was James Baldwin's *The Fire Next Time,* published during the 1963 centennial of Abraham Lincoln's Emancipation Proclamation. In seventeen years in rural Minnesota, I had never met a Black- or Brown-bodied person, and I was unprepared to appreciate Baldwin's appeal to take ownership of my nation's terrible legacy of racism. However, I am now trying hard to take stock of this shameful legacy. I now believe Baldwin when he says, "The story of the Negro in America is the story of America. It is not a pretty story."[1] I didn't know it then, but that first naive reading of Baldwin's essay marked the beginning of my fifty-seven-year pilgrimage to confront the scandal and traumatic effects of prejudice, essential to my formation as a human being and preacher.

In an essay about the creative process and words pertinent to preaching, James Baldwin once wrote about the artist's *lover's war* with society: "Societies never know it, but the war of an artist with society is a lover's war, and he does, at his best, what lovers do, which is to reveal the beloved to himself and, with that revelation, to make freedom real."[2] This koan-like passage can lead to many

---

1. James Baldwin, in *I Am Not Your Negro* (documentary film), Netflix.

2. James Baldwin, "The Creative Process," in James Baldwin, *The Price of the Ticket: Collected Nonfiction, 1948–1985* (Boston: Beacon, 2021), 324.

questions about the art, struggle, change of perception, and setting free of racial-equity preaching, all directed toward love.

Firm Up the Courage of Your Convictions

During the 1955 Montgomery Bus Boycott, Pastor Robert Graetz Jr. and his wife, Jeannie, a white-bodied couple, served the African American congregation of Unity Evangelical Lutheran Church in Montgomery. Rosa Parks lived with her husband, Raymond, across the street in a Cleveland Courts Apartments townhome. When Rosa and Raymond met in 1931, Raymond was a politically active barber working at significant risk on behalf of freeing nine "Scottsboro Boys" wrongfully convicted of raping two white women.[3] When Rosa was arrested in 1955, she and Raymond were active in the NAACP. As secretary of the local chapter, Rosa held meetings in the basement of Unity Evangelical Lutheran Church. The Parks and the Graetzes were friends.

Throughout the boycott, Robert Graetz served on the executive committee of the Montgomery Improvement Association and gave rides every day to Black folks boycotting the bus. During the boycott, Robert and Jeannie's home was bombed on August 25, 1956. Shortly after the Supreme Court ruling banning segregated seating on Montgomery buses, the Graetz home was bombed again, on January 10, 1957.[4] A hackberry tree planted in the crater of that bombing now stands tall as a living testimony of those difficult days. Robert and Jeannie Graetz are civil rights heroes—a white preacher and preacher's wife who devoted their entire ministry as champions of social justice.

I agree with Robert Graetz, who wrote in his autobiography: "I have never been particularly interested in 'how-to' books. To

---

3. Robert S. Graetz Jr., *A White Preacher's Message on Race and Reconciliation: Based on His Experiences Beginning with the Montgomery Bus Boycott* (Montgomery, AL: NewSouth Books, 2006), 60.

4. Graetz, *A White Preacher's Message,* 25–26.

me they seem much too simplistic."⁵ Racism is not a problem that can be quickly fixed. Instead, racism presents the preacher with a dilemma that questions long-held assumptions about people, institutions, and society. For a Christian to negotiate the horns of this dilemma, I see no other way but to make a fundamental option for justice come what may—to make a pilgrimage of resistance. A Spirit-guided option for justice with a preferential option for the poor affords the preacher the integrity to live in gospel tension with the blood-soaked trauma that racial enmity continues to pass from one generation to the next. Preachers of the social gospel of peace and justice, with God's help, learn the long game of living in "tensional integrity." God rewards this "tensegrity" with consequential opportunities and extraordinary companions along the pilgrim way.

Normalize Difference as the Center

The Christian life is a pilgrimage to the center of other people's lives. There, at that center, in the other, we meet Jesus. Only there can prejudice and hate be transformed by love.

Whenever we engage in the person-to-person transforming encounter of action for justice, we become friends and friends of God. The beloved community requires that we set aside pathological binary thinking about male or female, enslaved person or free, Jew or Greek. Only by the grace of God and the tensegrity of the cross can we be ministers of reconciliation. The tension of cruciform discipleship becomes a dangerous dynamo of vocational identity, stability, and integrity.

Before he was elected pope, Cardinal Jorge Bergoglio reportedly said to the college of cardinals:

> Evangelizing presupposes a boldness ("parrhesia") in the Church to go out from herself. The Church is called to go out from herself and to go to the peripheries, not only

5. Graetz, *A White Preacher's Message*, 255.

geographically, but also the existential peripheries; those of the mystery of sin, those of pain, those of injustice, those of ignorance and religious indifference, those of intellectual currents, and those of all misery.

When the Church does not go out from herself to evangelize, she becomes self-referential and then gets sick.[6]

Six months later, in his apostolic exhortation *The Joy of the Gospel,* Pope Francis wrote: "Each Christian and every community must discern the path that the Lord points out, but all of us are asked to obey his call to go forth from our own comfort zone in order to reach all the 'peripheries' in need of the light of the Gospel."[7]

The Latin American bishops have been firm in their message that the church sends us on a permanent mission as missionary disciples and evangelists through baptism, with a preferential option for the poor.[8] And so, our Latin American pope calls us to the peripheries. We can learn to approach our antiracism work in this way.

My breakthrough was to realize that the periphery is an elusive horizon. As we pursue this horizon, we surprisingly find ourselves in the center of other people's lives. I experienced this in 2016 when I first decided to visit St. Alphonsus Liguori Parish in St. Louis. Going to Black Catholic Mass initially stretched me in several superficial ways. Still, in making myself present at the worship center of my Black neighbors, I was surprised over the years to be lifted into worship within this community of friends of God.

---

6. Intervention by Cardinal Jorge Mario Bergoglio to the college of cardinals (March 9, 2013), in Gerard O'Connell, *The Election of Pope Francis: An Inside Account of the Conclave that Changed History* (Maryknoll, NY: Orbis Books, 2019), 154.

7. Pope Francis, Post-Synodal Apostolic Exhortation *Evangelii gaudium, The Joy of the Gospel* (November 24, 2013), www.vatican.va.

8. See Latin American Bishops Conference (CELAM) and Jorge Mario Bergoglio, *The Aparecida Document,* V General Conference of the Bishops of Latin America and the Caribbean (2007).

I was welcomed warmly and invited to return. I now feel more at home in Black Catholic worship, and the horizons of my Christian imagination certainly have expanded.

We Christians must keep asking what or whom we wish to place at the center of our lives and what pilgrim commitments we can make. Like a sailboat tacking back and forth, our work as Christians is to tack back and forth toward the elusive horizon at the peripheries. Actively extending our horizons in wider circles of encounter and empathy, we enter into the deep, intimate ties with individual Christians and Christian communities that keep us on a centered path.

Putting the cross in front of us, we go out to one another, witness the other's suffering, and encounter one another in a person-to-person transformation that leads to Christian love. Sometimes we struggle. The road may be steep, but we do not turn back. Divine Love longs to inspirit love within us. Breathing Love, we can do our bit to love, heal, and repair the world.

This pilgrimage of living by the gospel of peace and justice is a lifelong project. For me, these convictions have formed over nearly sixty years of discipleship. Early on, these convictions found expression in my commitment to live in the Galatian dilemma of "there is no longer male and female." Now I am trying to live in the tensegrity of "there is no longer slave or free" (Gal 3:28). Putting the cross in front of me, I have set out on a civil rights pilgrimage.

Think and Act Intersectionally

In the 1980s, after ten years of ordained ministry, I felt compelled to do a comprehensive survey of the hundred-year corpus of Catholic social teaching, the principles of which I now know to be so foundational to preaching for justice.

In 1892, a year after Pope Leo XIII's encyclical letter *Rerum novarum*, the first document of a corpus of Catholic social teaching that continues to this day, historian Anatole Leroy-Beaulieu presciently wrote:

A great struggle is preparing in our midst—a long and hard struggle. I do not think our children will witness the end of it. Social war is declared, and it will last for generations. It will not be a war of 30 years, confined to France and old Germano-Latin Europe, but a war of a hundred years and perhaps more, which will simultaneously set on fire the two extremes of the world.[9]

This quotation and the entire encyclical *Rerum novarum* were written in the social context of Karl Marx's class struggle. But to this day, there is great intersectionality in the struggle to confront, dismantle, and repair the effects of what activist author bell hooks calls "imperialist white supremacist capitalist patriarchy."[10]

One wonders if the church is equal to this struggle. In 1990, in his *Theology for the Third Millennium*, Hans Küng described the church as "*backward, anachronistic,* doctrinaire and authoritarian, its condition marked by narrowing, fixation, intimidation, and repression, which cause harm to both religion *and* society."[11] Pope Francis has warned against our being this kind of church, and countless Catholics disengage and disaffiliate from it.

Might Catholics react differently if we preachers were to preach with integrity out of the principles of Catholic social teaching and with the humility that knows we cannot dismiss racism, sexism, or classism? We can and must walk the tightrope of these dilemmas as disciples. As incoherent as our world experience is, we can extend the walls of our tents to meet one another with empathy, challenge one another as necessary, and do our part to improve things. In trying,

---

9. Anatole Leroy-Beaulieu, *Papacy, Socialism and Democracy, the Papal Encyclical on Human Labor*, trans. B. L. O'Donnell (London: Chapman & Hall, 1892), 189.

10. bell hooks, *The Will to Change: Men, Masculinity, and Love* (New York: Atria Books, 2004), 17; Mako Fitts, "Theorizing Transformative Revolutionary Action: The Contribution of bell hooks to Emancipatory Knowledge Production," *CRL James Journal* 17, no. 1 (Fall 2011): 112.

11. Hans Küng, *Theology for the Third Millennium* (New York: Doubleday, 1988), 221.

we give the Holy Spirit room to maneuver in the intersections of our troubled world. Then God only knows what God will do.

Build Intercultural Competence for Ministry

In 2014, Aquinas Institute of Theology became involved with the Archdiocese of St. Louis and the Missouri Dioceses of Kansas City and Springfield-Cape Girardeau to field an interdiocesan cultural competency training team. Our team was certified to use the USCCB *Building Intercultural Competence for Ministers* (BICM) workbook, published in 2012 by the Committee on Cultural Diversity in the Church under the leadership of Allan Figueroa Deck, SJ.[12] The workbook prioritized the rapidly growing population of Hispanics/Latinos in the Catholic Church in the United States and delineated five steps to building intercultural competency for ministry:

- Frame issues of diversity theologically in terms of the church's identity and mission to evangelize.
- Seek an understanding of culture and how it works.
- Develop intercultural communication skills in pastoral settings.
- Expand knowledge of the obstacles that impede effective intercultural relations.
- Foster ecclesial integration rather than assimilation in church settings with a spirituality of hospitality, reconciliation, and mission.

While we valued this team experience, over time, we questioned our ability during a one- or two-day BICM workshop to make a sufficiently transformative impact upon the mostly white participants mandated to attend. Eventually, the trainers drifted away, and we decided to quit.

---

12. Committee on Cultural Diversity in the Church, United States Conference of Catholic Bishops, *Building Intercultural Competence for Ministers* (Washington, DC: USCCB, 2012).

I agreed to let go of BICM, but the decision was difficult for me. I began filling this vacant space by reading about race and racism. I kept a reading list under seven headings: Biography, Black and White, Catholic, Fiction, History, Preaching, and Theology. There is much to read in each of these categories, and I believe it behooves preachers of a just word to tackle the requisite study. Below, I list three books that most have influenced my learning under each category; I could suggest many more, and I know many of this book's readers can, too.

Biography
- David W. Blight. *Frederick Douglass: Prophet of Freedom.* New York: Simon & Schuster, 2018.
- Frederick Douglass. *Narrative of the Life of Frederick Douglass.* 175th Anniversary Edition. Orinda, CA: Sea Wolf Press, 2020. 1845.
- Maurice J. Nutt. *Thea Bowman: Faithful and Free.* Collegeville, MN: Liturgical Press, 2019.

Black and White
- Ta-Nehisi Coates. *We Were Eight Years in Power: An American Tragedy.* London: One World Publishing, 2017.
- Resmaa Menakem. *My Grandmother's Hands: Racialized Trauma and the Pathway to Mending Our Hearts and Bodies.* Las Vegas, NV: Central Recovery Press, 2017.
- Isabel Wilkerson. *Caste: The Origins of Our Discontents.* New York: Random House, 2020.

Catholic
- Bryan N. Massingale. *Racial Justice in the Catholic Church.* Maryknoll, NY: Orbis Books, 2010.
- Maureen H. O'Connell. *Undoing the Knots: Five Generations of American Catholic Anti-Blackness.* Boston: Beacon Press, 2021.
- Bishop Mark Joseph Seitz, "Night Will Be No More," Pastoral Letter to the People of God in El Paso (October 13, 2019).

Fiction
- Nathan Harris. *The Sweetness of Water.* Boston: Little, Brown and Company, 2021.

- Harriet Beecher Stowe. *Uncle Tom's Cabin*. Durham, NC: Duke Classics, 2012 (orig., 1852).
- Colson Whitehead. *The Nickel Boys*. New York: Doubleday, 2019.

History

- David W. Blight. *Race and Reunion: The Civil War in American Memory*. Cambridge, MA: Harvard University Press, 2002.
- Martin Luther King Jr. *Stride toward Freedom: The Montgomery Story*. Boston: Beacon Press, 2010 (orig., 1958).
- Isabel Wilkerson. *The Warmth of Other Suns: The Epic Story of America's Great Migration*. New York: Vintage Books, 2010.

Preaching

- Clayborne Carlson and Peter Halloran, eds. *A Knock at Midnight: Inspiration from the Great Sermons of Reverend Martin Luther King, Jr.* New York: Warner Books, 1998.
- Kenyatta R. Gilbert. *The Journey and Promise of African American Preaching*. Minneapolis, MN: Fortress Press, 2011.
- James Henry Harris. *Black Suffering: Silent Pain, Hidden Hope*. Minneapolis, MN: Fortress Press, 2020.

Theology

- James H. Cone. *A Black Theology of Liberation*. 50th Anniversary Edition. Maryknoll, NY: Orbis Books. 2020 (orig., 1970).
- Shelly Rambo. *Spirit and Trauma: A Theology of Remaining*. Louisville, KY: Westminster John Knox Press, 2010.
- Howard Thurman. *Jesus and the Disinherited*. Boston: Beacon Press, 2012 (orig., 1949).

Find Your Way Forward
as a Racial Justice Preacher

In 2021, I enquired about whom I might invite to co-teach a summer graduate course on preaching about racism. Father Manuel Williams, CR, a Resurrectionist Black Catholic pastor in Montgomery, Alabama, enthusiastically agreed to my request. To tackle the contextually tricky task of preaching about racism with intentionality, we articulated four objectives: (1) to learn and apply the vocabulary of caste and trauma to understand racism in personal, congregational, ecclesial, and social contexts; (2) to bear witness to experiences of racial suffering; (3) to explore pastoral, prophetic, and theological strategies for constructive antiracism preaching; and (4) to pray to heal and repair the social fabric of a world torn by racism. In June 2021, sixteen students, including several Aquinas Institute alumni, participated in four Friday classes via Zoom.

As a pre-study, we listened to *Seeing White*, a remarkably instructive fourteen-episode podcast series about the origins and history of whiteness from the Center for Documentary Studies at Duke University. We also discussed four core texts: journalist Isabel Wilkerson's bestselling *Caste: The Origins of Our Discontents,* psychotherapist Resmaa Menakem's *My Grandmother's Hands: Racialized Trauma and the Pathway to Mending Our Hearts and Bodies,* Black theologian Howard Thurman's *Jesus and the Disinherited,* and African American homiletician Frank Thomas's *Surviving a Dangerous Sermon.* We read other shorter pieces as well. We wanted a vocabulary for talking and preaching with our congregations about race. Our core vocabulary became *caste* (Wilkerson), *trauma* (Menakem), and *preacher as pastor, prophet, and practical theologian* (Thomas). In our class conversations, the possibility of this book on preaching about racism came to light.

Make a Civil Rights Pilgrimage

My colleague Father Manuel Williams has served as pastor and director of Montgomery's Resurrectionist Catholic Missions of the South for thirty-some years. After teaching our Preaching and Racism class together, I arranged to visit Manuel to make a civil rights pilgrimage to Alabama. During the civil rights movement in the 1960s, I was a teenager who paid more attention to the anti-war movement than the civil rights movement. In the following decades, I remained woefully ignorant of the facts of racism in my homeland, or for that matter, in my home state. I needed to do some civil rights catch-up.

I bought a guidebook[13] and planned my trip. Home base was with Manuel in Montgomery. My pilgrimage included a day each in Selma and Birmingham, two days in Montgomery, and a stop in Memphis on my return to St. Louis.

Over these days, I made the following civil rights calendar to keep the events and the movements clear in my mind.

A Civil Rights Calendar[14]

May 17, 1954: *Brown v. Board of Education*, a Supreme Court ruling on the Fourteenth Amendment that outlawed school segregation

August 28, 1955: Emmitt Till (age fourteen) lynched for talking to a white woman in Money, Mississippi, with an open-casket funeral back home in Chicago

December 1, 1955: Rosa Parks (age forty-two) arrested on a bus that departed from Court Square, the site of Montgomery's slave market

December 5, 1955–December 20, 1956: Montgomery Bus Boycott, organized by the Montgomery Improvement Association, chaired by Martin Luther King Jr. (age twenty-six), pastor of Ebenezer Baptist Church

August 25, 1956: Bombing of the home of Rev. Robert Graetz, a leader in the Montgomery Improvement Association and white pastor of a Black congregation, United Evangelical Lutheran Church in Montgomery

November 13, 1956: Segregated seating on Montgomery buses banned by Supreme Court

---

13. Fraye Gauillard, *Alabama's Civil Rights Trail: An Illustrated Guide to the Cradle of Freedom* (Tuscaloosa: University of Alabama Press, 2010).

14. Many of these dates are inscribed on the black granite Civil Rights Memorial across the street from the Southern Poverty Law Center and around the corner from Dexter Avenue King Memorial Baptist Church, which is across the street from the Alabama state capitol in Montgomery.

December 25, 1956: Bombing of the home of Rev. Fred Shuttle-worth, pastor of Bethel Baptist Church in Birmingham

August 29, 1957: First Civil Rights Act passed by Congress since the Civil Rights Act of 1875 during Reconstruction

September 24, 1957: Federal troops ordered by President Dwight Eisenhower to enforce school desegregation in Little Rock, Arkansas

February 1, 1960: Sit-in by Black students at a whites-only lunch counter in Greensboro, North Carolina

December 5, 1960: Segregation banned in bus terminals by the Supreme Court

May 14, 1961: Freedom Ride bus bombed in Anniston, Alabama

May 20, 1961: Freedom Ride bus from Birmingham met by 200 Ku Klux Klan at Greyhound Bus Terminal in Montgomery

September 30, 1962: Riots when Black student James Meredith enrolled at Ole Miss (University of Mississippi)

1963: James Baldwin's *The Fire Next Time*

April 16, 1963: Martin Luther King Jr.'s "Letter from Birmingham Jail"

May 3, 1963: Marchers in the Children's Crusade met by police with dogs and firehoses at Kelly Ingram Park in central Birmingham

June 11, 1963: Alabama governor George Wallace stood in school-house door to stop university integration

June 12, 1963: NAACP activist Medgar Evers (age thirty-seven) assassinated in Jackson, Mississippi

August 28, 1963: 250,000 at March on Washington for Martin Luther King Jr.'s "I Have a Dream" speech

September 15, 1963: Four girls killed in the bombing of Sixteenth Baptist Church, Birmingham

July 2, 1964: Civil Rights Act signed by President Lyndon Johnson

February 21, 1965: Malcolm X (age thirty-nine) assassinated in New York City

March 7, 1965: Bloody Sunday, Edmund Pettus Bridge, Selma, Alabama

March 21–25, 1965: Selma to Montgomery March for voting
rights, fifty-four miles on Highway 80

August 6, 1965: Voting Rights Act signed by President Lyndon
Johnson

August 11–16, 1965: Watts Uprising, Los Angeles

October 2, 1967: Thurgood Marshall sworn in as the first Black
Supreme Court justice

April 4, 1968: Assassination of Martin Luther King Jr. (age thirty-
nine), Lorraine Hotel, Memphis

April 4, 1968: Robert Kennedy speech, Indianapolis

June 5, 1968: Assassination of Senator Robert Kennedy (age forty-
two), Ambassador Hotel, Los Angeles

The Edmund Pettus Bridge

Edmund Pettus was a Confederate officer, Grand Dragon of the
Alabama Ku Klux Klan, and United States senator from Alabama.
His name is prominently displayed on the massive Edmund Pettus
Bridge as US Highway 80 crosses the Alabama River into down-
town Selma. From Montgomery south to Mobile, the Alabama
River flows through the fertile Black Belt of cotton plantations of
the American South. Having driven from Montgomery, I crossed
the bridge and drove along Water Avenue with its nineteenth-
century businesses and hotels. Despite Selma's military-industrial
importance to the Civil War, my immediate impression was of a
city in economic and civic desolation that reaped what it had sown.

The civil rights movement was a charismatic breakthrough
movement led by a coalition of the young. On Bloody Sunday
in 1965, future congressman John Lewis, who suffered a fractured skull that day, was twenty-five. Martin Luther King Jr., who
crossed the bridge two weeks later at the beginning of the Selma to
Montgomery March, was thirty-five. Thousands of young Black-
bodied and white-bodied people converged on Selma and Montgomery to march for voting rights.

One of my civil rights heroes is Sister Mary Antona Ebo, a Black
Catholic Franciscan Sister of Mary from St. Louis. An iconic pho-

tograph shows Sister Antona marching alongside other religious sisters and clergy in Selma at a protest attended by Martin Luther King Jr. on March 10, 1965. When asked by the press why she had come to Selma, she answered, "I'm here because I'm a Negro, a nun, a Catholic, and because I want to bear witness."[15]

When Sister Antona died fifty-two years later at ninety-three, her funeral was celebrated at St. Alphonsus Liguori "Rock" Catholic Church in St. Louis. Though I had never met her, I occasionally preached at the Rock, and I did so on Sunday, November 18, 2017, the day before Sister Antona's funeral. I spoke about her youth during the Depression at the McLean County Home for Children in Bloomington, Illinois, her baptism as a Catholic at age eighteen, her search for a school of nursing that would accept her, her time at St. Mary's Infirmary School of Nursing in St. Louis, Missouri, a hospital for Black folk near the Mississippi River, and her subsequent welcome into the Sisters of Mary. She returned to school several times and eventually became the first African American hospital president in the United States in Baraboo, Wisconsin.

When she heard about the events that would come to be called Bloody Sunday, she and five other forty-something Catholic sisters in old-style black habits rented a small airplane to fly to Selma. The rest is history.

Think from Enslavement to Lynching to Segregation to Mass Incarceration

One of my visceral memories is the rush of terror I felt passing through the snarling dogs lunging from both sides of the Racist Dogs Sculpture in Kelly Ingram Park in central Birmingham. In May 1963, police assaulted one thousand students with dogs and high-pressure fire hoses during the Children's Crusade for voting rights. Four months later, across the street at Sixteenth Avenue Baptist Church, four girls died in a church bombing. Now, the

---

15. "The Nuns Who Witnessed the Life and Death of Martin Luther King Jr.," *Catholic News Agency*, January 17, 2022.

park and the church stand adjacent to the Civil Rights Institute, which tells the civil rights story of Birmingham.

After Birmingham, I spent two days in Montgomery. The red-brick Dexter Avenue King Memorial Baptist Church stands across from Alabama's state capitol in plain view from the governor's office. Behind the church stands the modernist headquarters of the Southern Poverty Law Center. At the other end of Dexter Avenue, the site of Montgomery's former slave market, Rosa Parks boarded the bus on the fateful day of her arrest in 1955, the day that propelled King into the national spotlight at age twenty-six.

Nothing prepared me for the visceral impact upon entering the Equal Justice Initiative's Heritage Museum and the National Memorial for Peace and Justice. In each location, slave sculptures by Ghanaian artist Kwame Akoto-Bamfo immediately draw visitors into such an immersive experience as words can hardly describe. In a disciplined narrative told in art, film, and detailed displays, the Heritage Museum tells the story of twelve million kidnapped and enslaved Black bodies, nine million Black bodies terrorized during Reconstruction, ten million Black bodies who endured segregation, and nine million Black bodies sentenced to mass incarceration. Less than a mile away, the National Memorial for Peace and Justice features over eight hundred weathered steel monuments listing, county by county, 4,400 named and unnamed men, women, and children victimized by racialized terror lynching. Thanks to the work of the Equal Justice Initiative, the civil rights pilgrim can see how the devastating echoes of chattel slavery continue to sound into our present day. The national sin of racism continues to pay itself forward.

My civil rights pilgrimage also took me to the National Civil Rights Museum at the Lorraine Motel in Memphis and, a few weeks later, to the Smithsonian Institution's National Museum of African American History and Culture on the National Mall in Washington, DC. Each museum adds to America's civil rights story. Yet, I say to an aspiring civil rights pilgrim without hesitation—first, go to Alabama.

Trust Yourself as a Pilgrim, and Make the Journey

At the beginning of the Montgomery Bus Boycott, Martin Luther King Jr. said, "Justice is love correcting that which revolts against love."[16] Here is what social activist bell hooks says about King's love ethic:

> Civil rights movement transformed society in the United States because it was fundamentally rooted in a love ethic. No leader has emphasized this ethic more than Martin Luther King, Jr. He had the prophetic insight to recognize that a revolution built on any other foundation would fail. Again and again, King testified that he had "decided to love" because he believed deeply that if we are "seeking the highest good" we "find it through love" because this is "the key that unlocks the door to the meaning of ultimate reality." And the point of being in touch with a transcendent reality is that we struggle for justice, all the while realizing that we are always more than our race, class, or sex.[17]

As I reflect on bell hooks's words, and as I journey back in memory to where my civil rights pilgrimage began, I couldn't agree more than with James Baldwin, who advised in 1985, "Go back to where you started, as far back as you can, examine all of it, travel your road again and tell the truth about it."[18] Your journey into racial justice preaching will be your own, with your starting points and shrines along the way. Trust yourself as a pilgrim, and make the journey!

---

16. Martin Luther King Jr., Address at the First Montgomery Improvement Association Mass Meeting at the Holt Street Baptist Church on the Eve of the Montgomery Bus Boycott, Montgomery, AL (December 5, 1955).

17. bell hooks, "Love as the Practice of Freedom," in *Outlaw Culture: Resisting Representations* (New York: Routledge Classics, 2006), 244.

18. James Baldwin, *The Price of the Ticket*, 11.

Part II
Black Lives Matter

Introduction by Maurice J. Nutt

Life is a gift from God—from our first breath as newborns to our last exhalation in death. We hear, especially from the Catholic Church, that every unborn human life must be respected, protected, and valued—that the unborn have a right to life. Amen! But what happens after the birth of God's sacred human creation? The questions are manifold: Is *all* human life treated equally? Are *all* human beings given the same advantages of health care, quality education, adequate housing, social, political, and economic opportunities, and equal justice under the law? Do we respect, protect, and value *all* human lives? Here in America, do *all* lives matter?

Theologian Kelly Brown Douglas believes, "There is no getting around it: an anti-Black narrative is pervasive in America's social-cultural mindset. The narrative has so impacted the nation's moral imaginary that 'letting Black people die' has virtually become an acceptable part of the nation's day-to-day reality."[1] Violence is inherent in the American ethos. We are a nation created from violence. From the genocide of Indigenous people to the enslavement of African people, America has perpetrated violence on all non-white ethnic groups. White supremacy, racism, and anti-Black violence have woven themselves into the fabric of America: in its laws and policies, religions, education and justice systems,

---

1. Kelly Brown Douglas, *Resurrection Hope: A Future where Black Lives Matter* (Maryknoll, NY: Orbis Books, 2021), 53.

77

and most especially in its attitudes and behaviors. This violence continues today, especially in the unwarranted and unnecessary murders of many known and unknown Black and Brown people. However, today the unrelenting violence against people of color is being exposed, recorded, and live-streamed on social media platforms. Across the country and around the globe, people protest in the streets against racial hatred and violence. We hear the reverberating shouts of "No justice, no peace," "Black Lives Matter," "Hands up, don't shoot," "I can't breathe," and "Say their names." The names of Trayvon Martin, Michael Brown, Breonna Taylor, Ahmaud Arbery, George Floyd, and countless others have cried out from the mouths of enraged protestors in a reverent litany of lament as they seek justice.

Contributors in this Black Lives Matter section engage our imaginations as they invite us to enter into the lives of, and have empathy with, those who experience and endure racial violence and injustice. I open the section by explaining the hashtag #*BlackLivesMatter* and how the nefarious nature of racism interrupts the ordinary daily lives of people of color, whether they are jogging, grocery shopping, sleeping, or at Bible study. I also include a homily that I preached about the sacredness of Black humanity and explore how my hearers responded. My Redemptorist confrere Peter Hill then invites us into his personal and transformative encounter with racism as a native of the Caribbean island of Dominica who has relocated to the United States. Thinking that he was somehow immune from racism because he was different from African Americans, Hill learned as a person and a preacher that he could not separate himself as a person or as a preacher from the profoundly different racial reality of the United States.

Dominican priest James Pierce Cavanaugh's essay gives the unique perspectives of two Black Catholic bishops on racism in the church and society. As auxiliary bishops from the North and South, Bishop Joseph N. Perry and Bishop Fernand J. Cheri, III, OFM, bring somewhat differing theological, ecclesiological, and liturgical appreciations to the experience of racism and the necessity of condemning racial injustice for the sake of reconciliation and unity among God's people. Bishop Perry expresses concern about how Catholics contribute to sustaining racial bias. Bishop Cheri unabashedly believes that, with honest and open dialogue, we can reconcile the Black Lives Matter movement with Catholic social teaching. (With sadness, we must note that several months after his interview for this book, Bishop Cheri died in New Orleans on March 21, 2023.)

Michael Meyer's essay explores preaching empathy as a path to conversion and liberation. A corporate attorney and permanent deacon in the Diocese of Metuchen, New Jersey, Meyer challenges white Catholics to personally confront their racism by empathizing with the devastation and injustices experienced by people of color and embarking on a journey from dominance to conversion and from oppression to liberation.

In the final essay of this section, Black Catholic womanist theologian Valerie Lewis-Mosley invites readers into her experience of being bridled by racism and misogyny within the Catholic Church. Her essay illuminates the process of liberating herself as a Black Catholic woman and Dominican lay associate to speak the necessary truth about how the church has harmed Black and Brown people and to preach prophetically with an unbridled tongue.

The corpus of these essays advocates preaching that demands that America honestly examine its conscience to see and accept its capacity to hate and destroy Black human life. By confessing its egregious sinfulness, abandoning its need for power and privilege, making amends to those unjustly harmed, and commencing transformational healing—then, and only then, will America become a place where Black lives really do matter.

6 Understanding and Preaching #BlackLivesMatter

Maurice J. Nutt

The proximity to which Jesus calls his followers requires concerted and sustained encounters with the Black experience that do not objectify Black people. Such encounters help foster a re-imagining of the Black body that will lead to eliciting responses of care and kindness as opposed to outrage and fear when encountering Black people in everyday life.

—Kelly Brown Douglas[1]

Black people continue to suffer at the hands of white supremacy. There is strong resistance to allowing Black people to attain a sense of full humanity or the ability to materially flourish. Black people continue to cling to their faith as a means of hope, longing for the day when life will be better, even though it seems having faith in God would be difficult in these circumstances.

—James Henry Harris[2]

On Sunday morning, July 14, 2013, I attended Mass at a small, nondescript Catholic church in an African American neighborhood on the south side of Chicago. The church was "Easter Sun-

---

1. Kelly Brown Douglas, *Resurrection Hope: A Future where Black Lives Matter* (Maryknoll, NY: Orbis Books, 2021), 163.

2. James Henry Harris, *Black Suffering: Silent Pain, Hidden Hope* (Minneapolis: Fortress Press, 2020), 225.

day packed." Yet unlike Easter, there were no new clothes or hats; instead, the congregants' faces showed signs of disgust, frustration, and sadness. The night before, the verdict had been rendered. George Zimmerman, the vigilante neighborhood watchman, was acquitted on all accounts of shooting and killing teenager Trayvon Martin in Sanford, Florida, because he allegedly was "standing his ground" and defending himself from the unarmed young Black man. In that small Chicago Catholic congregation, the parishioners gathered not only for a eucharistic liturgy on this Fifteenth Sunday in Ordinary Time but for a word of comfort and solace from the priest because, yet again, their ordinary lives were interrupted by a senseless death and a predictable acquittal. Undoubtedly, the Black priest presiding at the liturgy would have words that empathized with their anger and disappointment. Indeed, this was a safe place for them to be vulnerable and to express indignation, and indeed this was the time, space, and place where they would receive guidance and direction regarding this all-too-familiar happening—yet another unwarranted killing of an adolescent Black child.

The Gospel text for that Sunday was Luke 10:25–37. Jesus tells his disciples the parable of the Good Samaritan and enters into dialogue with a scholar of the law: "'Which of these three, do you think, was a neighbor to the man who fell into the hands of robbers?' He said, 'The one who showed him mercy.' Jesus said to him, 'Go and do likewise.'" It was a perfect Scripture text to address the current event of George Zimmerman's acquittal—a neighborhood watchman who did not treat his neighbor Trayvon Martin with mercy but rather with fatal violence.

However, the priest was silent on the matter—said absolutely nothing, not in his homily, not during the prayers of the faithful, and not even during his pastoral announcements! This Black priest pastor of this Black congregation was so unaware of their anguish and seemingly unconcerned. I have no defense for his homiletical infraction, insensitivity, and personal insolence. However, I will never forget the hurt on the face of an elderly Black woman, who throughout her life had undoubtedly suffered more than her share of racial violence, as she left the church building, shaking her head in disgust that the acquittal was never mentioned. She looked at me and said, "Father, that was a damn shame!"

The word *envisage* means to conceive of something not yet existing or known, to be able to form a mental picture of something. #BlackLivesMatter calls for the work of envisioning Black people. Black people exist; we are human beings; we are real. Black people must be seen as sacred humanity and not villainized and subjugated because we share this country, this planet, with white people. Black people are here, but do white people who socially, politically, and economically hold both privilege and power genuinely see them for who they are?

White people's unwillingness to see Black humanity is often cloaked in pseudo-liberal sentiments finding expression in statements such as, "I don't see color," "I'm color blind," and "Race isn't important; we're all human beings." Acknowledging, affirming, and authentically seeing Blackness can be difficult for white people because their race, ethnicity, history, identity, power, and privilege are inextricably tethered to the enslavement, subjugation, oppression, injustices, and violence endured by Black people. Unapologetically speaking the truth about anti-Blackness and white supremacy is not about making white people feel ashamed or guilty. Guilt-tripping does nothing to bring healing and restoration to Black people. Moreover, racial justice is not about white people's feelings. That's precisely the problem of white fragility and privilege. We must decenter whiteness and focus on solutions bringing healing, restoration, and equity to Black people.

Essentially, the phrase or hashtag "Black Lives Matter" is a heart-wrenching plea or lament. Created in July 2013 by Alicia Garza in a Facebook post called "Love Letter to Black People," Garza's intent was to affirm the distraught Black community after George Zimmerman's acquittal of shooting and killing unarmed Trayvon Martin. As reported in the *New Yorker:*

> Garza has a prodigious social-media presence, and on the day that the Zimmerman verdict was handed down she posted, "the sad part is, there's a section of America who is cheering

and celebrating right now. and that makes me sick to my stomach. we *GOTTA* get it together y'all." Later, she added, "btw stop saying we are not surprised. that's a damn shame in itself. I continue to be surprised at how little Black lives matter. And I will continue that. stop giving up on black life." She ended with "black people. I love you. I love us. Our lives matter."[3]

Her friend Patrisse Cullors amended the last words to create a hashtag: #BlackLivesMatter. Another associate, Opal Tometi, offered to build a social media platform on Facebook and Twitter, and they began promoting it and actualizing the hashtag into a movement. Many in the Catholic Church have castigated these Black queer women because some think they promote conflict with the church's teachings. Therefore, it is my intention to highlight the rhetorical lamentation and not specifically the movement. The import of the #BLM hashtag is "an affirmation of Black folks' humanity, our contributions to this society, and our resilience in the face of deadly oppression."[4]

Our nation was founded and exists today on a distorted construct of whiteness—meaning that what is deemed superior and normative is white—and those who are not white are considered inferior, inconsequential, or substandard. This delusional proposition, undergirded by white dominance and privilege, continues to sustain racial subjugation, injustice, and disenfranchisement in the church and society. The affirmation of #BLM by Black people and those of other ethnicities causes derision among some white people, and to ensure that their power is not undermined or confiscated, they counter with the declaration #AllLivesMatter.

---

3. Jelani Cobb, "The Matter of Black Lives," *The New Yorker,* March 14, 2016, www.newyorker.com. Also cited by Jelani Cobb in "The Matter of Black Lives," in *The Matter of Black Lives: Writing from The New Yorker,* ed. Jelani Cobb and David Remnick (New York: HarperCollins, 2021), 715.

4. Herstory, *Black Lives Matter,* www.blacklivesmatter.com/herstory/.

While every human life does matter, every life is not threatened by oppression or death. The irrational protestation of #ALM is an expression of white fragility, defined by Robin DiAngelo as "a state in which even a minimum amount of racial stress becomes intolerable, triggering a range of defensive moves. These moves include the outward display of emotions such as anger, fear, and guilt, and behaviors such as argumentation, silence, and leaving the stress-inducing situation."[5]

White fragility is at the core of many white parishioners feeling uncomfortable or angered should a preacher address racism from the pulpit. Therefore, many preachers avoid preaching about the sin of racism for fear that it will disturb their well-meaning white parishioners, who might leave the parish or withhold their financial support. Preachers are called to preach the truth of the gospel and not acquiesce to people's feelings of fragility. Their fragility does not consider how racism interrupts the ordinary lives of people of color. In every instance, people of color tried to live some semblance of normalcy when terrorizing racial hatred interrupted it. Consider Black people who were walking, jogging, grocery shopping, doing Bible study, at home sleeping, or eating a bowl of ice cream while watching television when their lives were interrupted by sudden death because of unreasonable fear or unrelenting hatred.

United Methodist bishop and homiletician Will Willimon writes, "Preaching's value is often in the subtle but powerful ways it forms us into people who have empathy for others, who assume responsibility for the needs of strangers, who feel that we are under judgment from a higher criterion than our own consciences, and who believe that, with the Holy Spirit set loose among us, we can be born again."[6] Willimon's assertion presupposes the congregation's willingness and capacity toward repentance, atonement,

---

5. Robin DiAngelo, "White Fragility," *International Journal of Critical Pedagogy* 3, no. 3 (2011): 54.

6. Will Willimon, *Who Lynched Willie Earl? Preaching to Confront Racism* (Nashville: Abingdon Press, 2017), 111.

transformation, and authentic discipleship. Anti-racism preaching demands that preachers honestly name racism as sin. Racism is antithetical to the teachings of Jesus Christ. Congregants are called to eradicate racism from their behavior and make genuine amends for their racist transgressions.

On February 20, 2022, I was invited to preach on one of the four Sundays during Black History Month in the Archdiocese of Newark. Cardinal Joseph W. Tobin, CSsR, archbishop of Newark, was keenly aware that mainly Black people were attending the archdiocese's annual Black History Month Mass. He felt that the spiritual and cultural gifts of Black people—all those from the African diaspora—should be shared with the entire archdiocese, most especially white people. For the four Sundays of Black History Month, under the auspices of the archdiocesan office for African, Caribbean, and Black ministry, Tobin invited Black or African priests locally and nationally to preach on the sin of racism at four predominantly white parishes in various counties throughout the archdiocese.

Presumably, the cardinal figured that if the white community wasn't coming to celebrate the richness of Black spirituality and culture at the cathedral, he would send the Black community to the white community, complete with Black preaching, gospel or African music, vesture, and dance. I offered the homily at a Sunday eucharistic liturgy in Jersey City at St. Aeden's Catholic Church, a Jesuit-staffed parish at St. Peter's University. The following is the Black History Month homily I preached on Luke 6:27–38.

Listen, Learn, and Love:
Honoring the Sacredness of Black Life

Divine providence has placed this Gospel text before us this afternoon, especially because of the incident that happened here in the Garden State of New Jersey at the Bridgewater Commons Mall, captured on a fifty-six-second smartphone video that went viral, an incident that happens far too often but is not often recorded.

The incident was a fight between an eighth-grade Black teenager named Zkyé, who defended an unnamed younger friend in the seventh grade being bullied by a Hispanic eleventh-grade teenager named Joey. The fight ensued, with pushing, shoving, and rolling on the ground until two police officers came.

While Zkyé was noble to stand up for his friend, the white officers immediately assumed that because of the color of his skin, Zkyé's noble act was not even in the realm of possibility. An officer pulled Joey from on top of Zkyé and handcuffed Zyké with his face down to the ground. The other officer offered Joey a comfortable seat on a couch. Joey offered to be handcuffed because he engaged in the fight, but that didn't happen. Joey later stated: "I know what the officers did was wrong, so there should be consequences."

James Baldwin speaks of this sort of incident in his 1963 book, *The Fire Next Time*. Baldwin reflected on the debilitating terror of racial hatred and violence that every Negro child has in preparing for the unknown. The child has no idea when that day will arrive but is assured by his or her parents that it will surely come.

God says: "But I say to you who listen, Love your enemies, do good to those who hate you, bless those who curse you, pray for those who abuse you" (Luke 6:27–28). Church, in every tense confrontation and unreasonable expectation and to every undeserved cry for help, Jesus asks us to respond with the compassion and mercy of God. We are called to break such cycles of irresponsibility and selfishness—to bring healing to another's pain and sorrow, to bring back the outcast and oppressed by seeking to re-create situations demonstrating God's universal and unconditional love.

Despite the violence done to us, despite the injustice and rejection we have suffered, Jesus demands that his disciples take that first difficult, awkward step to forgive. Our first objective must be God's work of reconciliation: to love the unlovable, to reach out to the marginalized, to dismantle whatever walls divide and isolate people, and to build bridges of hope that bring people together.

Church, Jesus challenges us to love our enemies. This is not loving some nebulous group determined by politics, sociology, or economics. It is not loving some distant sinner we will never have anything to do with. Today's text challenges us to love the people we live, work, and go to school with, whom we struggle with, and who get on our last nerve.

"To love our enemies" must be actively sought and perpetually promoted, not merely declaring a cease-fire but creating and maintaining genuine reconciliation. We Christians must recognize and receive the other not as someone foreign to us but as someone to see and acknowledge and honor as a human being truly. These children of God are our brothers and sisters. In today's text from Luke's Gospel, the Greek word for love is *agape*. This love is benevolent and charitable and expresses goodwill. The *agape* that Jesus asks us to have for our enemies means that no matter how they hurt us, we will never let bitterness close our hearts. We will seek nothing but good for that enemy. *Agape* recognizes the humanity we share with everyone, beginning within our own households and communities.

Oh, the words of Jesus in our Gospel passage this afternoon compel us to survey our Black history through the lens of solid gospel values because it would be easy to sink into despair without them. Everything the founding fathers claimed for humanity in the name of morality contradicted their attitude and treatment toward the descendants of Africa and the native inhabitants of this land. The enslavement of the Negro, the extermination of the Indigenous American, and the annexation of the Hispanics made the birth of the American nation a conception conceived in hypocrisy, dedicated to the twisted proposition that white people were somehow superior to non-white people and entitled to enslave, oppress, and destroy them.

We need the sacred words of Jesus: "Love your enemies, do good to those who hate you, bless those who curse you, pray for those who abuse you" (Luke 6:27–28) because it is a national tragedy and a national disgrace that nearly seven decades since the beginning of the civil rights movement, the progress toward racial justice is receding, not advancing. Where is the justice in health care when infant mortality rates, heart disease, and hypertension continue to drive mortality and morbidity tables in our communities? Where is the justice when our historically Black colleges and universities are underfunded or closed and when funding for student loans is reduced or eliminated? In the last month, thirty HBCUs have received bomb threats! Are you sure we are living in 2022 and not 1952? Where is equal opportunity when many of our most promising students find themselves as nomads with no place to go? Where is the justice that we worked and bled for when Black and Brown people make up 31 percent of the United States population but 80 percent of the prison population? Where is economic justice when African Americans, Asians, Latinx, and Indigenous peoples are condemned to the bottom of the pay scale, and the government reduces its commitment to affirmative action and employment and education?

Oh, those sacred words of Jesus must be adhered to when asked the poignant question, "If you love those who love you, what credit is that to you" (Luke 6:32)? Because whether it is the repugnant act of burning churches or desecrating synagogues in the dark of night, whether it is increased violence from white supremacist groups, or demonstrations against immigrants simply because they happen to be Black and Brown or do not speak as we do, compassion and acceptance have once again become dirty words. We, as a nation, have lost our ability to be compassionate and accepting regarding one's race, religion, or gender. This country that we love and built and whom our ancestors have fought and died for, from the Revolutionary War to the wars in Iraq and Afghanistan, needs to learn to love more and hate, not less, but not at all! Yes, Jim Crow Sr. may be dead, but Jim Crow Jr. is still alive and well.

To be clear, no one is born a racist. Racism is a learned behavior taught by our families, schools, and even our churches—taught by those we respect. Yet, Pope Francis admonishes us: "It is neither the culture of confrontation nor a culture of conflict which builds harmony within and between peoples, but rather a culture of encounter and a culture of dialogue; this is the only way to peace."[7]

---

7. Pope Francis, papal audience (September 1, 2013), www.vatican.va.

Jesus instructs us to love those who hate us and pray for those who persecute us. We disciples of Jesus Christ must put this admonition into practice more now than ever before. We hear hate speech, and hate groups attempt to divide this nation. Who would have ever imagined our nation's capitol building, built by Black folks, under siege? Books telling the true history of Black life in America are being banned in schools in specific states nationwide. White fragility has become so ensconced in the very fiber of our country that it is seemingly unacceptable to speak about the inhumane enslavement and lynching of people of the African diaspora or the unchallenged separate and unequal conditions Black people have endured, to speak of the horrendous racism perpetrated on Black and Brown people daily, or even to self-affirm ourselves as made in the image and beautiful Blackness of God by simply saying "Black Lives Matter." In an era of small vision, rampant apathy, and celebrated mediocrity, we so desperately need those who will stand up and speak against that which is wrong and embrace what is right. We desperately need to mean it when we say that racism, sexism, anti-Semitism, and anti-Muslim sentiments are wrong. These sentiments must be condemned from both the pews and pulpits of our Catholic churches!

It is untenable that some Catholic people do not and do not want to see that racism exists. Not only does it exist, but it is also America's original sin, and it is literally killing the sacred human lives of Black and Brown people. Racism is truncating and aborting sacred human lives of Black and Brown people. Some Catholics in this nation may not accept the reality of racism. Still, I am so glad that the leader of the Catholic Church universal sees it and challenges us to see and honor the sacredness of every human life. Let me pause and let the words of our Holy Father reverberate throughout this church. Pope Francis, expressing concern for George Floyd's murder, said, "I have witnessed with great concern the disturbing social unrest in your nation in these past days, following the tragic death of Mr. George Floyd." He said, "We cannot tolerate or turn a blind eye to racism and exclusion in any form and yet claim to defend the sacredness of every human life."[8]

Even before Pope Francis condemned racism in both society and the church, Newark Auxiliary Bishop Joseph A. Francis, SVD, the author of the 1979 United States Bishops' pastoral letter on racism, "Brothers and Sisters to Us," stated at the beginning of that letter, "Racism is an evil which endures in our society and in our church."[9] But is there anybody here who knows with God that trouble doesn't last?

And yet, as we look over our people's harrowing yet holy history and prepare to share Eucharist, we indeed have cause to be thankful. Thanks be to God for depositing within our ancestors the gifts and skills necessary to survive and forge a pathway through bitter struggle so that our history will be brighter. Thanks be to God for their legacy, blood, sweat, and tears. From their struggle, today's generation has inherited the strength of character, a vibrant culture of community, and a deep spirituality that knows God as a liberator and Jesus Christ as one who identifies with the oppressed! Thank God for the ancestors whose faith led them to pray in the words of James Weldon Johnson: "God of our weary years, God of our silent tears, Thou who hast brought us thus far along the way. Thou who has by Thy might led us into the light, keep us forever in the path, we pray."[10] Thank God for the ancestors! Thank God for their inspirational example of faith and their willingness to go deep and use the gifts and talents that God gave them for God's glory.

Thanks be to God for our African American Catholic heroes and heroines on the path to sainthood: Our holy Venerables: Pierre Toussaint, Mother Henriette Delille, SSF, Father Augustus Tolton,

---

8. Pope Francis, general audience (June 3, 2020), www.vatican news.va.

9. "Brothers and Sisters to Us: U.S. Catholic Bishops Pastoral Letter on Racism" (1979), no. 1, www.usccb.org.

10. James Weldon Johnson, "Lift Every Voice and Sing," www. jamesweldonjohnson.org. Public domain.

and our saintly Servants of God: Mother Mary Lange, OSP, Julia Greeley, and Sister Thea Bowman, FSPA. Then there's Daniel Rudd, Father Joseph Nearon, SSS, Bishop Harold Perry, SVD, Bishop Joseph Francis, SVD, Archbishop James P. Lyke, OFM, Dr. Nathan Jones, Father Bede Abrams, OFM Conv, Brother Booker Ashe, OFM Capuchin, Sister Beatrice Jeffries, SBS, Sister Antona Ebo, FSM, and Father Cyprian Davis, OSB, and all who found faith and freedom in Christ and convinced them no form of oppression could be tolerated. Their leadership, faithfulness, and vision have paved the way for us today!

Thanks be to God for Alice Walker, Lorraine Hansberry, and Zora Neale Hurston, who showed us real life through their creative writing, giving us *The Color Purple, A Raisin in the Sun*, and *Their Eyes Were Watching God*.

Thanks be to God for Martin, Malcolm, Marcus, and Medgar, who used their powerful voices to let us know we can have a dream that Black is beautiful, and it's beautiful to be Black!

Thanks be to God for W. E. B. DuBois, E. Franklin Frazier, Thurgood Marshall, John Hope Franklin, and Cornel West, who used their massive intellects to chart the right course for the advancement of the Black race.

Thanks be unto God for all the grandmas, grandpas, aunts, and uncles, whom the history books may never record yet were influential in paving the way—doing what they could with what they had so that today's youth would have a brighter future. Indeed, my grandfather, Edward Louis Duvall, a devout Black Catholic man, paved the way for me to be standing before you today. He was born just ten years after slavery in 1875 in St. Mary, Missouri. At age twelve, he expressed to his pastor that he felt called to the priesthood. Though his pastor kept putting him off, my grandfather became a catechist. He was the godfather of many in his Black community who wanted to be baptized. He took care of the needy. Yet, he waited to one day enter the seminary. That day never came. His pastor never told him that he wouldn't be accepted to the seminary because of the color of his skin. My grandfather didn't marry until he was forty years old, still hoping to become a priest.

Being a good married Catholic man, he made up for lost time and had eight children: five boys and three girls. In 1936, he wanted to attend the weekly novena of Our Mother of Perpetual Help at St. Alphonsus Liguori "Rock" Catholic Church in St. Louis. The ushers met him at the door and told him, "Colored folks weren't welcome in this church to pray before the icon of Our Mother of Perpetual Help." Of course, I wasn't there that day. Still, in my spiritual imagination, knowing that my grandfather was a praying man, I'd like to believe that my grandfather prayed, "Lord, I may not be able to enter into this church today, but one day my descendants will be able to worship here." God, being God, not only allowed his descendants to worship there, but his grandson also became a Redemptorist priest and was appointed the first African American pastor of that church. And not only that, but Black folks at that St. Louis church also prepared another young Redemptorist seminarian for the priesthood during his summer ministry assignments. Black folks prayed for and helped prepare Joseph Cardinal Tobin, CSsR, to one day shepherd the people of God of this Archdiocese of Newark. Did you hear me? Black folks prayed for and prepared your archbishop to minister to you!

Won't God do it? Is there anybody here who knows that God will make a way out of no way? Is there anybody here who knows that if God is for us, who can be against us? Is there anybody here who knows that God is an ever-present help in times of trouble? Is there anybody here who knows that no weapon formed against you shall prosper? Won't God do it? I asked, won't God do it? Say yeah. Say yeah. Say yeah! Listen. Learn. Love. Amen.

*   *   *   *

Typically, preachers do not receive substantial or immediate feedback on their homilies. However, the pastor of St. Aedan's told me that a parishioner of the parish, when leaving the church, asked her pastor (referring to my homily), "What was *that* supposed to be?" The pastor responded, "*That* was the preaching of the gospel!"

Another parishioner located me on social media and sent the following message:

Father Nutt, I'm a St. Aedan's Parish member in Jersey City, NJ. I attended the Black History Month Mass yesterday, and I must say your sermon genuinely moved me. The way you emphasized Luke's Gospel message of love and forgiveness while also bluntly acknowledging the racial injustices faced by marginalized groups in this country was powerful to me. Despite the hypocrisy of how the government or even the church has sometimes historically treated us, you implored us to follow Jesus's way to love our "enemies," forgive and, more importantly, persevere. I felt heard, and I felt seen.

Although I'm a devout Catholic who loves the church's theology, liturgy, and rituals, my family and friends have always discussed certain blind spots that exist within the church as it relates to [Black people]. You touched on all of that yesterday, and I thank you. I immediately spread the word to my family and friends and shared the church service video with them. Everyone was just as enraptured as me by your beautiful message and delivery. The passion and honesty with which you laid out everything in the pulpit was invigorating. Thank you for being you and for everything you do to continue to spread Jesus's message of love and forgiveness, despite our trials and tribulations. I pray that God's love and protection continue to cover you, and may his grace and mercy continue to shine down upon you!

It is vital to notice how two people received my preaching of racial justice and the need to listen, learn, love, forgive, and advocate for a more just and humane church and society and heard it differently. A lady was annoyed by my message and delivery, and a young man was invigorated and "felt seen." Essentially, even though a preacher can be emphatically clear with their message, the listener receives and filters the message through their cultural background and lived experiences. I can only assume that both parishioners were catechized by church teaching and understood the teachings of Jesus, yet had different emotional responses to my homily. A singular homily on the sin of racism heard simultaneously and in the same place can be both challenging and affirming. I assert that Catholic preachers must do a better job of preaching about the sin of racism.

Effective twenty-first-century prophetic preaching demands a more perceptive understanding of race and Christian faith. Within the context of prophetic preaching, the preacher has the dual task of condemning the evils of racism and its perpetrators and bringing hope and healing to those oppressed. Every Sunday, Black people sit in the pews of Catholic churches encumbered by their anxious questions and urgent pastoral needs; this is especially true for those maligned by racial hatred. They sit there hoping that perhaps today, through the preacher, there will be a word from the Lord that will make sense of their harsh realities. Perhaps today they will not only receive spiritual sustenance from the Eucharist amid life's challenges but a word that liberates, affirms #BlackLivesMatter, and demands justice for all. Then and only then can they leave their church pews hopeful, knowing that they have genuinely been envisaged—seen, known, and valued by the preacher as beautiful Black children of God whose lives really do matter.

7 Preaching to a Wounded World

Peter D. Hill

When, at age eight, in the summer of 1989, I made my first trip from the Caribbean island of Dominica to New York City, I loved everything about the Big Apple: the flashy lights of Times Square, the massive skyscrapers, the sounds of the subway, the smell of fresh fruit on the sidewalk stalls, the sound of children keeping cool under the open fire hydrants, and feasting on a McDonald's Big Mac. Little did I know how different New York would seem after I moved to the city ten years later to begin religious formation with the Congregation of the Most Holy Redeemer (the Redemptorists).

Before moving to the United States, I grew up sheltered on a small island home to roughly eighty thousand inhabitants, most of whom are Black. Black people on my island held positions of privilege and power. The small and predominantly Black population instilled confidence that would later be invaluable. I was privileged to attend some of the best schools on my island and to travel throughout the Caribbean, the United Kingdom, and the United States from an early age. I never saw my Blackness as a limitation, as Blackness was all around me. In my majority-Black Caribbean nation, race relations are different. I could not relate to the word *minority* until I moved to New York.

What was and is operational in my home society is *colorism*, what Alice Walker terms "prejudicial or preferential treatment of

95

same-race people based solely on their color."[1] Although I was unfamiliar with the term growing up, I did believe that lighter-skinned children were attractive, and I witnessed and took part in teasing darker-skinned children by calling them names such as *Black as tar* or *Black and ugly*. Colorism also came through in my music playlist, where one song etched in memory is Nardo Ranks's "Dem a Bleach," which examines the reality of women using a variety of skin-lightening creams to lighten their skin. Unfortunately, colorism is still very much active on the island. However, I never felt skin color to be a liability or limitation as much as I experienced after moving to the United States.

Life in America

"See me and come live with me are two different things." This Caribbean adage summarizes the difference in my experience between visiting New York City at age eight and living in the same city ten years later as a young Redemptorist. As a boy in New York City, I had remained shielded from the realities of American life. As a boy, the people I interacted with, the foods I ate, and the churches where I worshiped were predominantly Caribbean. Vacationing among the Caribbean diaspora in New York did not fundamentally challenge that experience. Not until I lived in the United States did I come to experience and witness—though only partially understand—the complexities of race relations and racism in America. When I was first called the N-word, I thought this blatant disrespect and silencing of my voice was simply people being rude and ignorant, not realizing the deeper machinations at work.

Years later, I can now say that the work of Catholic priest and theologian Father Bryan Massingale has enlightened and broadened my thinking in this area. Massingale believes that most

---

1. Alice Walker, *In Search of Our Mothers' Gardens: Womanist Prose* (New York: Harcourt, 1983), 290.

Americans have a "commonsense" understanding of racism: "Person A (usually, but not always, white) consciously, deliberately, and intentionally does something negative to person B (usually, but not always, Black or Latino) because of the color of his or her skin."[2] This understanding was the lens I used at first to interpret my experiences. I saw racism "as personal acts of rudeness, hostility or discrimination usually but not always directed against persons of color."[3] When I was called derogatory names and told to go back to Africa, I interpreted this as people being ignorant.

However, Massingale challenges us to go deeper in understanding racism to recognize its broader implications. He speaks of a "culture of racism" at work in the United States. He writes, "Racism functions as a culture, that is, a set of shared beliefs and assumptions that undergirds the economic, social, and political disparities experienced by different racial groups."[4] This culture of racism perpetuates a belief that whites are superior to non-whites. Without interrogating this racist culture in depth, one can too easily fall prey to this pervasive system of false thinking. My interpretative journey from commonsense racism to a culture of racism takes time, but this journey is necessary.

A Unique Challenge

When I came as a young adult to New York, whites loved my exotic accent, distinguishing me from African Americans. As I now try to drill deeper into my experience of this cultural cue as a Black man from the Caribbean in America, I can affirm the following insight reported in a research article in the *Journal of Black Studies*: "Many Black Caribbeans may experience a segmented assimilation due in large part to their being something like a model minority,

---

2. Bryan N. Massingale, *Racial Justice and the Catholic Church* (Maryknoll, NY: Orbis Books, 2010), 13.

3. Massingale, *Racial Justice*, 14.

4. Massingale, *Racial Justice*, 24.

. . . an elevated minority status, where they and many others consider Black Caribbeans as 'above' African Americans. This is seen in Black Caribbeans stressing the foreignness in contacts with others, keeping the accents and accentuating cultural cues to distinguish them from African Americans."[5]

The culture of racism in America has preconceived notions of how a Black person should act and sound, and I do not fit that mold. The white supremacist system can grab onto this difference and do what it does best: separate, divide, and conquer. As a friend remarks, white people sometimes believe that enslaved Africans went to the Caribbean on British Airways, while enslaved Africans went to the North American continent on slave ships. The magnetic power of this racist thinking would have me believe that I am better than my African American brothers and sisters. This culture of racism stinking thinking is part and parcel of what theologian Kelly Brown Douglas calls the anti-Black narrative:

> Whiteness as a construct exists only in opposition to that which is non-white. In this regard, it finds its most oppositional counterpart in Blackness. The construct of whiteness thus provides fertile soil for what is perhaps the inevitable flourishing of an anti-Black narrative. Whether inevitable or not, it is only in appreciating the pervasive and distinctive presence and dehumanizing presuppositions of an anti-Black narrative ensconced within this country's collective psyche that we can begin to understand the intensity of white repulsion when it comes to Black bodies.[6]

Comprehending the power and pervasiveness of the anti-Black narrative has been pivotal in my journey. Once my eyes opened,

5. Michael C. Thornton, Robert Joseph Taylor, and Linda Chatters, "African American and Black Caribbean Mutual Feelings of Closeness: Findings from National Probability Survey," *Journal of Black Studies* 44, no. 8 (2013): 802.

6. Kelly Brown Douglas, *Resurrection Hope* (Maryknoll, NY: Orbis Books, 2021), 10.

I began to see the workings of the anti-Black narrative all around me. This narrative dictated the non-BIPOC art on the walls of my religious institution.[7] The readings of white European male authors assigned at my various educational institutions needed desperately to be decolonized. The spirituality and ritual of church services offered little to non-white worshipers. Ultimately, the anti-Black narrative opened my eyes to see how systematically society has erased and painted Blackness as subhuman to its normative white standard of humanity.

I am from the Caribbean and Black, and my Caribbean Blackness speaks. However, what is said is irrelevant to white people, as they see only Blackness. The white person who called the police while I was walking down my street from the bookstore did not care that I was a seminarian from the Caribbean—only that I was Black. The professor who kept calling me by another name did not care who I was—other than Black. White persons look at me and see not African American or Caribbean or African—they see Black.

I can only be Black and never white. I cannot and do not want to change my Blackness, and therefore the struggles of my African American brothers and sisters are also my struggles. When I walk into a store and am followed by the clerk assuming I am a thief, when the police stop me for no apparent reason, when my words are not believed versus the same words of my white friends and colleagues, systemic racism cares little that I am a Caribbean Black. The effort I took to be polished and properly dressed, the energy I exhibited in navigating white spaces to accentuate my difference from African Americans, and my intentionality in not befriending African Americans could never make me accepted in the eyes of systemic racism. Therefore, my African American brothers' and sisters' pain, trauma, and woundedness are mine and must be mine.

However, my African American sisters' and brothers' struggles are my struggles not simply because we are Black but because we are human beings. I lived in New York City during the 9/11 attacks. The days immediately after the attacks were some of

---

7. BIPOC: Black, Indigenous, People of Color.

the best days in the city. Though it was a brutal tragedy, people came together beautifully to help others in need. People prayed together, went out in search and rescue, and showed genuine care and concern. We showed the best of our humanity. Likewise, we all are affected by racism because of our humanity. Author, poet, and civil rights activist Dr. Maya Angelou can be found online quoting the Roman playwright Terence: "I am human, and nothing human can be alien to me."[8] This teaching is and must be the crux of our living together. Racism does not only do damage to Black people; racism harms everyone. Our common humanity and the dignity of each human person compel us to preach on racism.

As a Black Caribbean male, the temptation is to say that I am not from this country and this issue is not mine; however, this attitude perpetuates the racist system. This issue is my issue because I belong to the human family. It is everyone's issue because we all constitute the human family. We all hold the imprint of God. Racism seeks to eliminate the humanity of non-white people. It also destroys the humanity of white people. To be effective preachers against racism, a belief in our common humanity is, therefore, of the essence.

Working Gospel

Living in the United States has exposed me to some of the brutalities of racism and the wounds it causes. I have titled this chapter "Preaching to a Wounded World" because our world is wounded and in need of healing. The sin of racism destroys all of us, and preachers, anointed by the Holy Spirit and the power of God, are called to proclaim the Good News of Christ to this broken world. To do so, preachers need to ask this fundamental question: Who is the God we preach?

Although the task may sound pedestrian, I believe all preachers would do well to articulate their operative understanding of God proclaimed in the pulpit. African American homiletician Frank

---

8. Terencius Lucanus, *"Homo sum, humani nihil a me alienum puto."*

Thomas addresses this reality, and his observation is worth pondering at length:

> My goal is to help preachers become honest about the fact that all preachers have a "working gospel" and, if they are not careful, their working gospel becomes embedded in the cultural and religious dominance hierarchy. When we present our working gospel as "the gospel" and thereby seek to make our interpretation normative for all people, we make a working gospel part of our dominance hierarchy. We operate out of a pseudo-legitimacy as definers of the authoritative interpretation of the text and ignore the fact that there is such a thing as heresy. From the perspective of marginalized people, heresy is a working gospel that serves to justify privilege, racism, institutional discrimination, conquest, seizing of land, extermination and enslaving of people, the theft of resources of empire, and the like. A tremendous amount of conflict and violence is caused by a belief in the superiority of one's own gospel as the complete and conclusive Gospel.[9]

My working gospel comes from two primary sources. First, I am formed and steeped in the religious charism of my Redemptorist Congregation. In 1732, St. Alphonsus Liguori founded the Congregation of the Most Holy Redeemer in Scala, Italy, with Luke 4:18 as its foundational text: "The Spirit of the Lord is upon me, because he has anointed me to bring good news to the poor. He has sent me to proclaim release to the captives and recovery of sight to the blind, to let the oppressed go free." My working gospel as a preacher prioritizes the poor and the oppressed in society. More so, it communicates a message of healing and hope, as Luke's Jesus comes to usher in a new way to live and be in God's kingdom. I seek to preach this liberating God to a wounded world—God on the side of the oppressed, marginalized, and poor, but also God who is madly in love with all humanity. Not all homilies and

---

9. Frank A. Thomas, *Surviving a Dangerous Sermon* (Nashville: Abingdon Press, 2020), 3.

sermons that I preach will be on the wounds of racism; however, keeping Luke 4 in mind serves as an interpretive lens of reading Scripture and a reminder of my call to preach a message of Good News to the world.

Second, I have been formed in my preaching life by Henri Nouwen's *The Wounded Healer.* In this classic text, Nouwen reflects on what it means to be a minister in contemporary society: "Since it is his task to make visible the first vestiges of liberation for others, he must bind his own wounds carefully in anticipation of the moment when he will be needed. He is called to be the wounded healer, the one who must look after his own wounds but at the same time be prepared to heal the wounds of others."[10] Although Nouwen does not specifically address the topic of preaching, I think he would agree that effective preachers must come in touch with their wounds.

Preaching to a Wounded World

Systemic racism is one of the deep wounds plaguing American society. Its harmful effects targeting Black people are everywhere. The senseless murder of twenty-five-year-old Ahmaud Arbery while jogging in the Satilla Shores neighborhood of coastal Georgia, the murder of George Floyd by a police officer in Minneapolis, also in 2020, and the 2022 mass shooting of ten Black people in a supermarket in Buffalo are only a few examples. We all can list so many more.

How does one preach the Good News of Jesus Christ to a world wounded by systemic racism? As a Black Caribbean male, how do I preach the Good News of Jesus Christ in my adopted home? My working gospel compels me to bring together my formation as a Redemptorist and my ministerial posture as a wounded healer while firmly rooted in my Dominican-Caribbean heritage.

As a moral theologian, St. Alphonsus believed in the inherent dignity of each human being. He taught that God is "madly" in

---

10. Henri J. M. Nouwen, *The Wounded Healer* (New York: Image Books Doubleday, 1979), 82.

love with all God's children. Preaching to a wounded world starts with this conviction that God created us all in his image and likeness and that God is madly in love with us. No one is excluded, and no one has a monopoly on God's love. As Jesus announces his mission to go out and preach the Good News to the oppressed, I also share in this mission of Christ flowing from my anointing at baptism and ordination.

In addition to recognizing all people's inherent value and dignity, I believe knowing and spending time with poor, marginalized, oppressed, and BIPOC people is necessary so that we can experience, know, and understand their lives. In my last semester of studies to obtain my master of divinity degree, I was required to take a course outside my Roman Catholic tradition. I chose to take a course in Black studies at Howard University School of Divinity in my consortium. All fifteen students were Black—my first time sitting in an all-Black classroom since I left my home country seven years prior. I had become used to sitting in majority-white classrooms with different rules. I learned so much as I interacted in this all-Black class—listening to their stories of racism, their joys and hopes, and the future they dreamed of for America. This physical closeness provided a source of personal growth and understanding that could not have happened otherwise. Massingale reminds us: "Racism fractures the unity of the human family, violates the human rights of individuals and groups, and mocks the God-given equal dignity of human beings."[11] Conversely, genuinely interacting with everyone, especially those who are different from us, can help us recognize our shared humanity.

Nouwen believes that one's wounds are a source of community and healing for others when we truly embrace our brokenness:

A Christian community is therefore a healing community not because wounds are cured and pains are alleviated, but because wounds and pains become openings or occasions for a new vision. Mutual confession then becomes a

---

11. Massingale, *Racial Justice,* 127.

mutual deepening of hope, and sharing weakness becomes a reminder to one and all of the coming strength. . . . Community arises where the sharing of pain takes place, not as a stifling form of self-complaint, but as a recognition of God's saving promises.[12]

We preach as wounded healers when we can directly point to the sin of racism and call out the pain and damage that racism does to BIPOC. As a young Black male from the Caribbean, I came to the United States identifying as a Caribbean individual. I initially did everything to distance myself from being seen as an African American. In my mind, this was something good. I felt unique, special, and better than African Americans. I quickly learned that in a world where white supremacy and structural racism rule, whatever type of Black one is does not matter. As someone who came to this country naive about race relations, I became wounded and scarred by the numerous racist encounters I experienced.

However, these wounds have made me highly conscious and proud of my Blackness and heritage. These wounds made me proud to research my ancestry, to learn that I am 29 percent Togolese, 26 percent Nigerian, and 21 percent Cameroonian. These wounds also triggered an excitement to engage with the Black Catholic intellectual tradition by joining the Black Catholic Theological Symposium, a society dedicated to the fundamental humanity of all persons within the Black Catholic experience. Instead of destroying me by making me doubt my identity and worth, these wounds have planted my feet firmly in the richness of my Blackness. In the words of Sister Thea Bowman, these wounds woke me to realize that I come to my church "fully functioning."[13] Furthermore, as a Black person, I should never be ashamed or made to apologize for my Blackness; instead, I should always take pride and share the richness of the Black tradition with everyone.

---

12. Nouwen, *The Wounded Healer*, 94.

13. Thea Bowman, address to the United States Conference of Catholic Bishops (June 17, 1989), www.usccb.org.

Therefore, as a wounded-healer preacher, I constantly strive to be attentive to the places of pain and suffering in society—to the suffering mothers whose sons die because of police brutality, the women of color attacked for no apparent reason, or the families losing homes to gentrification. All these examples illustrate the real wounds caused by systemic racism.

Ultimately, preaching to the wounded world is all about preaching hope. Racism steals hope from people. Our hope is Jesus Christ. Amid our world's woundedness, we preachers point to places of life, healing, and newness in Christ. Coming from the Caribbean, where the racial situation is not the same as in America, I grew up witnessing Caribbean people, white people, Indigenous people, and people of European and Middle Eastern backgrounds all get along and work and play in the same spaces, respected and contributing each in their own way to society. So much is possible for us if only we embrace God's call to be children of God. This image of togetherness fuels my hope.

I come to the project of preaching racial justice as a Black male from the Caribbean with a particular history and background. I am not African American, though I have descended from enslaved African people. I do not have the experience of listening to my ancestors telling stories of horrid systemic racism, lynching, and other atrocities committed against Black people. Growing up Black in my island home of Dominica was not without its blind spots, but I had access to opportunities. Moving to America sensitized me to a very different racial reality in which racism is a profound and deep social wound. Racism not only wounds; it kills. Racism obliterates the Black human spirit, and it kills Black bodies. To preach the Good News of Jesus Christ and offer words of hope in this deadly world is to unequivocally affirm the beauty and blessing of Blackness and to prophetically and unapologetically proclaim that Black lives matter. However, we, as preachers, must first be in touch with our wounds, the wounds of our people, and the ways we wound one another. Most of all, we must become open to the healing and liberating mercies of Jesus Christ so that we might witness his saving power in our lives and our world.

8 The Counsel of Two Black Bishops

James Pierce Cavanaugh

Several years ago, when I was still in formation to become a priest, Bishop Edward Braxton came to speak at Aquinas Institute of Theology, our Dominican school of theology in St. Louis, Missouri. He addressed the racial divide in the Catholic Church and possible ways to bridge it. I remember being especially eager to hear what he had to say, his being one of our few Black bishops in America. Two years later, the summer following George Floyd's horrific death, I was assigned as a transitional deacon to St. Katharine Drexel Parish, a vibrant Black parish in Chicago's South Side. I cannot possibly convey fully and with justice here the tremendous impact such an experience had on my preaching formation. What I *can* say, however, is that I am sure that the St. Katherine's community was far more generous with me than I ever could have been with them. The summer next, I returned to celebrate one of my first Masses of Thanksgiving in that same community as a newly ordained priest. You can be sure that the event was joyful and boisterous, and I am certain I will always look upon it warmly in memory. In these experiences and others, what strikes me particularly is the vibrancy and strong and wise faith of Black Catholics. And yet the Black Catholic community—in particular the African American Catholic community—is *doubly* marginalized in the United States today. Black Catholics make up about 4 percent of the Catholic population in the United States; what is more, within the broader Black *Christian* community, only 8 percent are Catholic.[1] This double marginalization is a source of sadness and pain for Black Catholics today: doubly indeed are their voices muffled out in this large chamber of voices we call a free society. For this reason, I wish to address specifically their voices, to learn the wisdom of their experiences, by turning to two of the few Black Catholic bishops in America today, whose experiences as shepherds must reflect theirs.

The Role and Witness of Bishops

The Catholic Church's governing structure makes the Black episcopacy's perspective particularly important. The church is a two-handed sort of entity; one hand represents the collective influence of all the baptized, and the other hand represents the governance of the church by its episcopacy. Without a doubt, all Black Catholics, by virtue of their baptism, are called to exercise leadership broadly in the church and world. Our church is a church of *two* priesthoods: the priesthood of the laity and the priesthood of the ordained, the one ever at the service of the other. As the episcopacy (the bishops) are to be representatives and witnesses to the faith of their communities, Black bishops are essential for our understanding the experiences of Black Catholics in general. Of the men consecrated to this order of bishops in the United States, only twelve are Black. Given the space limitations of this chapter, two will be represented here. For help in choosing, I turned to two Black Catholic priests—Father Paul Whittington, OP, and Father Maurice J. Nutt, CSsR—in determining which two bishops to converse with. I remain grateful to these two excellent men for their invaluable support and advice in constructing these pages.

Bishops Joseph Perry and Fernand Cheri, the two bishops I was privileged to speak with, communicated to me the importance of the Black Catholic experience in America today. Their words serve as witnesses not only to this overall experience, but also to their

---

1. Bryan N. Massingale, *Racial Justice and the Catholic Church* (Maryknoll, NY: Orbis Books, 2010), 94.

pastoral responsibility as designated guardians of Catholic faith and teaching. In particular, they have weighed in on the racial divide of our church, and also on racism in America. The only way to heal these wounds and erase the error and sin of racism in our midst forever is if we allow such Black leaders to show us the way. This chapter is meant to underscore and amplify their voices in the midst of our society and culture.

Bishop Joseph N. Perry

Bishop Perry, an auxiliary bishop of Chicago, is a man with a deep and thoughtful disposition, exceptionally patient and obviously wise. He speaks clearly and concisely; I have the sense that he is a man who thinks out whatever he will say before ever saying it.

Bishop Perry was inclined to focus on the problem at hand through a theoretical rather than a personal lens. Yet he *did* provide a story from his days as a young priest when he was concelebrating Mass with an auxiliary bishop—a story I believe worth sharing. He and the bishop were with a mainly white congregation in the diocese. At some point early in the Mass, the bishop stated that a certain segment of the population, namely, a population of color, was missing from their number. Perry said that the congregation "froze up" at that point; in fact, he describes himself freezing up a bit, as well. The comment, it seems, did not have the overall effect the bishop had desired, and this experience stayed with Perry. While he is staunchly committed to the prophetic role of the bishop and the need for such a witness in today's church, Perry thinks other techniques are far more effective at getting such a point across. Perry has spent his life considering what methods work. For me, this spells out another significant characteristic of Perry: his sensitivity to thought and language and its effects on the various communities in his care. His solicitude in this way allows him to speak successfully and with nuance to all peoples, even when, in his role as bishop, he rises to prophetic speech.

For Perry, original sin is the one and true obstacle to racial reconciliation. "Humans being humans," he says, "the human condition fosters in us an inclination out of which people still are prompted to say, 'I don't want these people *next door*; I don't want them in *my* space; no one can tell *me* how to live.' It amounts," he adds, wistfully, "to sinfulness in the human condition." Bishop Perry does not speak from the vantage point of despair; this is where grace, "God's medicine," can work to transform the human soul toward holiness. Racism is not unassailable, according to Perry; only God's grace can break the deep inclination toward sin and undermine the racism in our hearts and in our culture.

"Systemic racism" is a term that has entered into common parlance in recent years. For Perry, it is a term that sets the agenda for much of the discussion concerning race relations. "When you use the term *systemic racism*," he says, "you're talking ultimately about a bias rooted in life; a bias that wants to ensure that not all can reap the fruits of life equally." In the United States, the roots of systemic racism stretch as far back as slavery. "In this country," he says, "going back to the enslavement of Africans, it has been a Black and white issue that even today we haven't gotten over, even despite laws we've enacted." Perry says it is impossible for us to treat systemic racism without acknowledging the role of Christians, including Catholics, in sustaining it. However, in his view, there were, fortunately, *some* limitations set on racism. "When Blacks were brought over, slave masters brought the slaves into their religious experience. Baptism didn't necessarily win other privileges for them; it didn't win their personal freedom or self-determination, but it in any case provided some fundamental understanding that these people *had souls*."

With the eventual abolition of slavery in the United States, there came an opportunity for the evangelization of a people who had together borne this evil and suffering. Indeed, the Vatican saw the opportunity clearly, but its encouragement to evangelize the formerly enslaved peoples was not heeded nearly enough. "Rome wanted the U.S. bishops to attend to the evangelization of former slaves," Perry notes, "but this did not occur to the extent Rome thought it should. The church had priests, brothers, and nuns who ministered to the Black community. But there was no corporate program for evangelization of Blacks by the Catholic Church in America."

Moreover, there was a resistance to incorporating Black Catholics into the clergy and hierarchy. "Certain visionary priests and nuns foresaw that Blacks needed their own clergy," Perry says. "But the system didn't allow Blacks to be received into many things. And so, the promotion of Black clergy didn't get underway until late." Indeed, the heritage of such resistance is visible in the Catholic Church in America today.

The lack of Black clergy, along with the slow growth of Catholicism in the Black community, has resulted in many Blacks turning toward other Black Christian denominations for the interpretation of a Christian expression. For this reason, Perry thinks, the Black Catholic community still bears more of the trappings of Protestant theology and liturgy than other Catholic communities today do. "The Catholic Church was not attractive enough to the freed slaves," Perry says. "So they created their traditions based on the style of the Protestant faith. Among such as these, ministers emerged according to that ecclesiology and style, whereas the Catholic Church had a much more stringent structure and style. And not receiving Black clergy didn't help." This picture presented is a dire one, and Bishop Perry puts it succinctly in saying: "We have the idea today that most Black Christians are of a Protestant persuasion, and we are."

Yet there is a gap, too, between Black Catholics and Protestants. Nor is this gap, as Perry puts it, insignificant. "With the way that approaches to ecumenism and religious liberty have gone," he says, "the whole landscape and terrain has multiplied, grown. Over time, the Catholic Church has not been seen as the denomination *attractive* to Blacks. And so, on the one hand, we have had to create our own style and culture. Even though the Catholic structure has largely remained un-open to that."

On the other hand, he continues, Black churches have continued to morph into many styles and traditions. "The Christian menu is now very broad. Today, the Black church is culturally defined. It has a freedom and individuality different from sacramental churches, so it is here to stay." And thus, discrepancies between the traditions, Catholic and Protestant, have been allowed to continue to grow. In other words, the gaps between these traditions continue to widen. Such discrepancies ultimately prevent Black churches from speaking with one voice. How can Black Christians maintain a unified voice in speaking about race in such a doctrinally decentralized setting? It is a question with no easy answer and (according to Perry) a distinct obstacle.

Yet even with the acknowledgment of such an obstacle, a further difficulty remains—how to integrate the worship experiences of predominantly Black communities with mostly white ones. Considered separately from questions of ecumenism and Christian unity, the division between the Black and white churches creates a further obstacle to Christian churches together speaking with one voice. "Cardinal George," Perry says, referencing the late cardinal of Chicago, "used to talk about spatial racism; where we've commandeered a space for ourselves and determined that there are people who cannot or should not enter that space, whether public or private." According to such a limitation, people of different races are prevented from being able to encounter one another as mediators of grace. Perry frames the point about grace as a point about space. Once upon a time, Black and white spaces were formally separated by law. Fortunately, such acts of government as the U.S. Supreme Court ruling on *Brown v. Board of Education* in 1954 and the U.S. Congress passing the Civil Rights Act of 1964 have acted to make segregation illegal. Today's spatial separation is not identical to the forced segregation of the past, but the roots of today's separation cannot be easily disentangled from such past practices. According to Perry, an ignored or overlooked spatial segregation still exists in our houses of worship.

"When we get comfortable in our own cocoon," he says, "it takes some courage to break through natural barriers. And when a different group comes in, we think our spaces are invaded. A team of Black students comes into a neighborhood to play white students in school; people in the neighborhood *still* get uncomfortable. But this discomfort . . . it is un-Christian." Perry is clear that the sharing of spaces is a sure path to the reconciliation needed in our society; he is also clear that some shared spaces promote this end more effectively than others. He believes spaces of worship are the most effective of all such spaces: "People can still say that Sunday worship is one of the most segregated spaces among Americans. No one questions this, but it is not Christian." He says this not to demean or dismiss various communities' worship or faith experiences but to emphasize the missed opportunity when people of different backgrounds find it impossible to embrace Christian worship together. Promoting such integrated worship, for Perry, is a necessary path toward reconciliation and also true Christian unity.

But how to integrate worship among various peoples in a day and age that pushes public worship ever more toward the margins? In Perry's view, the culture's de-emphasis of religion or institutional practice of religion is an underappreciated culprit in the enduring racial divide. He calls secularization a kind of sprint toward "complete autonomy" and a disregard of common worship, which remains an unconditional good. He believes secularization, rather than empowering people on the margins (as a common narrative would have it), only further entrenches the racial divide. "Formerly," he says, "Sunday was understood as a shared kind of activity given to God. When we use Sunday for something entirely other than what it was meant for, we take that gift away from God. We focus on the individual at the expense of the community, at the expense of our common duty to God." For Perry, only our Christian heritage is effective enough to undermine the evil and menace of racism, only Christianity and the teachings of Christ. "The Sabbath was created for God, not us," he says. "We're supposed to rest on that day, but it belongs to God first. Give him honor and praise for who he is, and then rest for the remainder of the day. Instead, we have a hyperprivacy that invades our American culture, turning us inward, not outward."

Yet Perry believes that the church retains a powerful instrument: in its institutions of Catholic education. He views Catholic education as a bastion against this secularization, even if the strength of this bastion in recent years has waned. The sort of evangelization and reconciliation that can occur in Catholic schools and educational institutions has proved to be among the most influential forces in our culture at undermining sin and moral decadence. With a decline in its strength, the church's power to work against racism becomes more and more compromised. However, Perry remains hopeful that in the next several decades, Catholics will steadily resolve to strengthen these institutions. Along with evangelization and the promotion of shared worship spaces, he believes Catholic education remains a powerful force against systemic racism in America in our times.

Bishop Fernand J. Cheri III, OFM

I first met Bishop Cheri when he ordained a classmate of mine in New Orleans, where he served as a dynamic auxiliary bishop. I was impressed by his charisma and charm, which shone brilliantly in his excellent and courageous preaching and teaching. Such traits were essential to him in his ministry in New Orleans, where he spent much of his life as a priest and bishop before his death in 2023. Whereas Bishop Perry tended to think structurally and theoretically about racism in our times, Bishop Cheri was much more inclined to consider the problem from the perspective of his own experiences.[2] "I was born and raised in New Orleans," he says affectionately, "in Epiphany Parish. It was run by the Josephites, and I was taught by the Sisters of the Blessed Sacrament. It was a middle-class, Black parish. Most of the folk were masonwork people, carpenters, or in construction work. It was a very protective and supportive community."

Such a protectiveness in his community is of special interest, Cheri says, because that very upbringing in a faithful Black Catholic community insulated him as a boy from experiences of racism. "I didn't have a *real* experience of racism until seminary," he says

---

2. Despite his death several months after this interview, I have chosen to honor Bishop Cheri by reporting his words in the present tense.

matter-of-factly. His youth, rather, belonged to a community of warmth and support, family and friends. "I went to school with a lot of relatives," he says, "so if I got into trouble in school, it got to my mom's house even before I got there, you know?" This network of support and care was essential for his formative years, and these experiences combined to form a deep Catholic faith in a very personal way. "My eighth-grade teacher, for example, was instrumental in my going to seminary," he recalls. Good, loving relationships were the foundation for his faith. An upbringing such as he had points to the essential role of Christian formation outside the home as well as within it. Furthermore, this formation helped build within him a bulwark against the wounds he might have received from experiences of racism later on. This underscores the importance of Christian formation, not only from the perspective of eradicating racism in our midst but also for protecting those people from it, such as those it ordinarily aggrieves.

Racism, however, raised its ugly head when Cheri entered seminary among predominantly white peers. "One weekend, at the college seminary, I wanted to go home and see one of my brothers play football. I asked a classmate to take me to town, as I knew he lived about two or three miles from me. He told me he'd take me across the Causeway, but that he couldn't take me into the city. He was afraid to be seen with me in the city, *because I was Black.*" It was surprisingly only then that Cheri experienced his Blackness as an obstacle to interpersonal relationships. Unfortunately, the incident was not an isolated one. "As a seminarian, I couldn't go into certain churches in New Orleans even," Cheri says. "It was quite clear in those places. I was not welcome." The experience was not exclusive to Cheri, and he readily tells stories of others known to him. "Harold Perry," he recalls, "who was the first Black man in the United States known to be a Catholic bishop, wasn't even allowed to confirm in certain churches. If you want to know how that was allowed, the buck stopped with Archbishop Hannan. *He* let [Perry's exclusion from certain churches] go on." Cheri explained that the church calls for prophets, but so many instead prefer the status quo. "Perry was installed in 1966, and I don't know if you know, but there was picketing outside the cathedral, saying, '*God doesn't want Black bishops.*' And even more explicit than that. Oh yes, he went through a lot as a leader of the church in the South," Cheri adds. "If he was any different as a person and as a Black bishop, I don't think there would have been any more Black bishops than there were. Because of his character and strength, it gave the church the courage to name Black bishops at a time when it was clearly unpopular."

For Cheri, systemic racism is best observed as the destructive force it is in all the various discrimination laws and the enduring enforcement and promotion of spatial separation along the lines that Bishop Perry describes above. For Cheri, this separation is a feature not only of the South but also observable across the whole country. "You'd think it would be different in different places in the country," he says. "But it was pretty much the same, in fact. Martin Luther King Jr. said the people of Chicago could teach the people of the South some things about how to be a racist. Jim Crow–style discrimination was all over the place." Unfortunately, spatial separation became a common experience among the Christian community, especially in houses of worship, and has remained a feature of Catholic worship until today. "There were a lot of Black churches built because Blacks were not welcome in some of these white parishes," Cheri explains. "From Houston to Mobile, you had these Black parishes and schools, partially because of the assistance of Katharine Drexel, partially because of others. These schools and parishes in the South *created* the Black Catholic community." Despite obstacles, Cheri says the Black Catholic community thrived. Distinct ways of looking at the world and even styles of theology grew up within these creative settings. The continued marginalization of such viewpoints prevents the unleashing of such powerful charisms, including the Black charism of healing. Theological viewpoint, Bishop Cheri notes, is often restricted to the perspective of the clergy, among whom Black men are still underrepresented. This underrepresentation still serves as a significant obstacle to the church's prophetic voice.

Furthermore, Cheri thinks that the church hierarchy's sorts of concerns are often not so pertinent to the Black community. "I attend the workshops," he says, "and as a Black Catholic, not one of them is especially significant to me, and it is not a surprise. What does the team of bishops and USCCB staff look like for a typical committee? There are fifteen staff members; fourteen of whom are white, and the other one Hispanic." Representation at the top level is key for promoting reconciliation across the racial divide. The Catholic experience cannot be so narrowly understood, Cheri thinks; only when consideration of that experience widens will greater reconciliation take place. "So, in one meeting, I say the issues don't really address me," Cheri recounts, "and it's a dead silence. Another bishop says to me, 'This'll cause scandal if you pursue this here,' and so I let it go." But he does not, in fact, let it go altogether. "Here's what I mean," he explains. "They say 38 percent of a given diocese is Black. Show me that 38 percent represented in the chancery or on a committee or a council or a board. Show me that, and there's a basis to talk. But if not, there's just such a lack." Cheri speaks this way out of love for the church, a love rooted in his youth, which impels him to speak thus for the sake of the church's overall sanctity. He thinks the church is a powerfully compelling and necessary voice but that it squanders much of its power when it chooses the status quo rather than a prophetic voice. In his view, the church's too-narrow theological frame too often leads to a church that proves unwilling or unable to dialogue with perspectives outside the church's own.

Yet, in Cheri's view, the church's rich anthropology and teachings about the dignity of the human person set it on unassailable ground to speak prophetically. He doubts that the church makes the most of opportunities to employ this anthropology and these teachings. For example, he cites the church's relationship with the Black Lives Matter movement. "I'll tell you," he says, "what we need is to sit down with BLM, and try to understand what their call for justice is all about. We have to see what's truly Christian in the movement and what we as church can proclaim, instead of (for example) merely holding the movement in contempt for its socialist mentality." He firmly believes that much of the Black Lives Matter's understanding of justice can be reconciled with our Catholic sense of justice; in fact, he believes such a Catholic sense could *strengthen* such movements as BLM in their definition and pursuit of human virtue. In Bishop Cheri is a confidence that the Catholic Church's theological heritage and moral teaching have much to offer the current world. His only fear is that if we disregard such movements that are especially popular among young people, we lose the opportunity to speak persuasively and convincingly to the next generation and lose (in their eyes) even more relevance in our world. Instead of fearing ideas or values that are foreign or opposed to our own, we should try to strengthen the *shared* values and infuse a Catholic consciousness into these values to create both greater ground for collaboration and greater opportunity for evangelization. In these ways, whether inside or out, the church can carry out its prophetic mission in the world today and undermine such evils as racism in our midst.

Synthesis

While there may be differences in emphasis or perspective among bishops like Perry and Cheri, my objective here is to provide a brief synthesis of their views in order to spell out a method for the church to engage the culture, if not a solution to the problem of racism.

In a nutshell: the church must better embody that "perfect society"[3] that Paul VI calls forth in *Sollicitudo omnium ecclesiarum*. A "perfect society," on this count, does not mean that the church is somehow morally without fault. Indeed, the *humanity* in our church makes such a "perfection" unrealistic, if not impossible. Rather, it means that the church lives as a *complete* society according to its own sufficient lights. These lights consist in gospel

---

3. See the introduction to Pope Paul VI, Apostolic Letter in the Form of Moto Propio *Sollicitudo omnium ecclesiarum* (June 24, 1969), www.vatican.va.

truths. The church must be a society that strenuously strives to embody these gospel truths and to make these truths manifest in our cultures and societies through convincing and powerful words on the one hand (Matt 28:18–20), and through tireless, compassionate witness on the other (2 Thess 3:13). As such, the church in the twenty-first century must show forth as *prophet* and as *moderator*. In speaking with Bishops Perry and Cheri, what they especially emphasize is the church's call (1) to critique the status quo and cultural "orthodoxies" that run against gospel truth while also (2) to serve as a fair-minded, engaged mediator in the exchange and flow of ideas. As prophet, the church must object to behaviors and customs that run contrary to gospel truth and the human call to holiness; and as listening and fair-minded moderator, the church must preside over conversations in such a way as to draw forth whatever is good in them.

The church, as "perfect society," scatters its reflection throughout all the nations. In eschewing any *contemptus mundi* attitude, the church draws all peoples to itself and promotes free and fair discussion; in serving as a chastening power that re-kindles the conscience—the voice of God in our hearts—the church can undermine unholiness in our midst. For racism, we must recollect, is at root unholy; it is ungodly; it is an affront to the Holy Spirit who dwells in each of us (Matt 5:22). Both Bishops Perry and Cheri suggest that the church, if it is to be the dynamic force it is called to be in our world, must first strengthen itself *from within*. In this way, it will impress its visage on all societies and reflect its image throughout all nations.

9 Preaching Empathy to a White Congregation

Michael A. Meyer

A February 2021 Pew Research Center study confirms what most preachers already know: racism is one of the pulpit's most avoided topics, especially in predominantly white congregations. According to the report, just 42 percent of Blacks have heard a sermon, lecture, or discussion about race relations or racial inequality in the past year. That figure rises to 47 percent in Black Protestant churches but falls to 41 percent in Catholic churches and 35 percent in white/other Protestant churches.[1] A more recent Pew study identifies a more sobering statistic: only 18 percent of white Catholics say that they had heard a sermon, lecture, or discussion about race in church in the prior year.[2]

Few preachers would deny a moral obligation to address the sin of racism from the pulpit. Indeed, in *Open Wide Our Hearts*, the United States Conference of Catholic Bishops committed themselves to preach *regularly* on racism and *directed* priests and deacons to do the same.[3] Yet, the Pew studies confirm that their

---

1. Pew Research Center, *Faith among Black Americans* (Washington, DC: Pew Research Center, 2021), 12.

2. Pew Research Center, *Black Catholics in America* (Washington, DC: Pew Research Center, 2022), 13.

3. United States Conference of Catholic Bishops, *Open Wide Our Hearts: The Enduring Call to Love—A Pastoral Letter against Racism* (Washington, DC: United States Conference of Catholic Bishops, 2018), 28, www.usccb.org.

commitments and directives remain unfulfilled. While racism, indifference, and fear undoubtedly contribute to the sorry state of preaching about racism, the most significant contributor may be that most preachers do not know *how* to address the sin of racism from the pulpit of a predominantly white community.

This chapter proposes preaching empathy as a path to conversion and liberation from the sin of racism. Overviews of racism in a predominantly white church and the psychology and theology of empathy establish a framework for the subsequent discussions of empathic, transformational preaching and the role of the preacher as a leader. A sample homily closes the chapter, offering an example of how preachers might address a much-neglected topic, the sin of racism, from the pulpit of a predominantly white assembly.

Racism in the Predominantly White Congregation

The predominantly white congregation, like the church, is one body consisting of many parts. As a result, at least four attitudes about race are typically present: egalitarianism, explicit racism, unconscious bias, and indifference. Egalitarianism refers to the attitude of people who genuinely believe in and actively promote the equality and dignity of all human beings. Egalitarians acknowledge racism as a sin and work to eradicate it. Unfortunately, this level of moral development is extremely rare,[4] so one can presume the same low presence in a mostly white congregation.

Predominantly white assemblies have their share of racists. Explicit racism is an attitude of racial superiority expressed through racial prejudice, bias, and the active promotion of outcomes that benefit one's race to the detriment of another. While explicit racists certainly exist in the predominantly white church, their numbers are hard to quantify. "Crude and blatant expressions of racist sentiment, though they occasionally exist, are today

---

4. Hing Keung Ma, "The Moral Development of the Child: An Integrated Model," *Frontiers in Public Health* 1, no. 57 (November 2013): 4.

considered bad form,"[5] so explicit racists often mask their true sentiments publicly.

Individuals with unconscious biases toward people of other races likely comprise a more significant component of the predominantly white church community than egalitarians and racists. Unconscious bias is an indeliberate preference for or aversion to a particular race that influences one's perceptions, attitudes, and actions. Unaware of their prejudices, which developed over time through exposure to racist attitudes and social structures, the unconsciously biased usually express publicly the more egalitarian or neutral attitudes they consciously hold. As a result, they, too, are hard to quantify.

Sadly, indifference may be the most common attitude toward racism in the predominantly white congregation. A 1989 National Research Council report indicates that most whites are simply ambivalent toward Blacks.[6] The indifferent do not see themselves as racists and, therefore, view racism as an issue that does not concern them. Indifference *is* racism, however, when we fail to extend to people of another race "the same recognition of humanity, and hence the same sympathy and care, given as a matter of course to one's own group."[7] This attitudinal pluralism exacerbates the challenge of addressing racism in a predominantly white congregation. Preaching about racism to egalitarians would be very different from preaching to racists or individuals who harbor unconscious bias or indifference, leaving the preacher to negotiate how to reach the many parts of the one Body of Christ.

Racism is a thorny subject among white Americans. Most whites have not experienced racism to any meaningful degree.

---

5. National Conference of Catholic Bishops, *Brothers and Sisters to Us: U.S. Bishops' Pastoral Letter on Racism in Our Day* (Washington, DC: United States Catholic Conference, 1979), 6, www.usccb.org.

6. National Research Council, *A Common Destiny: Blacks and American Society* (Washington, DC: National Academy Press, 1989), 138.

7. Paul Brest, foreword to "The Supreme Court, 1975 Term: In Defense of the Antidiscrimination Principle," *Harvard Law Review* 90, no. 1 (November 1976): 7–8.

We typically are indifferent to, unaware, or suspicious of racism's soul-crushing impact on people of color and how whites benefit from social structures founded on racist attitudes. As a result, discussions of racism often trigger a range of uncomfortable emotions that both preachers and listeners prefer to avoid—defensiveness, embarrassment, anger, and resentment, to name a few. In the end, many whites find themselves "suspended between these opposing attitudes. They are uneasy with injustice but unwilling yet to pay a significant price to eradicate it."[8] Empathy can convert that uneasiness into compassionate action aimed at eradicating racism.

Empathy as a Path to Conversion and Liberation

Empathy is an emotional intelligence competency that helps people connect and show compassion toward others. When we empathize, we step into and, at some level, understand another person's situation without having experienced it ourselves. We appreciate other people's circumstances from *their* perspectives. Empathy adds emotion to sympathy. When we sympathize, we feel bad for people without becoming invested emotionally in their plight. Empathy, by contrast, "requires intimate comprehension of others' inner lives, the context in which they live, and their resulting actions."[9] It fosters positive regard for the predicament of others and a willingness to respond compassionately.

The Psychology of Empathy

Empathy is a relatively new area of study in psychology. German psychologist Theodore Lipps first identified it as a psychological phenomenon in the late nineteenth century, and American psy-

---

8. Martin Luther King Jr., *Where Do We Go from Here: Chaos or Community?* (Boston: Beacon, 1968), 12.

9. Helen Riess, *The Empathy Effect: Seven Neuroscience-Based Keys for Transforming the Way We Live, Love, Work, and Connect across Differences* (Boulder, CO: Sounds True, 2018), 14.

chologist Carl Rogers's pioneering research in the mid- to late twentieth century fostered greater interest in its psycho-social benefits. Today, empathy is the focus of many psychological studies relating to the development of interpersonal relationships and leadership skills.

Empathy involves "a sophisticated integration of many brain regions," including perceptive channels that receive an experience and responsive channels that motivate action.[10] Human beings are hardwired for empathy. Mirror neurons, distinctive nerve cells that fire when we perform an action *and* when we witness someone else acting, are crucial to empathy generation. They make us smile when a baby smiles and hurt when a loved one hurts, though to a lesser degree than if we felt it ourselves. This remarkable characteristic helps us experience other people's pain vicariously without becoming so overwhelmed that we cannot assist them.[11] Empathy teaches us to avoid harmful situations and motivates us to help those physically, psychologically, or emotionally in need.

While we often think of empathy as a state, a phenomenon, or an emotion, it is more like a three-stage continuum—cognitive, emotional, and compassionate—that "moves human beings from observation to action."[12] The cognitive phase of empathy involves knowing and understanding another's experiences, thinking about feelings, and putting them into perspective. The more curious a person is, the more cognitive empathy they likely will have. Yet, cognitive empathy alone can result in a "too-cold-to-care phenomenon," the failure to internalize perceived experiences that causes us to become so detached that we are not motivated to act on them.[13] Cognitive empathy, then, is most beneficial when it triggers emotional empathy.

---

10. Riess, *Empathy Effect,* 14, 15.

11. Riess, *Empathy Effect,* 18.

12. Helen Riess, "The Science of Empathy," *Journal of Patient Experience* 4, no. 2 (June 2017): 76.

13. Daniel Goleman, "Hot to Help: When Can Empathy Move Us to Action?," *Greater Good Magazine* (March 1, 2008).

Emotional empathy arises when perceived experiences become, to some extent, the perceiver's experiences. This stage of the empathic continuum arouses the physical, emotional, and psychological states of others in our bodies.[14] We feel other people's pain, though not to the extent that it inhibits the action that arises in empathy's compassionate phase. Compassionate empathy is the "tender response" to the perception and internalization of another's suffering.[15] It is empathy in action—the critical, motivating aspect of empathy.

From an evolutionary perspective, Helen Riess explains that empathy inspires people to reciprocate helpful behaviors that promote the species' survival.[16] It connects people, fosters pro-social behavior, and develops critical interpersonal and societal support systems. While most people exhibit some degree of empathy, we are not always empathic. Empathy fluctuates, and overexposure to certain conditions can numb our empathic responses.[17] We also tend to offer our most profound empathic concern to people with whom we share the most in common, so-called in-group bias. This affinity toward people of the same ethnicity, religion, class, level of education, and political affiliation can limit our empathy for and willingness to offer compassionate assistance to people with whom we have less in common—so-called out-groups.[18] In-group bias is empathy's most criticized weakness and a root cause of racism.

Fortunately, empathy can be taught most effectively by example. Empathic behavior "can change the brain chemistry of both leaders and followers by creating an interconnectedness of thoughts and feelings."[19] As Carl Rogers observes, "A high degree of empathy

---

14. Daniel Goleman, "What Is Empathy?," in *Empathy*, ed. Harvard Business Review (Boston: Harvard Business School Publishing, 2017), 5.
15. Riess, "The Science of Empathy," 76.
16. Riess, *Empathy Effect*, 18.
17. Riess, *Empathy Effect*, 25.
18. Riess, *Empathy Effect*, 33.
19. Riess, *Empathy Effect*, 149.

in a relationship is possibly *the* most potent factor in bringing about change and learning."[20] Based upon Rogers's groundbreaking work, psychologists have developed myriad training programs to cultivate empathy in teachers, medical doctors, therapists, and business leaders. The theology of empathy shows that preachers should be empathic leaders, too.

The Theology of Empathy

The theology of empathy begins with divine empathy, God's merciful activity toward humanity. Divine empathy encompasses the classic biblical expressions of divine action, including *chesed*—merciful love; *agape*—unconditional love; compassion—suffering with; and redemption—deliverance from evil. As Edward Farley explains, if redemption is "a reconciling love imparted to human relations, and an emancipating norm of justice for oppressed groups, that which redeems is a kind of compassion, an acting on behalf of needy others." [21] Our redemptive God, therefore, is perfectly empathic. Divine empathy is boundless and universal—it extends to all who suffer without regard to privilege, class, gender, or race. It fosters cooperative relationships among God, humanity, and all of creation in the image of the Holy Trinity's cooperative relationship. It reveals itself most fully in Jesus Christ.

Jesus Christ is divine empathy in the flesh. Through the incarnation, God draws close to the weak and helpless, becomes one of us, takes our oppression as God's own, and transforms our slavery into liberated existence.[22] As fully human, Jesus experienced illness, pain, oppression, marginalization, suffering, and death not simply as an observer but in his very being. As fully divine, Jesus expresses

---

20. Carl R. Rogers, *A Way of Being* (Boston: Houghton Mifflin, 1995), 139.

21. Edward Farley, *Divine Empathy: A Theology of God* (Minneapolis: Fortress Press, 1996), 295.

22. James H. Cone, *God of the Oppressed*, rev. ed. (Maryknoll, NY: Orbis Books, 1997), 71.

divine empathy without qualification or restriction. In Jesus, then, divine empathy and human empathy are "inconfusedly, unchangeably, indivisibly, inseparably" joined.[23]

This intimate interplay of divine and human empathy is most evident in Christ's limitless compassion for all. Compassion is empathy in action, the willingness to "suffer with" and do all in one's power to offer comfort and ease the suffering. Without compassion, "the Jesus story is incoherent, and a life inspired by the Gospels is impossible."[24] Moved to compassion by the suffering of others, Jesus cures the sick, heals the lame, and makes the blind see, often crossing social boundaries to do so. Jesus's healing miracles do not come from mere sympathy. As Bryan Massingale observes, "Compassion arises not through an avoidance of suffering, but from a deeper entering into it."[25] For this reason, Jesus *suffers with* humanity, most profoundly and definitively in his passion and cross. As we read in Scripture, there is no greater compassion than "to lay down one's life for one's friends" (John 15:13).

A theology of empathy would be incomplete without the Holy Spirit, the love, and the agapeic concern that courses through the empathic continuum. The Holy Spirit is the motivating force that inspires us to understand and internalize the emotions of others and moves us to act compassionately toward the needy. In the empathic continuum, the Holy Spirit speaks to the soul, which Polish philosopher Edith Stein understood as the immutable component of the psychophysical person created for empathy.[26] The Spirit actualizes the soul's latent potential "to allow the psychophysical person to become the fully realized manifestation of their actual spiritual person."[27] It inspires us to shed all presuppositions

---

23. Farley, *Divine Empathy,* 283.

24. Bryan N. Massingale, *Racial Justice and the Catholic Church* (Maryknoll, NY: Orbis Books, 2010), 115–16.

25. Massingale, *Racial Justice,* 114.

26. Edith Stein, *On the Problem of Empathy*, trans. Waltraut Stein; 3rd rev. ed. (Washington, DC: ICS Publications, 1989), 110, 109.

27. Eric McClellan, "Edith Stein: Her Empathic Theology of the Human Person," *Pacifica* 30, no. 1 (2017): 27.

and prejudices that interfere with empathy. This transformative process is the salvific conversion that moves us from racist attitudes to empathic compassion.

The gospel of Jesus Christ demands conversion. The familiar words "repent, and believe in the Good News" (Mark 1:15) reflect the essential human response to the life, passion, death, and resurrection of Jesus Christ. It is the "ever-present task of each Christian."[28] Indeed, as homiletician James Henry Harris observes, "The resurrection is the most powerful symbol of liberation because it implies transformation and change in the most comprehensive and enduring way possible."[29]

While "repent" is an accurate translation of the original Greek word used in Mark, *metanoeite* further signifies conversion, a change of heart, and a radical turnabout that invites a new way of life.[30] Harris explains that this call to conversion "means that we are to change attitudes, change hearts, change our focus, our traditional thoughts, change our understanding, our perspective, change our practices and the way we understand our relationship to others."[31] We see this radical change in the conversion of St. Paul, who, following an encounter with Jesus, turned away from his life as a foremost Christian persecutor to become the Apostle of Christ to the Gentiles. As Harris explains, "One can't authentically hear the gospel and not change. The gospel demands it!"[32]

The empathic continuum is all about change. Each phase of the continuum presents an opportunity for radical change: from ignorance to awareness of other people's suffering (cognitive); from insensitivity to feeling their pain (emotional); and from hostility or indifference to "suffering with" and offering assistance (compassionate). Indeed, compassion is the sure sign that the empathic

---

28. NCCB, *Brothers and Sisters to Us*, 10.
29. James H. Harris, *Preaching Liberation* (Minneapolis: Fortress Press, 1995), 31–32.
30. Jim Wallis, *The Call to Conversion: Why Faith Is Always Personal but Never Private*, rev. ed. (New York: HarperCollins, 2005), 4.
31. Harris, *Preaching Liberation*, 20.
32. Harris, *Preaching Liberation*, 21.

continuum has been completed, that the radical conversion demanded by the gospel has come about. Every Christian preacher, in one way or another, preaches conversion. Preaching against racism deserves no less. The psychology and theology of empathy lay the groundwork for preachers to address this challenging subject from the pulpit. We next consider how.

Preaching Empathy for Conversion and Liberation from the Sin of Racism

Preaching, at its core, strives to foster an encounter with God that leads to the conversion of minds and hearts. The Word proclaimed and preached plays an indispensable role in actualizing that encounter because preaching is a revelatory act. It identifies the real presence of the trinitarian God among the assembly in its particular context. Preaching empathy to address the sin of racism in a predominantly white congregation, then, seeks to reveal the real presence of divine empathy in the community and cultivate empathy among the members of the congregation empathically. It does so through preachers who are empathic leaders.

Preaching to Cultivate Empathy

Cultivating empathy requires considerable sensitivity and time. While one or more preachings can speak to divine empathy and promote the understanding, emotion, and compassion that foster empathy toward people of other races, the successful journey through the empathic continuum requires continuous interpersonal dialogue and relationship building. Leah Schade's sermon-dialogue-sermon process, developed to address challenging subjects from the pulpit, like racism, offers a model that encourages both.[33]

Schade's approach begins with a church forum that introduces a difficult topic's key concepts and challenges, followed by prophetic preaching that places the subject in its scriptural and

---

33. Leah D. Schade, *Preaching in the Purple Zone: Ministry in the Red-Blue Divide* (Lanham, MD: Rowman & Littlefield, 2019), 73–140.

congregational contexts. This phase develops the knowledge and understanding associated with the cognitive stage of the empathic continuum. Next, the congregation and the preacher engage in deliberative dialogue, discussing the issue, expressing and listening to concerns, assessing courses of action, and formulating a community response. This step kindles the emotional component of empathy, where community members learn to experience the issue as others experience it. Lastly, follow-on preachings prophetically proclaim the community's stance on the subject and its commitment to address it, reflecting the development of empathic concern and leading to a compassionate, communal response. This sermon-dialogue-sermon model helps address racism in a predominantly white community by encouraging dialogue and interpersonal relationships where knowledge, emotional investment, and compassionate response can incubate and grow.

Certain theological and doctrinal principles are essential to developing empathy in a predominantly white congregation through preaching. They include:

- God loves all people equally, regardless of race.
- Every human being is created in the image and likeness of God.
- Jesus's commandment to love our neighbor as God loves us is unconditional.
- Racism is a sin, a failure to honor the God-given dignity of all people and heed God's commandments.
- Individual racist acts, over time, have created unjust social structures that contradict gospel values and perpetuate racism.
- The prevalence of racist acts and systems diminishes us and renders us accomplices to the sin of racism when we fail to act against it.
- The absence of personal culpability for individual racist acts does not absolve us of our Christian responsibility to eradicate racism.

These principles establish the core Christian values that expose racism for the sin that it is. They contribute faith-based knowledge to the cognitive phase of the empathic continuum and provide a foundation from which preachers can address racism and cultivate empathy from the pulpit.

Preaching empathy as a catalyst for conversion from the sin of racism necessarily means preaching God's Word. Jesus *is* divine empathy, and Scripture is replete with God's empathic compassion for all humanity, especially the marginalized. Jesus's words and deeds are our model, and Jesus's model is always divine empathic love. "Love compels each of us to resist racism courageously. It requires us to reach out generously to the victims of this evil, to assist the conversion needed in those who still harbor racism, and to begin to change policies and structures that allow racism to persist."[34]

Empathic Preaching

Love also compels preachers to preach about racism empathically. Racism is a grave matter that demands robust and unequivocal preaching. Yet, like Jesus, preachers are pastors first, pastors who meet the members of their congregations where they are. Preachers, therefore, must have an intimate understanding of their parishioners' inner lives, experience their pain, and offer them the Good Shepherd's compassion even if they are racists, unconsciously biased, or indifferent.

Racism wounds all, including white members of the community. Harris observes, "Oppressors are also oppressed and need to be liberated from the will to dominate others."[35] Thus, preachers in a largely white congregation must empathize with *all* members of the community—the oppressed and the oppressors, the egalitarians, the unconsciously biased, and the indifferent. As the U.S. bishops emphasize, "We must create opportunities to hear, with open hearts, the tragic stories that are deeply imprinted on the lives of our brothers and sisters, if we are to be moved with empathy

---

34. USCCB, *Open Wide Our Hearts*, 18.
35. Harris, *Preaching Liberation*, 25.

to promote justice."[36] While the bishops are speaking about the victims of racism, preachers must listen to all members of a racially and attitudinally diverse assembly because all suffer in their own ways. Standing in the shoes and assuming the emotions of these diverse populations is a tall order but essential to unifying all parts of the Body of Christ against racism.

Empathic preachers must listen *and* choose their words carefully. Preaching is speaking the truth in love (see Eph 4:15). Speaking the truth means not avoiding the harsh reality of racism in our society. Preaching in love means resisting the temptation to wield denigrating, accusatory rhetoric from the pulpit. It means judiciously using words like "white privilege" and "white frailty," which many whites find offensive. While these terms have their place in the dialogue about racism, not all will appreciate the truths that these words reflect. Preachers may need to lead their congregations through the empathic continuum before the members of a mostly white community will be able to receive them empathically.

The Preacher as Leader

Theologians cast the preacher in many varied roles, including prophet, pastor, storyteller, and poet, and each has a place in preaching against racism. Yet, preaching empathy as a catalyst for conversion from the sin of racism especially calls the preacher to be a leader.

Empathic leaders transmit empathy throughout their organizations like a virus[37] because groups tend to behave toward others the way their leader behaves toward them.[38] Empathy begets empathy. Preachers must lead their congregations out of the sin of racism through the empathic continuum and toward the Spirit-

---

36. USCCB, *Open Wide Our Hearts*, 10.

37. Riess, *Empathy Effect*, 150.

38. Carl R. Rogers, *Client-Centered Therapy: Its Current Practice, Implications and Theory*, 70th anniv. ed. (London: Little, Brown Book Group, 2020), 348.

driven conversion that manifests itself in fervent compassion and a willingness to right this senseless injustice. How do preachers lead in this way? Walter Burghardt explains: "Our people should sense from our words and our faces, from our gestures and our whole posture, that we love the crucified communities with a crucifying passion; that we agonize over the hardness of our hearts, our ability to 'eat, drink, and be merry' while a billion humans go to bed hungry; that the heavy-burdened can look to us not so much for answers as for empathy, for compassion."[39]

Preachers lead by example. They lead by steadfastly trusting that God will liberate them from their own suffering, guilt, and lamentation toward empathy and conversion. Preachers must lead as Moses did, "trusting that God will indeed enable and empower us to speak the truth about the trials and tribulations of our own people to whoever needs to hear it."[40]

Preaching against racism in a predominantly white assembly can be uncomfortable and even dangerous, but our congregations need to hear it. We need empathic leaders in the pulpit willing to confront racism by promoting empathy among all community members. We need preachers who join their congregations on a mutual journey from dominance and oppression to conversion and liberation. Preaching racism in a predominantly white parish *is* challenging and uncomfortable, which I learned firsthand when I delivered the following homily on Divine Mercy Sunday at the parish where I serve as a deacon. I also learned, however, that the dire need to address racism from the pulpit and the eternal joy of God's liberating grace made manifest in the proclamation of the Word far outweigh any hardships that may accompany preaching the Good News.

---

39. Walter J. Burghardt, *Preaching the Just Word* (New Haven, CT: Yale University Press, 1996), 78.

40. Harris, *Preaching Liberation,* 26.

Divine Mercy[41]

Dallas police officer Amber Guyger returned home after a fourteen-hour shift. Tired and distracted by a phone call, she parked her car in the garage and walked to her apartment. When she opened the door, Officer Guyger was startled by a man sitting in the living room. Ignoring police protocol, she drew her gun and shot Botham Jean twice in the chest, killing him. Botham Jean was sitting in *his* living room eating ice cream. Amber Guyger was in the wrong apartment.

Officer Guyger was tried and convicted of murder a year later. At her sentencing, Botham Jean's younger brother Brandt spoke to Amber from the witness stand. He forgave her and told her he loved her as a person, wanted the best for her, and didn't want her to go to jail. Then, in a remarkable gesture of grace, Brandt Jean asked for permission to hug Amber Guyger. The judge agreed, and the two exchanged a long embrace punctuated by words of remorse and forgiveness, comfort and gratitude. Brandt Jean extended mercy to Amber Guyger. Jesus calls every one of us to do the same.

Today is Divine Mercy Sunday, the day we celebrate the great gift of God's abundant mercy. So what is Divine Mercy, and why does it deserve its own day? Our readings offer some insight. In our Gospel (John 20:19–31), the disciples are terrified, hiding behind locked doors for fear of persecution. Jesus appears to them and mercifully offers them peace—not just any old peace, but *shalom*, the eternal peace that reconciles us with God and gives us the strength and courage to carry that same mercy and peace out into the world. And what happened? Peter and the disciples emerged from hiding, preached the Good News, and cured the sick (Acts 5:12–16). They carried God's mercy to the ends of the earth.

Mercy is the beautiful virtue that extends lovingkindness, compassion, and forbearance to all in need. The Latin word for mercy,

---

41. Homily by the author on Divine Mercy Sunday, Saint Catherine of Siena Church, Pittstown, NJ (April 24, 2022).

misericordia, consists of two root words: *miseria*, which means misery or affliction, and *cor*, which means heart. So, the merciful carry the affliction of others in their hearts. We *receive* the gift of Divine Mercy first from God, whose mercy endures forever. We *witness* Divine Mercy in Jesus Christ, who healed the sick, made the blind see and the lame walk, suffered, died, and rose again to free us from sin and suffering. We *share* Divine Mercy when we "open our eyes and see the misery of the world, the wounds of our brothers and sisters who are denied their dignity, and . . . heed their cry for help!"[42]

The world cries for help in so many ways, but I'd like to address one wound that demands our merciful attention today: racism. While our country has seen much progress over the past sixty years, racists and racist systems continue to disregard the God-given dignity of certain people based on their race, limiting their opportunities and threatening their well-being and even their lives every day.

Racism is a sin. It "blots out the image of God among specific members of [the human] family, and violates the fundamental human dignity of those called to be children of the same Father."[43] As a predominantly white parish, it can be easy for us to overlook racism—most of us have never experienced it directly, and we do our best not to cooperate in it or perpetuate it. Racism, then, may seem like a problem that's out there but not our problem. But we can't forget that some of our brothers and sisters here at St. Catherine's suffer the effects of racism every day. While many of us may not see it or hear about it, they're *living* it.

For Christians, racism is never someone else's problem. As St. Paul tells us, when one part of the body suffers, all the parts suffer (1 Cor 12:26), so the absence of personal fault for racism doesn't absolve us of responsibility for eliminating it. Racism is *our* problem because Jesus calls every one of us to resist and undo

---

42. Francis, *Misericordiae vultus*, Bull of Indiction of the Extraordinary Jubilee of Mercy (April 11, 2015), no. 15.

43. NCCB, *Brothers and Sisters to Us,* 3.

injustices, "lest we become bystanders who tacitly endorse evil and so share in guilt for it."[44] Racism is *our* problem because Jesus calls every one of us to be merciful just as our Father is merciful (Luke 6:36).

How do we do that? We start with a long embrace punctuated by words of remorse and forgiveness, comfort and gratitude. We educate ourselves to better understand the suffering racism inflicts. We pray for Divine Mercy to kindle that spark of understanding into the flame of empathic concern, to help us welcome *their* affliction into *our* hearts. With the help of Divine Mercy, we'll grow to appreciate that not cooperating in or perpetuating racism isn't enough. We won't tolerate it; we'll call it out for the sin that it is whenever we see it, and we'll work to build systems that respect every person's God-given dignity, regardless of race. With the help of Divine Mercy, we will end racism for good. That's why Divine Mercy deserves its own day.

---

44. National Conference of Catholic Bishops, *To Live in Christ Jesus: A Pastoral Reflection on the Moral Life* (Washington, DC: United States Catholic Conference, 1976), 25.

10 Preaching with an Unbridled Tongue

Valerie D. Lewis-Mosley

Woman. Black. Catholic. How do I properly order and unpack these words to describe to my reader the fruits, both bitter and sweet, by which I proclaim the gospel? As a woman, I both witness to my faith and experience the impact of racism through the intersectional lens of Catholicism and the Black church experience. I am called to be fully active and functional in a church that, in practice, does not see me as a reflection of the *Imago Dei*. I am perceived as sacrilegious because my spirituality sees through the eyes of the African diaspora. I am perceived as superstitious because Catholicism is not a mainstream practice within the African American community. I am perceived as scandalous because I am a Black woman, with all the myths that continue to define Black womanhood. I exist in a world that does not value my testimony of faith, my cultural and spiritual experience, or my gender.

With other Black authors in this book, I am on a lifelong journey of reckoning with the sin of racism and exclusion, which theologian Miroslav Volf describes as "undaughtering and unsonning."[1] Nonetheless, my ability to speak with agency has become my platform to praise, bless, and preach through the Dominican spirituality and charism of the Order of Preachers. Black Catholic spirituality motivates my contemplative prayer to active proclamation.

---

1. Miroslav Volf, *Exclusion and Embrace: A Theological Exploration of Identity, Otherness, and Reconciliation* (Nashville: Abingdon Press, 1996), 158.

My Jesuit education has formed my conscience for justice. The matriarchal ancestral roots of my South Carolina Gullah Geechee African ancestors inspire me to speak with an uncompromised voice in the presence of injustice.

I focus here on racism as an impediment to my presence as a Black Catholic woman in the life of the Catholic Church and how "a bridled tongue" hinders the authentic preaching and teaching of a gospel of social justice. Preaching with an unbridled tongue is the action needed to dismantle the silence on racism—a necessary voice crying out in the darkness of the church's silence from the pulpit and lack of action from the pews. Preaching with an unbridled tongue tells the story of what racism does to the mind, body, and spirit. It is the shared narrative of the experiences of being invisible in the Catholic identity. I am not seen and not heard. The church is blind and deaf. Yet, I will speak with a longing to be heard.

What Does It Mean to Preach with an Unbridled Tongue?

We Black Catholic laywomen come to our church with the mantra "fully functioning" and knowing "who we are and whose we are." Black women struggle with identity, ownership, empowerment, and leadership, and racism impedes our visibility and voice in the Catholic Church. These concerns are not new, so I am on this journey to preach with an unbridled tongue. I wish to speak in a voice that does not stammer at the truth of how the church has harmed Black and Brown peoples by the institutionalized and individual practices of racism.

By faith, I wish to challenge the cultural divide within a church fractured by the sin of racism and fueled by a false narrative that Black lives do not matter. This narrative, perpetuated by white supremacy and the church and our country's idolatry of whiteness, prevents my personhood from being visible and negates the legitimacy of my existence. Though ministers of the gospel receive a charge to preach and teach truth, I rarely hear a sermon in a

Catholic Church on racism. When I do hear racism discussed, it is by Black clergy. As a cradle Catholic, I can say that for sixty-five years, I have not heard preaching and teaching engage in a dialogue about race. I have countless experiences of coming to Mass hoping to receive refuge from the trauma experienced by the onslaught of attacks on Black bodies, but with no promise of justice. I leave those liturgies feeling even more downtrodden than when I arrived.

The public square is more in tune than our preachers, telling the truth about oppression and exclusion. Church voices have been on mute. We hear a sanitized proclamation of the gospel—a mouthing of pleasantries in homilies that do not disturb. When a preacher does speak about racism, we hear an outcry of objection instead of an Amen. I have experienced white parishioners walking out of church on these occasions. Black priests have been transferred out of dioceses and sent back to their religious societies for daring to preach a gospel of social justice that proclaims Black Lives Matter. Preaching on human dignity and the sanctity of life disregards Black lives who are at risk because of racism, police brutality, inequitable access to health care, inadequate education, and disproportionate imprisonment.

What Does It Mean to Be Authentically Black and Catholic?

This question precipitated my return to the church. Three generations of Black Catholic ancestors precede me. They were instrumental in building a historically Black Catholic parish in Jersey City in 1930 during the Great Migration. I am the great-granddaughter of matriarchs who took action as Catholic laywomen to create a haven where the sin of racism could not hinder them from sacramental participation in the life of the church. Still, they were excluded and denied the sacraments in Catholic parishes. The agency of my matriarchs was not enough to protect me from the experiences of racism. I did not expect to be shielded from the racism in the world, but I did believe that my church would provide a secure zone for me to practice and witness my faith without impediment. This naive belief changed for me in the early 1970s.

In October 1968, *Ebony* magazine published an interview of former Black Catholic religious sisters. Patricia Grey (formerly Sister M. Martin de Porres, RSM) revealed the trauma and injury these sisters experienced within Catholic convents because of racism and hate.[2] A subsequent article by Saundra Ann Willingham (formerly Sister M. Melanie, SNDdeN) was published by *Ebony* in December 1968: "Why I Quit the Convent."[3] Reading about this experience shattered my heart and left a profound rift within my spirit. I began to question my high regard for the Catholic Church, and over the course of years, I began to drift away from the institutionalized church.

Unseen as a Black woman in the sacred spaces of the church and unheard in its homilies, I felt *undaughtered* by the church. I struggled internally to preserve my mental health. How could I be truly Catholic in an institution that seemed to have erased me as a Black woman from its sacred narrative? My spirituality and faith in Jesus and the sacramental life of the church did not waiver. Yet my desire to give public witness to that faith came to a complete pause.

The Black Catholic Clergy Caucus released this statement in 1968: "The Catholic Church in the United States, primarily a white racist institution, has addressed itself primarily to white society and is definitely a part of that society. On the contrary, we feel that her primary, though not exclusive work, should be in the area of institutional, attitudinal and societal change."[4] Reading this years later provided me some solace in knowing that I had

---

2. "An Awakening of Catholic Nun Power," *Ebony* (October 1968): 44–50.

3. Sandra Ann Willingham, "Why I Quit the Convent," *Ebony* (December 1968): 64–74.

4. Black Catholic Clergy Caucus, "A Statement of the Black Catholic Clergy Caucus," in *Black Theology: A Documentary History, Volume I, 1966–1979,* ed. James H. Cone and Gayraud S. Wilmore (Maryknoll, NY: Orbis Books, 1993), 230, www.wherepeteris.com/statement-of-the-black-catholic-clergy-caucus-1968.

not imagined the emotions and isolation I had felt. As theologian James Cone observed, "The document was ignored by the Catholic hierarchy, apparently with the hope that its authors would come to their senses. But the Black Catholic Clergy Caucus refused to accept silence."[5] If this statement had been readily available to the laity in 1968, it might have changed the exodus of so many Black Catholics from the faith.

My struggle with living my faith as a Black woman who is Catholic was one that I battled in silence. I loved the spirituality of my Catholic faith and witness. It became a question mark when I became conscious of the church's complicity and silence on racism. The lack of pastoral care made me question my presence as a Black woman in the Catholic Church. I was a young adolescent in the sixties, the era of Vietnam, civil rights, and Black Power, where Black was Beautiful. I developed a consciousness of being young, gifted, and Black. I perceived a disconnect between my culture of Blackness and my faith tradition of Catholicism. The everyday experiences within the overall Catholic culture reflected invisibility when it came to the presence of young Black girls or women. Catholic experiences were synonymous with whiteness. This idolatry of whiteness suggests that the only way to be Catholic is to embrace whiteness. Herein lie the seeds for white racism and Black self-annihilation. By contrast, I needed to forge an identity centered on my Blackness and my voice as a woman. Otherwise, I would have fallen prey to what W. E. B. Dubois terms *double consciousness* (*The Souls of Black Folk*, 1903), Frantz Fanon calls *Black skin, white masks* (*Black Skin, White Masks*, 1952), or Charisse Jones and Kumea Shorter-Gooden call *code switching* (*Shifting: The Double Lives of Black Women in America*, 2004).

The alienation, isolation, and exclusion were not figments of my imagination. I observed that my godparents, who stood at the waters of baptism with me, had left the Catholic Church. They became involved in their adopted Protestant faith traditions as

---

5. James H. Cone, *For My People: Black Theology and the Black Church* (Maryknoll, NY: Orbis Books, 1984), 49.

Baptist and Pentecostal ministers. Their singular response to my question of why they were no longer Catholic was, "Racism is the reason." Racism also almost led me to give up on my faith of origin. Yet my love for the Eucharist sustained me, and it was not something I could give up.

The Black Catholic legacy of having a voice, action, and agency to challenge racism in the church also runs deep within my bones. I had nearly forgotten that. The voice of Sister Thea Bowman raising the question "What does it mean to be Black and Catholic?" motivated and inspired me to become fully active and participatory in the life of the church. The power of her words came from an unbridled tongue seeking to provide pastoral care to the church and its Black Catholics. In her famous address to the Catholic bishops, she said, "It means that I come to my church fully functioning. I bring myself, my Black self, all that I am, all that I have, all that I'm worth, all that I hope to become. . . . I bring my whole history, my traditions, my experience, my culture, my African American song and dance and gesture and movement and teaching and preaching and healing and responsibility as gift to the church."[6]

The racism that almost robbed me of my faith impedes the evangelization mission of the church. To be radically Catholic goes beyond passive acceptance to bring about a discourse of reckoning. Radical Catholics take action and challenge the church with a spirit of renewal. Radical Catholics teach and preach with a spirit of conviction, feeling empathy for the challenges that oppress Black and Brown peoples so that, in Bernard Lonergan's words, "What hitherto was unnoticed becomes vivid and present . . . what had been of no concern becomes a matter of high import."[7]

Black Catholic laywomen's voices, action, and agency are vital. Both society and the church have marginalized us. Statistical data

---

6. Sister Thea Bowman, address to the United States Conference of Catholic Bishops, Seton Hall University, South Orange, NJ (June 17, 1989), www.usccb.org.

7. Bernard Lonergan, *A Second Collection: Papers* (Philadelphia: Westminster Press, 1974), 65–66.

and intellectual dialogues do not provide the embodied experience of our suffering, isolation, and exclusion. The scarring caused by racism goes deep into the marrow of our bones and the core of our souls. The trauma is intergenerational, as noted by the exodus of my godparents from the Catholic Church. This hurt needs to be acknowledged. Our experiences and aspirations need pastoral care and concern.

What Does It Mean to Be Radically Catholic?

Understanding how racism harms the church requires a radically Catholic perspective and identity. The traditional Catholic identity has not created space for the suffering and alienation of Black people. The myopic expectation that there is only one way to be Catholic has contributed to excluding those who look like, think, and feel like me and hurt and suffer like me. To be radically Catholic is a paradigm shift. It means to be fully active in the pulpit and from the pew. I have chosen to adopt a radically Catholic persona. A radically Catholic persona requires a new field of vision, a conversion of one's spiritual eye so that we do not look for a one-size-fits-all idea of what it means to be Catholic. Radical Catholicism is not complacent. We must challenge the perception that excludes Black bodies from being integral to Catholic identity. If I am perceived as not belonging as a Black woman, I am invisible as a vital part of the Catholic community. Whatever gifts or contributions I may have to offer go unnoticed and unwanted.

Still, I bear the responsibility of being a free Black Catholic woman. As Toni Morrison, another Black Catholic woman, once said, "Your real job is that if you are free, you need to free somebody else."[8] This uncompromising work of freedom is captured by the words of Deuteronomy 16:20: "Justice, and only justice, you shall pursue, so that you may live and occupy the land the LORD your God, is giving you." I also take inspiration from the wisdom

---

8. "Toni Morrison Talks Love," *O, The Oprah Magazine* (November 2003): 4.

of Pope Francis, who, in response to the George Floyd killing, said: "My friends, we cannot tolerate or turn a blind eye to racism and exclusion in any form and yet claim to defend the sacredness of every human life."[9]

To preach with an unbridled tongue involves sharing the embodied experiences of what racism is. We also need an appropriate biblical hermeneutic for this project because Scripture is the foundation for the preacher. We must formulate a Christian imagination and moral disposition in applying the Scripture that opens our lips to preach justice so that we may praise God in truth. Aligning the narrative of our lives with that of Scripture, we hope to tell the story of racism and its traumatic impact within the Body of Christ, the church, with a redemptive impact. An unbridled tongue and a radically Catholic identity go hand in hand. Without compromise, we call out sin and challenge injustice. By so doing in us, God lifts us from destruction, rends our hearts, and allows for intellectual and emotional conversion. God casts off our fear so that with an unbridled tongue and a radically Catholic identity, we can speak courageously to rectify the sin and heal the brokenness. Racism exists because the church has failed to dismantle it!

Radical faith in action is needed—radical in the sense of being energetic toward change and addressing the church's participation in the ongoing attitudes that foster racism, white privilege, and white supremacy. This robust faith fully and actively participates in the work and prayer of scrutinizing the thoughts, words, actions, and attitudes exhibited in our day-to-day behaviors. To be radically Catholic goes beyond passive acceptance to initiate a discourse of reckoning with the sin of racism. In a spirit of renewal, how do we rise to the challenge of witnessing to what the church says it is? Our faith requires us to teach and preach with a spirit of conviction and a feeling of empathy for the challenges that bind up and oppress Black and Brown peoples.

---

9. Pope Francis, general audience (June 3, 2020), www.vatican.va.

What Does It Mean to Be Radically Womanist?

Every day, Black women suffer the micro- and macroaggressions of our culture's ingrained prejudice, dislike, and contempt for Black women. These sinful insults and assaults must be spoken of, shared, and unpacked. How will people know and come to understand unless they are informed and made aware of these everyday transgressions? Feminist scholar Moya Bailey describes *misogynoir* as "where racism and sexism meet, an understanding of anti-Black misogyny. The concept is grounded in the theory of intersectionality which analyzes how various social identities such as race, gender, class, and sexual orientation interrelate in systems of oppression."[10]

The attempt to silence the voice of Black people is historical. A bridled tongue has a bit in it to restrain movement and speech. Once bridled, the mouth is controlled and restrained. A physical image of a bridled mouth is that of enslaved Africans whose mouths were affixed with metal apparatus to restrict the speech of defiance and protest. The voice is the vehicle of empowerment through self-determination. It is the mechanism of being able to speak my truth, defend and define that which is vital for my existence. Any time Black Catholic women dare to act in our own agency and voice our concerns in our best interest, even for our survival, it comes at a price. In the words of womanist Catholic theologian Diana Hayes:

> A womanist sees herself both individually and in community, but that individuality, in keeping with her wholistic African heritage, arises from the community in which she was born, shaped and formed. Her goal of liberation, therefore, which is both spiritual and physical, is not simply for herself but for all of her people and, beyond that, for all who are also oppressed by reason, of race, sex, and/or class.[11]

---

10. Moya Bailey, *Misogynoir Transformed: Black Women's Digital Resistance* (New York: New York University Press, 2021), 1.

11. Diana L. Hayes, *And Still We Rise* (New York: Paulist Press, 1996), 140.

We must challenge the perception that excludes Black bodies and voices from being integral to the Catholic identity. The presumption that I am not Catholic because I am a Black woman excludes me from active and full participation in the church. I become invisible. Whatever gifts or contributions I may have to offer go unnoticed and unwanted. Undaughtered, unseen, and unheard, this is what it feels like to be a Black Catholic laywoman in the church.

In choosing to be radically Catholic, I am shifting the paradigm so that my Black Catholic womanist tongue is no longer silent but unbridled as a sincere gift of self to the church. If not by me and others like me, who will raise their voice to boldly speak the necessary truth about how the church has harmed Black and Brown peoples? Preaching with an unbridled tongue, we call for honest scrutiny and discussion about racism in its corporate, institutionalized, and personal manifestations as embodied by the church. Racism is about making Black people invisible, not seeing us, and not hearing our laments of marginalization and suffering. Preaching with an unbridled tongue brings the truth of these experiences to the forefront. We will not be content to merely whisper about them or share them as a signifying lament.

Womanist theologian Kelly Brown Douglas defines a signifying lament as "one that allows an otherwise powerless people to speak the truth about life and their own oppression in a coded way that hides the real message from those for whom it was not intended."[12] Whenever the elders of my home parish discussed how their faith community of Christ the King was formed, they would lower their voices almost as if whispering to say, "You know this church was built because of racism. We were rejected at many of the Catholic churches, so we built our own church." The elders muffled their voices when speaking about racism. Was it fear or shame? Was it

---

12. Kelly Brown Douglas, "Black and Blues God-Talk/Body-Talk for the Black Church," in *Womanist Theological Ethics*, ed. Katie Geneva Canon, Emilie Townes, and Angela Sims (Louisville, KY: Westminster John Knox Press, 2011), 118.

an inability to call out the sin of racism, or was it conditioning to not speak out in protest against the church?

Now is the time for prophetic lament. Although we did not create the sin, nor are we ultimately responsible for fixing the problem, we must come to terms with any complacent complicity that embodies racism and contributes to self-annihilation. The silence and whispers are no longer acceptable. Appropriating the language of a poem from an anonymous slave narrative, I declare we must cut loose the stammering tongue that hesitates from calling out the cognitive dissonance between the faith professed and the faithless actions practiced in the pulpit and the pew. The mission of preaching with an unbridled tongue and being radically Catholic is a call to put the concerns of those unsonned and undaughtered by racism at the center of the church's concern.

> Go in peace, fearing no man, for lo! I have cut loose your stammering tongue and unstopped your deaf ears. A witness shalt thou be, and thou shalt speak to multitudes, and they shall hear. My word has gone forth, and it is power. Be strong and lo! I am with you even until the world shall end. Amen.[13]

13. From an anonymous slave narrative, epigraph to *Cut Loose Your Stammering Tongue: Black Theology in the Slave Narrative*, ed. Dwight N. Hopkins and George Cummings (Maryknoll, NY: Orbis Books, 1991), v.

Part III
Ancestors and Stories

Introduction by Deborah L. Wilhelm

But this is the covenant that I will make with the house of Israel after those days, says the LORD: I will put my law within them, and I will write it on their hearts; and I will be their God, and they shall be my people.

—Jeremiah 31:33

One day our neighbor, a firefighter, was called at the last minute to help with a wildfire, and her kids came over to spend the day. The fire's smoke kept us all indoors, so we made zucchini bread, worked a puzzle, and talked a lot about dogs—but even after all that, we still had hours that needed filling with something that didn't involve their worrying about their mom. So scrounging up some leftover scrapbook paper in various colors and patterns, I offered to teach Dax, Karly, and Cady how to fold an origami heart. Why a heart? Well, that's the only thing I know how to fold! For the next two hours, we sat around the kitchen table, drinking many sodas (part of the joy of being not-the-mom), making hearts of all sizes and colors, and then writing little messages on the fronts. When the kids left, they had a paper bag full of hearts-with-words to give to Mom and their other family and friends.

So when the prophet Jeremiah speaks God's message about a new covenant for Israel, with the Lord saying, "I will put my law within them, and I will write it on their hearts" (31:33b), I hear those words in a literal and bodily way. But immediately and surprisingly, God also says, "No longer shall they teach one another,

147

or say to each other, 'Know the LORD,' for they shall all know me, from the least of them to the greatest" (31:34a), and that statement unsettles me. *No teaching*? Those words are not what I expect. After all, I'm a teacher. I'm a preacher. If your kids need to come to my house, I will teach them to fold the one origami item I know how to make (more or less): a heart.

Upon reflection, however, the idea of not needing to teach others how to know God makes sense. And it sounds inviting. The Hebrew word here is a form of *torah*: a word of teaching and heritage, of growing maturity and family relationship. When we truly hear God's teaching—through nature, Scripture, and other people—we recognize it as what-has-always-been-there. God's teaching comes to us in our Scriptures, proclaimed truthfully and boldly. It comes to us in our stories and songs, cherished and shared in our families and communities. It comes to us from our ancestors, some of whom still wait, with voices that may have been long silenced but are not dead, only sleeping. We don't discover this teaching; we only recognize its truth. And that recognition is the focus of this final section.

We are who we are in part because our ancestors were who they were. Therefore, the concluding chapters of this book invite us to look backward, around, and forward, all simultaneously. Writing from the ancestral land of the Kalapuya peoples in Oregon, I invite preachers, teachers, and ministry leaders to consider the influence of our ancestors' stories on our own lives and identities—and to read our Scriptures in ways that listen for the voices of the silenced and create space for them to speak for themselves. Vincent Pastro, a priest who has served the Hispanic community of the Archdiocese of Seattle, speaks to the church's institutional ecclesial racism through his reflection on Our Lady of Guadalupe, the Preaching Woman, who "announces consolation and denounces injustice." He offers a vision of the church that, like the Preaching Woman herself, is strong and beautiful, and who "*is* what she proclaims." A. Anita Vincent follows, giving postcolonial insight for preachers and teachers, drawn from history, Scripture, and her own experience of otherness as a Catholic woman immigrant of color. She offers a fresh interpretation of several Scripture passages as a way of illustrating her invitation to accomplish our own reading through an "other" lens. Lay Episcopal catechist Beth Blackburn assesses the relationship between the developing science of epigenetics and a theology of original sin. She examines the effects of generational trauma throughout our human story and calls us to remember what it means to be one body, the Body of Christ. Bringing the section and the book itself to a close, Resurrectionist Black Catholic pastor Manuel Williams gathers words and songs—"African American songs of resistance and hope"—from his grandmothers. He then challenges us to use both words and music to dismantle white supremacy so that nation and church can finally be free and just.

It's time to learn that God's word has already been written on our hearts. Metaphorically speaking, we *are* ourselves hearts with words—God's words. Only when we recognize that truth can we begin to live it. Just for a moment, envision a world where we know in our bodies that God's word is written on our hearts—yours and mine and our beloved ones and even our less-beloved ones—that God's words inform every heartbeat everywhere. Perhaps that vision sounds naive or foolishly optimistic, but it turns our eyes to see our connection to the divine mystery that breathes us into life and calls us back to its eternal self. It is real but not yet complete. So we teach and preach and lead until the days arrive when these ministries are no longer necessary, and we live God's word as written on every heart, starting with our own. As you read this final section of the book, its contributors offer that prayer for you today: that God's word, written on your heart, comes alive in your prayer, in your comings and goings, in your preachings and teachings, in your conversations and your interactions and your daily grind and your moments of awe. Please, then, read on.

11 A Holy and Sacred Journey

Deborah L. Wilhelm

Today I write from the Willamette valley in western Oregon, ancestral land and home of the Kalapuya peoples—among them the Chemapho, Tsankupi, Chelamela, Winefelly, and Mohawk. These people have lived here since time immemorial and still live here today. In the words of this text, I hope to honor with gratitude the land itself and the Kalapuyans—those who live here today and those who were forced from their sacred homelands. I also hope to honor other displaced Indigenous peoples who now call this valley their home.

The headline stretches across the first page of the society section in a small-city newspaper: "Daughter of Pioneer Family Wedded." The photo beneath shows a pale, slender bride clothed in a white, long-sleeved, silk taffeta dress, pearl-drop earrings, and a movie-star smile. In her hands, she holds a small white Bible and a crystal heirloom rosary. The year is 1960. The place is Oregon. The bride is my mother. And I? I'm barely an idea in my parents' minds yet, but I am already a "someone" without even yet having to exist. Asleep in the future dreams of my parents, I will awaken into birth as another generation of this pioneering family.

Like my mother, I am a daughter of pioneers. Or a daughter of colonizers. Take your pick.

Sleeping alongside the Ancestors

Learning Oregon history in Mrs. Daniels's fourth-grade classroom, I was proud of my daughter-ness. My people were hardworking.

Courageous. Intelligent, ambitious, generous, forward-thinking. My great-great-grandmother and her physician husband had completed the perilous journey West along the Oregon Trail in 1850. They had adventured in wagon trains because the Donation Land Act of 1850 had offered free land to white settlers (a single white male could claim 320 acres; a married man, an additional 320). My ancestors came to get their share, 640 acres of Willamette Valley beauty and fertility.

Once here, the family flourished. They grew crops, milled lumber and grain, built businesses, and re-shaped the Willamette Valley into their Edenic vision and the agricultural powerhouse it is today. They blossomed into generations of faithful, observant Catholics.

But as you already know, the land that Congress "donated" to white settlers wasn't the government's to give. It had been home to others for many thousands of years. Nevertheless, nearly half a million white settlers undertook the journey West over the next two decades, with perhaps eighty thousand arriving in Oregon Territory to claim their piece of the "donation." By 1851, just one year after my great-great-grandparents arrived, the entire Willamette Valley had been parceled out. My pioneering ancestors staked their claims on the land of the Kalapuya peoples: Chafan, Chemapho, Mohawk, Winefelly. The newcomers' efforts at farming and milling were richly rewarded by a Willamette Valley lushness that existed primarily because the Kalapuyans had been managing the bountiful watersheds throughout their history. My ancestors arrived and built their homes on tracts of land that had been neatly carved up and assigned numbers, without regard for the features of the land nor its dignity as part of God's good creation, let alone the dignity of its people.

It did not take long for all the people who lived here first—fishing, gathering, and hunting in the homelands of their ancestors for fourteen thousand years—either to perish or to survive as a remnant, landless on their own lands.[1]

_____

1. Before contact with white people, Oregon's Kalapuyans numbered perhaps as many as 20,000. Disease reduced their numbers to

Schoolchildren of my era studied the Oregon Trail, but not the genocide at trail's end. Nor did we learn that Oregon, admitted to the Union in 1859, was the only state to enter with an exclusion law already in its constitution, forbidding Black persons to move to the state.[2] We were white children in a white school in a white state. Yes, we eventually learned about the slave trade (junior high school) and the civil rights movement (high school), and of course, we all agreed that prejudice and discrimination were wrong. Naively, as a child I thought, *Well, I'm glad that I don't have any stereotypes about others—and especially glad that I'm not prejudiced.* I was certain that I'd meet some Black people someday and that those people would affirm my not-a-racist self-conviction. The First Peoples, by the way? Those whose land my own ancestors had taken? They never even entered my mind. No wonder: All of those sovereign nations added together formed only a tiny percentage of Oregon's 1970s-era population.[3] Oregon was white, and who can be a racist when everyone is white? After all, isn't my personal attitude of openness and acceptance enough? Maybe you've asked yourself the same question.

The answer: No, it is not.

Listening: *The Move from Somnambulant Unawareness to True Hearing*

It takes a long time to open oneself to the idea that being raised as a courageous, hardworking, generous, forward-thinking person of

---

around 1,000 by 1850, and 344 by 1856. See David G. Lewis, "Counts and Bands of the Kalapuyans to 1856," *Quartux: Journal of Critical Indigenous Anthropology* (2019), www.ndnhistoryresearch.com.

2. Oregon State Bar, "Storywall," *Diversity and Inclusion in the Oregon Legal Profession,* https://storywall.osbar.org.

3. The 2020 United States Census indicates that 1.5 percent of Oregonians self-identified as "American Indian and Alaska Native," and another 2.9 percent as "American Indian and Alaska Native in combination." Another 2 percent self-identified as "Black or African American," and another 1.2 percent as "Black or African American in combination." See www.census.gov.

faith is not a sufficient response to the call of Christ. And the listeners at our liturgies, the students in our classes, and the people in our faith formation programs who see themselves, as I did, in this thank-God-I'm-not-a-racist light (and who doesn't, really?) may not know that God requires us to see beyond ourselves. Instead, they—and we—may live in a state of somnambulant unawareness, holding the kinds of ideas that at first glance might not seem privileged but are:

I've worked hard for everything I have.

I've had to take bold risks throughout life, and I've earned my way.

I'm generous with my time and money to those less fortunate.

My ancestors were discriminated against, too.

I pray diligently that the needs of the poor and oppressed will be met.

I'm not bothering anyone and don't want to be bothered in return.

My family didn't own slaves, so this stuff doesn't apply to me.

The Native Americans' way of life was doomed to fail; they required too much space.

Indigenous peoples weren't exactly perfect; they waged wars and kept slaves, too.

We preachers and teachers, meanwhile, might be tempted to add these:

I don't need to speak about race and racism, or address people of color, because they're not really in my parish or congregation or among my students.

We welcome people of color, and everyone already gets along quite well.

I'd be run out of town if I preached about racism.

Nobody taught me how to do this.

Coupled with *I'm not a racist,* these thoughts allow us to hide out in an untroubled, comforting ignorance. They allow us to avoid facing the truth that simply being born in a certain place, at a certain time, to certain people, bestows or withholds *privilege*—a word that may seem accusatory but that means here, simply, to benefit from these accidents of our birth—even though the descendants of colonizers and the descendants of the colonized are sisters and brothers.

Untroubled unawareness, however, is treacherous. It allows us to look away from the ongoing suffering of those whose lands and cultures, languages and bodies were conquered. It allows us to look away even from our own self-understanding, where we might have to confront our privilege. Untroubled unawareness also allows us to hide from the truth that sin is not only individual but also communal—and, importantly, to avoid examining the culpability of the former in the latter. Naming individual sins (for example, *I lied, I gossiped, I took the Lord's name in vain six times last week, I had impure thoughts*) can create a comforting distance from our communal sins (for example, *my willingness to participate in the widespread disregard for the integrity of our common home, my acceptance of our institutional, cultural, organizational, and ecclesial sexism and racism*). That intellectual distance may ease our minds at the surface, but underneath, we know better. We know that communal sin is still sin. And we know that it's deadly.

And yet, these parallel truths are integral to our Christian heritage and salvation story. From the very beginning of Genesis, the Bible asks us to notice that God creates a place—an actual place, the ancestral homeland and ground for the very first story of our faith. Then God creates people to tend this place. And God provides abundantly for the people, their home, and their descendants. The Genesis story sets up a theological understanding of relationship that hums as a theme throughout Scripture. We preachers, who love Scripture, study it, reflect on it, and dare to speak it among God's people, can become too comfortable with our as-usual understandings and interpretations. These may then settle into mere artifacts instead of living words from the Living God, becoming ossified assumptions that limit God's voice and turn our understandings into idols.

As a preacher and teacher, I have had to take responsibility for recognizing and transforming my unquestioned assumptions about racism, because my journey of faith has stripped them away. I did not go willingly. A few years ago, a group of protestors at our large public university pulled down two statues on campus, a pioneer man and a pioneer woman. For me, a daughter of pioneers, those statues spoke of my heritage. I'd played before them as a child. I'd pointed them out to visitors. The protestors, however, saw those same statues differently: as symbols of a conquering culture that thrived at the expense of the people who lived here first. I didn't want to think of my family as part of a colonizing culture, but the protestors confronted me with a challenge to look harder, listen deeper. This challenge was especially painful because of my longtime work as a preacher, teacher, and writer. *I'm not a racist* (sound familiar?), I thought, *but this protest is wrong.* However, I was deeply reading the Pentateuch at the time, and I began to hear our sacred stories of wandering, warring, and conquering afresh, in ways that invited me to hear the protesters' voices. Ancient Scriptures became new, because I was reading with eyes to see and listening with ears to hear. Perhaps if I (if we) had begun to listen earlier, those whose voices have been ignored wouldn't have to shout.

Awakening through True Listening: Spirit, Scripture, Hearers, Cosmos

Consider, as one illustration, the covenant between God and Abram. God promises Abram that he will be blessed, that he will become a great nation, and that God himself will lead the people to a new homeland—a capacious, fertile land, flowing with milk and honey, promised to Abram and his descendants forever (Genesis 12). Interestingly, the promised home is already filled with peoples: Kenites, Kenizzites, Kadmonites, Hittites, Perizzites, Rephaim, Amorites, Canaanites, Girgashites, and Jebusites—that is, children, women, and men who call it home. At this point, the story begins for me to feel uncomfortably familiar, and my ears hear echoes of the names of the Kalapuya: Chemapho, Tsankupi,

Chelamela, Winefelly, and Mohawk. So I listen more deeply, as a daughter of colonizing settlers, to what is being said, and to what is not being said, to those who are speaking, and to those who are silent. Or silenced.

In our Judeo-Christian heritage, we properly read the Exodus stories as God's liberating intervention in human history. An obscure community of little ones, *anawim*, chosen by God as God's special people, is freed from slavery into the fullness of life, beloved by God. God's promise is providence, progeny, and place—and this motif has lifted and comforted oppressed peoples since the days of its writing. Nevertheless, as scholars, academics, and speakers of the word, we know that our interpretations are never the final word, that they will experience ongoing interrogation—by others and ourselves—and must be open to change.

Our own hearers can help, if we will listen. For example, you might preach about the covenant, the exodus, or the promised land. The member of your assembly whose family has lived in your area for many generations may hear the journey as one of manifest destiny, with the un-chosen or de-chosen people being "othered," for whatever reason, as a necessary sacrifice so the chosen can succeed. Meanwhile, people in your assembly who are descended from enslaved persons may hear the same textual journey as liberation, the saving intervention of God in history to call forward the forgotten and lift the downtrodden. Others may hear the journey as a chance to ponder the dignity of the unheard, perhaps wondering what Sarah thought about all of this covenanting, or maybe even ignoring your carefully crafted homily to wander away on their own interpretive paths. And an Indigenous person in your assembly might identify with the First Peoples of the land of Canaan, reading the journey as an invasion of their sovereign lands by a foreign people and their foreign God. The possibilities are many. We err gravely if we assume that God does not speak through the silent ones in our assemblies, our histories, or our Scriptures, or if we presume to speak for them.

You and I do not cause our listeners to change. God does that.

Nevertheless, preachers are enormously privileged (especially in Catholicism, where half of the potential ministerial population is born pre-disqualified from clerical vocation—and thus the vast majority of Catholic homiletics—because it is female). When any of us stand up to preach, teach, or lead, the entire room is (theoretically) listening—at least until we bore, offend, or otherwise alienate them. As those charged with proclaiming God's Good News, we are also charged with what Vincent Pastro in his chapter calls "denouncing." As a preacher, I understand denouncing as resisting what *is*, in service of what *is good*. We may fret that the situation is hopeless, that structural sin is too big for us to tackle, or maybe that people aren't spending enough time praying the rosary. Such distractions may allow us to forget that the suffering ones are our sisters and brothers and that all of us are commanded to resist this suffering in our thoughts, words, and actions, following the Christ who lived that message among us. We resist people and organizations that are unjust. If we are privileged, we resist relaxing into that privilege or descending into a lazy, ineffective, guilt-ridden, liberal (especially white) self-recrimination. We resist our own fear, and preach instead boldly, truthfully. With God's word breathed into our lungs, our speech must come from and return to listening, so that the voices of all God's beloved community can be heard.

The Soteriology of Waking: Restored, Fed, and Unbound

This message is a hopeful one! Our words and examples can become icons of transformation and relationship, and the connections among words, place, life, and identity are vital for this awakening. Here in Oregon, Esther Stutzman, a Kalapuya and Coos storyteller, says that one reason to learn an old language is its connection to the place it was spoken. "We believe," she says, "that languages are the breath of life and the breath of identity, and the more [of] your own language you can speak, the more it connects you with the land and your ancestors."[4] People—white people with the authority of place in higher education—had said that the Kalapuyans were gone and that the Kalapuyan language was dead. Neither statement is true. Kalapuyans are reclaiming their identity and their language, which Esther Stutzman and others describe as merely sleeping. They are working to awaken it by cataloging transcripts of old conversations, listening to a few priceless audio recordings, and releasing a multivolume Kalapuyan dictionary.

In other words, they are listening to the voices of their ancestors. They are waking the sleeping words, re-claiming the names of their geographic markers, re-writing themselves into the books of history through their own lens, because a language is so much more than just words. Language reflects reality and embodies culture. But it does more: language creates reality, creates culture. And even more: language addresses time—it connects us to the generations who preceded us, to the world around us that is our home, and to our hopes and dreams for the future.

Listening to ancestors is what we do, too—it is our Judeo-Christian heritage to hear and share the "breath of life and the breath of identity."[5] We believe in the God whose word spoke into being everything that is, who came as Word in flesh, who is still speaking to us today. From silence came everything, through the word. And words are still what we preachers have, to speak our own lives into a message for the world. The privilege of speech is effective only to the extent that it proclaims the gospel in the voice of the entire community on behalf of those who most need good news. As the Kalapuya peoples reclaim their sleeping language, its breath of life and identity, we all awaken to the knowledge that, ultimately, our own language is God's very self.

Indeed, waking the sleeping is a salvific metaphor. It is God's plan, echoed over and over in Scripture, and as such becomes a

---

4. Karen Richards, "Ancient Oregon Languages Being Nudged Awake" (December 18, 2018), KLCC NPR for Oregonians, https://www.klcc.org.

5. Richards, "Ancient Oregon Languages."

point of access for those of us who teach and preach. The metaphor illuminates God's saving desire for restoration and the interworking of God and human beings and their communities.

The Word of God is a powerful instrument in our struggle to free ourselves from the comfort of injustice for the healing of our sisters and brothers. Consider, for example, two famous raisings from death in the Hebrew Scriptures. The ancient peoples, in death, "slept with the ancestors," and the miraculous raising of two children includes pointed restoration to their mothers: When Elijah restores life to the widow of Zarephath's son, the text says that Elijah "gave him to his mother" (1 Kgs 17:23). Later, when Elisha restores life to the Shunammite woman's son, he calls the mother to him, saying, "Take your son" (2 Kgs 4:36). This restoration to the mother is a foreshadowing of our return to the God who gave us life—and, in a continued metaphorical reading, a restoration to the living ancestors and the living place of God's providence.

The concept of restoration to the mother continues in the New Testament. When Jesus restores life to the widow of Nain's son, Luke notes that "Jesus gave him to his mother" (Luke 7:15). And when Jesus raises Jairus's daughter, he restores her to her mother and father both. We begin then to see the intimate interworking between God and humanity, for as soon as the child awakens, Jesus says to her parents, "Give her something to eat" (Luke 8:55). The interworking is perhaps even stronger in John's Gospel, where Jesus goes to the tomb of his beloved friend Lazarus, and before the miracle tells the people, "Take away the stone" (John 11:39). He calls forth the dead and then gives another command to the mourners: "Unbind him, and let him go" (John 11:44).

But perhaps one of the most vivid restoration stories in Scripture is that of the dry bones in Ezekiel. In his vision, Ezekiel, the mortal one, is commanded by the Lord God, the Holy One, to call a valley of dry bones to hear God's word. Ezekiel does as he is told, but it is God who brings the bones to life, giving sinew, flesh, and breath. God, who has promised them new hearts, new spirits, pulls them from their graves: "'I will put my spirit within you, and you shall live, and I will place you on your own soil; then you shall know that I, the LORD, have spoken and will act,' says the LORD" (Ezek 37:14).

We are, all of us, sleepers in need of waking, especially those of us who have benefited from the privilege of whiteness and who have not yet heeded the call to hear God's words. Pulled from our graves, from hearts of stone we receive hearts of flesh. And the gospel message is equally clear: Once we are awakened, God commands us to roll away the stones that keep others in their graves. We are to unbind the ties that bind them, that hide them away in tombs, that limit them, that deprive them of their freedom and grace as beloved children of God.

Whose voices are we not hearing? This is the question that every preacher should bring to every preaching. These voices are not dead, but merely sleeping, like the little girl healed by Jesus. We don't have to put words in their mouths, nor should we. But we do have to ask the question and listen for the answer. And when we ask, the human cognitive imperative requires us to ponder—and to wait, patiently and humbly, for the sleeping voices to awaken, to provide the space for these voices to test the range and lyricism of their words, to create the environment that encourages them to speak with an expectation of being heard rather than harmed. We cannot remain in untroubled unawareness. Rather, we listen for God to speak from the silence, creating over and over again with just a word. When our brothers and sisters are suffering, then Christ is suffering. We name that suffering and its causes and call people to do better. The task is difficult. It is also our vocation.

My understanding of the gospel of Jesus Christ is that the burden of responsibility for justice falls upon the privileged. When Zechariah, for example, questions the angel's prophecy about the upcoming birth of John, the angel takes away his voice. But when Mary asks the angel announcing her pregnancy, "How can this be?," she receives assurance and responds with the Magnificat. Why the difference? Zechariah lives the privilege of maleness and priestly identity; he should know better. If he doesn't lift his voice in praise of God and on behalf of the lowly, he's not doing his job. (Just sayin'.) The words that the privileged one *should* have said are given instead to the poor one (and I cannot help but hear the voices of the statue-removing protestors as I write that sentence). Mary's Magnificat, prayed nightly in our Liturgy of the Hours, is a little-recognized icon of transformation for Christian community.

As a poor person in an occupied land, Jesus could easily have taken the strategy of the revolutionary. But nowhere in his life and teaching does he tell the poor to revolt. Instead, in harmony with all of Scripture, he calls the privileged to yield. If you are in a white body, that means you. If you are in a male body, that means you. If you are in a healthy body, that means you. If you are a preacher or a teacher or a leader in ministry, that means you. And even when the Good News seems bad, it's actually good, because we cannot continue as we have been. All of the sleepers—all of us—are commanded to restore children to their mothers, to give the recently dead something to eat, to roll away stones and unbind burial cloths.

We live in a realized eschatology, the understanding that the reign of God is both "right here" and "not yet." This means more than the basic idea that salvation history is still unfolding (although that is true). It means that—liberated from time and space—past and present and future no longer exist. Our stories, the breath of life and the breath of identity, permeate us. They are awake and alive, just as we are. The sacred journey is for each of us alone, all of us together, and all of God's good creation, and the preacher's work is part of God's holy call to restore us to our ancestors, our stories, our homes with God. Some ancestors have been privileged to speak, while others long to have their words heard, just as some of us today have been privileged to speak while others long to be heard. Have we been listening to only our own ancestors, or to *all* of the ancestors? To paraphrase a thematic question of this book, *Whose ancestors matter?*

A postscript: While this chapter was still in its infancy, my mother died. The daughter of pioneers whose wedding photo opens this essay now rests with her ancestors. We all rest with our ancestors, and in them. And they rest in us. The journey is a holy one, sacred, with preachers to help restore us to God our Home.

A Sample Daily Homily: "To the Victors"
(March 23, 2022, Deuteronomy 4:1, 5–9)[6]

Today I find these lines from Deuteronomy deeply troubling. Maybe it's the word "occupy," which in Hebrew implies possession by force and seems especially distasteful as we watch the ongoing brutality of the Russian war against Ukraine. Moses has just narrated Israel's military victories—and distributed the conquered lands among the conquerors—before this admonishing of the people to obey God's law. What's also disturbing is the promise that the nations will admire the victors and their God, as if religious practice justifies invasion. Today's Scripture sounds a little too much like today's news.

Is occupation really God's directive? Or our interpretation of what God's reign is? What I do know is that this story carries gut-wrenching similarities to ever-worsening stories of the war in Ukraine. Gut-wrenching similarities, actually, to all of the invasions and occupations of one people by another throughout human history. Gut-wrenching similarities, if we're honest, to the genocide and land theft of the First Peoples throughout the United States—including right here where I live in the Willamette Valley, home of the Kalapuya peoples from time immemorial. And now that I think about it: gut-wrenching similarities to every single time that we humans have stood in silence as our sisters and brothers suffer, or as we've used some sick and wrong self-understanding of superiority or God's will to justify oppression or privilege.

Today I can't look away. Neither can you. *We* can't look away. Because feeling gut-wrenched isn't enough. If that doesn't sound

---

6. Deborah Wilhelm, "To the Victors," *The Word: Daily Homilies from the Order of Preachers* (March 23, 2022), https://word.op.org. Used with permission.

like good news, maybe it's because sometimes the Good News is a smack upside the head that we need to change for the better. Jesus himself lived in an occupied land. He knew what happens to the conquered, the outsider, the other. He knew what would happen to him. He spoke God's truth and healed the broken anyway. Being gut-wrenched—that is, compassionate—is a start. Conversion is next, as we actively work to transform our privilege into healing and wholeness for all. Only then can we say that we have truly heard God.

12 Guadalupe and the Beloved Pueblo

Vincent J. Pastro

The town of Santa María del Tule, in the state of Oaxaca, Mexico, is a small settlement on the main highway leading from Oaxaca City to Mitla. Directly off the road, the central plaza holds the feature that gives the town its name—the Tule tree. In sheer bulk, the tree is perhaps one of the largest in the world (more than 170 feet wide) and certainly one of the oldest (at least two thousand years old). This large Moctezuma cypress, which I have seen myself, is known in the Indigenous language as the *ahuehuete*, the word for "cypress," meaning *upright drum in water*.[1] The Tule is a tree of life, having witnessed more than two thousand years of the *Zapoteca* Indigenous culture.[2] It has also witnessed death from genocide: Shortly after the Spaniards arrived in Mexico in 1519, they began a war of attrition that wiped out an estimated twenty-three million Indigenous in Mexico alone within about sixty years.[3] The European invasion of "conquest" was one of the most egregious events in world history. The number of dead for Latin America, through the war of conquest and European diseases such as smallpox, is mind-boggling: up to some ninety million human beings. We also remember twenty million African people sold into slavery who

---

1. See *New Britain Museum of American Art*, www.nbmaa.org/artists/vistas-del-sur/ahuehuete.

2. The two largest Indigenous groups (among thirteen) in Oaxaca are the *Mixteca* (*Alta* and *Baja*) and the *Zapoteca*.

3. Javier Garibay Gómez, *Nepantla, Situados en Medio: Estudio Histórico-Teológico de la Realidad Indiana* (Mexico City: Centro de Reflexión Teológica, 2000), 207.

did not survive the Middle Passage[4] and six million Jewish people killed by the Nazis during World War II. The diabolical structural evil of genocide continues in regions of our world today.

Those honored by the dominant culture as the great European "discoverers" of the Americas—Christopher Columbus, Hernán Cortéz (Mexico), and Francisco Pizzaro (Peru)—were, in fact, assassins who maimed, raped, robbed, and killed their way through the great multitude of the Indigenous races and lands of the Americas.

The Tule tree of Santa María stands as a silent witness[5] to what happened during those years. Silent witnesses are *martyrs* who shout the truth. This truth, moreover, is not limited to human barbarism. The barren hills, along with the natural beauty presently seen in Oaxaca, are the result of the "conquest of Mother Earth," for the Europeans stripped the land of trees, thousands of cypresses, for their project of subjugation. The Tule tree was too large to destroy, so it was left. This great tree of Santa María, symbolic of humanity and creation, stands as a witness to the atrocities that happened then and to this day at the hands of new *conquistadores*.

Tree of death, tree of life. . . .[6]

The Crucified Pueblo

Though geographically distinct, I have often thought that Tepeyac and Golgotha are the same hill. The *Dolorosa* who stood at the foot of the cross on Calvary is Santa María Tonantzin Guadalupe, the Preaching Woman who stands at the foot of the cross of the *pueblo* on Tepeyac. Tonantzin is the Náhuatl word for "Divine Mother."

4. M. Shawn Copeland, *Knowing Christ Crucified: The Witness of African American Religious Experience* (Maryknoll, NY: Orbis Books, 2018), 73.

5. I borrow the phrase from Dietrich Bonhoeffer.

6. James H. Cone, *The Cross and the Lynching Tree* (Maryknoll, NY: Orbis Books, 2013). Although I do not directly cite James Cone's seminal work, this book informs the title of my essay and all that follows.

Tepeyac is the hill in Mexico City where Our Lady of Guadalupe manifested the divine consolation of her gracious accompaniment of the Mexican *pueblo*—the people—and, indeed, of all Latino and Latina immigrants and their children in the United States. Tepeyac, Guadalupe, and the cross are intimately intertwined so that they form a Trinity: *Tepeyac*, the gracious Mother-Father God who accompanies the poor and afflicts the oppressor; the *cross* taken upon the divine shoulders out of love by the Son; and the *Guadalupana*, the Preaching Woman, the divine presence of the Spirit of God who moves where she wills and goes where the *pueblo* follows. This Preaching Woman proclaims the living Word she carries deep within. She is the gospel bearer of the *pueblo*.

I am often asked by liberal white people (of which I am one in skin color—the heart is a different story!) why the crucifixes in Mexico are so vivid, tortured, and bloodied. The answer is that the poor not only *imagine* the crucifixion; they also *live* it—a crucified people, the *pueblo crucificado* in Jesuit martyr Ignacio Ellacuría's powerful words. The poor throughout the world form a solidarity of the oppressed, too many to be enumerated: women, men, children, Mexican, Indigenous and Latin American, African American and Black, Asian, and Brown, Hispanic-Latina and youthful Latinx, gay and LGBTQ, abused women suffering from domestic violence, seniors on fixed incomes, Africans, refugees from war-torn Ukraine. This solidarity has a face: Brown, Indigenous, and beautiful—the face of Our Lady of Guadalupe, the *Morenita* (the beloved Brown One), Santa María Tonantzin Guadalupe to the Indigenous peoples of Mexico.[7] They stand, with the Preaching Woman, at the foot of the *pueblo crucificado* of the world, asking for her loving consolation and *acompañamiento en la lucha*—accompaniment in the struggle. The words of M. Shawn Copeland regarding enslaved African Americans summarize what the *pueblo Latino* feel about the cross of Jesus:

---

7. See Virgilio Elizondo, *La Morenita: Evangelizer of the Americas* (Clayton, MO: Ligouri Publications, 1981).

Jesus identified with and preached the gospel to those who were poor and afflicted, oppressed and dispossessed: "*Did you ever see the like before, King Jesus preaching to the poor.*" The enslaved people understood the similarity of their condition with that of the Bible's outcast and despised . . . because Jesus himself was beaten, tortured, and murdered, the enslaved people believed that he understood them and their suffering like no one else. They believed that he was one with them in their otherness and affliction, that he would help them to negotiate this world with righteous anger and dignity. They were motivated not out of despair but out of love and faith . . . black people fixed their eyes on Jesus and his cross as they grappled with the absurdity of enslavement. They took Jesus to themselves as one of them; the innocence, agony, and cruelty of his suffering was so very like their own.[8]

We cannot lose sight of the absolute scandal of the cross and the scandal of racism against Brown people and immigrants. As Ellacuría points out, "The death of Jesus and the crucifixion of the people are historical events and the result of historical actions."[9]

Latin American poor have a particular affinity for the cross, bearing in their wounded hearts the genocidal conquest that marks their identity. They carry in their bodies the Pauline stigmata—the marks of Jesus crucified: "From now on, let no one make trouble for me; for I carry the marks of Jesus branded on my body" (Gal 6:17). The cross is vivid. It *lives*. It is one with the crucified Jesus, not only metaphor but reality. In Latin American theology, then, the poor *pueblo* is not only saved. It is also *savior*, for it is the crucified Body of Christ:

The crucified people have a double significance: they are victims of the sin of the world but also those who cooperate

8. Copeland, *Knowing Christ Crucified,* 49.

9. Ignacio Ellacuría, "El pueblo crucificado: Ensayo de soteriología histórica," *Revista Latinoamericana de Teología* 6, no. 18 (1989): 309, https://doi.org/10.51378/rlt.v6i18.5933.

in (its) salvation. The last aspect of the Pauline affirmation "died for our sins and risen for our justification" we will not develop now because [this] study, which looks at the crucifixion, only presents the first stage. The second stage centered in the resurrection of the people will be to demonstrate how the One crucified for sin can bring about in his resurrection the salvation of the world. There is no salvation from the simple event of the cross and death; only a people that lives, because they have risen from the death inflicted upon them, are able to save the world.[10]

Santa María Tonantzin Guadalupe, Preaching Woman *par excellence*, stands at the foot of the cross of the *pueblo* and is one with them in their crucifixion. She manifests the divine Spirit that raises the Crucified One to life—*vida*—in the *pueblo*. The Preaching Woman has two roles with the *pueblo crucificado*. First, she stands at the foot of the cross of Jesus and the *pueblo*. She is *consuelo, auxilio, y defensa*, divine consolation and protection. Second, she denounces the ones who crucify and invites to *metanoia*, conversion, change of heart: "Go tell the bishop," she says to Juan Diego Cuauhtlatoatzin, the One Who Speaks Like an Eagle, the one chosen for her manifestation. *Consuelo y defensa* for St. Cuauhtlatoatzin; *metanoia* for the bishop. She is the Preaching Woman full of the Spirit.

Preaching Racial Justice

My concern in this chapter is institutional ecclesial racism. Preachers, because we are ecclesial, denounce the racism in the church and console the victims of racism. I have been privileged throughout my ministry to take up the Holy Preaching, to denounce and console on behalf of the *pueblo crucificado* Brown immigrants and their children in the United States. Like the Tule tree, I have witnessed oppression—sadly, an *ecclesial* oppression. The Brown

---

10. Ellacuría, *El pueblo crucificado*, 15.

immigrant is "invited" to be a part of the community but on the conditions mandated by the dominant: speak "our" language; live "our" culture; be "church" like we are "church." "We accept them, Father, but they need to learn 'our' language, so there should be no Mass in Spanish." How often have I heard and seen this racism in our parishes. After a Guadalupe celebration that left the church building in perceived "disorder," the white person who was pastoral associate complained about the "mess." We exchanged words, and she accused me of calling her a racist. I responded, "You are not a racist, but your attitudes are." This kind of racism is ecclesial and it is institutional. It comes from people who are part of the church community and are not aware of the racism that permeates the white ecclesial institution.

The ecclesial academy is no different. Recently, I witnessed the indiscriminate pause of a highly effective program of Hispanic-Latino formation that had benefited the immigrant Latino community for over thirty years. The Holy Preaching that we proclaim requires us to name the racism underlying such actions for what it is. In this small way, we also participate in the cross that Brown immigrants and their children bear. As the Preaching Woman, Santa María Tonantzin Guadalupe, *Sedes Sapientiae*, accompanies us with her Spirit-filled wisdom. Anyone who ministers with Latino communities in the United States is familiar with her story and importance to the *pueblo*. But often, we overlook the most essential parts: her actions of consoling and denouncing.

When Hernán Cortéz arrived on the shores of Veracruz in 1519, he and his group quickly forged their way to Tenochtitlan, the center of the Mexica Empire. They were at first repelled. But Cortéz returned with a larger group of *conquistadores*, and by 1521 the Spaniards had imposed their rule on the *pueblo*. The friars arrived, accompanying the military *conquista* with the imposition of a new, foreign religion. The sad story of the encounter of the *Doce Apóstoles*—the "Twelve Apostles" who were the first Franciscans in Mexico—and the *papahuaque* (the Mexica priests) of the *pueblo* is vividly told by José Luis Guerrero. When the priests understood that the dialogue was really a monologue, they said,

"Do with us as you will."[11] A religious genocide began. The *Doce Apóstoles* blasphemed against the faith of the ancestors. The *conquistadores*, acting at the behest of Catholic authorities, destroyed the sacred places of worship, razing to rubble temples that had stood for centuries.

Tepeyac was the center of popular devotion to Tonantzin, the "Precious Divine Mother." Dominant Western anthropology classifies her as a "god," but the proper word is *teotl*, meaning a manifestation of the divine. Indigenous theologians today call her pre-Columbian presence on Tepeyac the *semilla de la palabra* (patristic-matristic "seed of the Word"),[12] or better, *la presencia de la palabra* (presence of the Word).[13] Jesus and the Spirit of God were present in Latin America long before the friars' arrival. Tonantzin dwelled on Tepeyac for centuries before the European arrival. Generations of Mexica people worshiped on Tepeyac, where there was a temple to Tonantzin, Mother of *Ipalnemohuani*, the Giver of Life.[14] Exotic flowers and birds, cypress trees, and various lush green plants must have adorned the summit of Tepeyac where the temple stood. Unfortunately, we will never know, for shortly after the battle between Cortéz and Cuauhtémoc, the *conquistadores* destroyed all the temples in the area of Tenochtitlan, including the temple to Tonantzin. They also deforested the hill so that nothing remained but emptiness.

It must have been a surprise to Juan Diego Cuauhtlatoatzin, who regularly crossed Tepeyac, when he heard birds singing on a cold December morning in 1531. He wondered whether he was

11. José Luis Guerrero, *El Nican Mopohua: Un intento de exégesis, tomo I* (Mexico City: Universidad Pontificia de México, 1996), 61–67.

12. Manuel Arias Montes, *Y la palabra de Dios se hizo Indio: Teología y practica de una catequesis inculturada y liberadora, una propuesta desde Oaxaca, México* (Mexico City: Editoriales Dabar, 1998).

13. I am indebted to Father José Marins for this phrase.

14. Miguel León-Portilla, *Tonantzin Guadalupe: Pensamiento Náhuatl y mensaje cristiano en el "Nican Mopohua"* (Mexico City: El Colegio Nacional, Fondo de Cultura Económica, 2000), 84.

in *Ilhuicatlalpan*, the "Paradise of the Ancestors."[15] He pondered what this birdsong meant when a woman called him by name. She was Mexica like him, dressed in the clothing of Mexica royalty and wearing the traditional black band of pregnancy around her hands. She spoke to him in Náhuatl, calling him "my most beloved son." He called her "my most beloved daughter." She sent him to the bishop, requesting a "little house" on Tepeyac to accompany the people with her "love, compassion, help, and protection."

This woman, Santa María Tonantzin Guadalupe, is "The Preaching Woman." She preaches consolation to the Mexica and desolation to the oppressor, and the *pueblo* becomes, like her, Holy Preachers, saving divine presence in the world. Copeland says the African American people are "justified by Jesus" to be his saving presence to the racist. Likewise, the Hispanic-Latino people in the United States, "justified by Jesus," are to be his saving sacramental presence. They have a mission—*Iglesia en salida*, as Pope Francis says. They proclaim the Good News of justice to the dominant privileged in the United States. The preaching is a dialogue of "Word" and "Answer." In a theology of the Word setting the tone for Vatican II, Otto Semmelroth, SJ, speaks of the Scripture and the preaching in the Liturgy of the Word as God's Word to the people. The Liturgy of the Eucharist invites the people to a dialogue with the Triune God, for as eucharistic community, they "answer" God in the "return" of Jesus to God in the Eucharist.[16] The Holy Preaching is a dialogue, an intimate conversation among the Triune God, the Enfleshed Word, the community, and the preacher. In the case of Santa María Tonantzin Guadalupe, the

---

15. León-Portilla, *Tonantzin Guadalupe*, 87.

16. See Paul Janowiak, *The Holy Preaching: The Sacramentality of the Word in the Liturgical Assembly* (Collegeville, MN: Liturgical Press, 2000), and Otto Semmelroth, *The Preaching Word: On the Theology of Proclamation*, trans. John Jay Hughes (New York: Herder & Herder, 1965). I am grateful to Janowiak for introducing me to Semmelroth's theology many years ago. The phrase "Holy Preaching" used through this essay is taken from Janowiak's reference to St. Dominic's *Sacra Praedicatio*, the Sacred Preaching.

dialogue is a dance of many partners, much like the trinitarian dance of the Divine Three in *perichoresis*. The Preaching Woman is the Sacrament of the Dance, for the Holy Preaching is, at its core, a dance in which we intimately partner with the Holy Three. Santa María Tonantzin Guadalupe dances with the divine presence of the Trinity, the Mexica, the poor, Brown immigrants, and their descendants "numerous as the stars of the sky" (see Genesis 15), and, indeed, the entire cosmos. Indigenous cosmology especially remembers Mother Earth, *Pachamama*, so deeply wounded by global warming. The Dance's climax is the Holy Preaching—the Sunday event in poor communities, conversations in the base ecclesial communities, marches where the poor demand rights and dignity, or a prophetic Holy Preaching among the powerful and the wealthy.

To better understand what the Preaching Woman reveals, we must look at the language she uses. The first obvious thing is that verbal language is culture and race specific. In the case of Santa María Tonantzin Guadalupe, the language is the Mexica race and culture. The words are tender and compassionate, like the words of Indigenous races worldwide. She does not come speaking the Spanish of the European *conquistadores*. Though the Guadalupe event happened in 1531, its language is the "Eternal Now" of Meister Eckhart. The Indigenous Náhuatl is not only bound to Tepeyac, Cuauhtlatoatzin, and the Mexica of five hundred years past. The language of the Preaching Woman is fresh and new each day. It is spoken to Mexican people who know nothing of the original Indigenous languages and to the Indigenous who have retained the autochthonic language. It is spoken to Mexican communities in the United States, where she most commonly speaks Spanish—but also to the Guatemalan Indigenous community in the Mam language. Her language is universal, spoken to African Americans suffering police brutality, to LBGTQ people ostracized by the dominant, to single mothers, to migrants on boats in the Mediterranean or in the desert of the Southwestern United States. She speaks English, Chinese, Swahili, Spanish, Japanese, Thai, Purépecha, Zapoteco, Mixteco, Danish, German, French, and Italian—every language is a means of divine grace. Most significantly, the Preaching Woman speaks consolation and defense to poor communities and rebukes the wealthy and powerful. The language is never exclusive and always inclusive—particularly of gender. The Preaching Woman is Sacrament of the Inclusive God, speaking one way to the Mexican immigrant community, another to African Americans, another to Indigenous peoples, another to women who suffer domestic violence, and another to the LGBTQ community. The preaching language is always different and always the same, for it is the message of consolation (Isaiah 40) for peoples sorely oppressed.

Her language is also that of service and presence. In Indigenous cultures of Oaxaca, the *yya* (pronounced "eeh-yah") is central. The *yya serves* the community.[17] Today, anyone can be *yya*—teachers, mechanics, techs, pastoral agents, or politicians concerned for the dignity of the *pueblo*. *Curanderas* serve through herbs, prayers, and touch, and medical doctors dispense healing antibiotics. The *yya* can be the town catechist or preacher. The Preaching Woman is the *yya par excellence*. Hers is the service of accompaniment, *acompañamiento*, of the *pueblo*. Her image is standard iconography in every Mexican home. She is healing, serving presence, consoling the *pueblo*, carrying the Word wherever divine consolation—or denunciation—is most needed. Her preaching is *prophetic*. It *announces* consolation and *denounces* injustice, racism, and oppression. Prophetic preaching is often associated with denunciation, but the prophets also announced divine consolation: "Comfort, O comfort my people, says your God. Speak tenderly to Jerusalem, and cry to her that she has served her term, that her penalty is paid, that she has received from the LORD's hand double for all

---

17. Andrés Moctezuma Barragán, *Historia de Yanhuitlán y la Mixteca Alta antes de 7 Mono* (Mexico City: Instituto Nacional de Antropología e Historia, 2001), 81–85. Historically, the *yya* was the major leader of the community. The leadership was hereditary. Nowadays, anyone can be *yya*. I am grateful to María Teresa Montes Lara, OP, for her wisdom regarding the meaning of *yya*.

her sins" (Isa 40:1–3). The Preaching Woman consoles the poor
and afflicts the comfortable: "But woe to you who are rich, for you
have received your consolation. Woe to you who are full now, for
you will be hungry. Woe to you who are laughing now, for you
will mourn and weep. Woe to you when all speak well of you,
for that is what their ancestors did to the false prophets" (Luke
6:24–26). This final "woe" of the Lukan Beatitudes is a warning
for preachers. We fear criticism and look for honor, but preaching
is a double-edged sword. Like God's Word, it cuts to the quick:
"Indeed, the word of God is living and active, sharper than any
two-edged sword, piercing until it divides soul from spirit, joints
from marrow; it is able to judge the thoughts and intentions of
the heart" (Heb 4:12). Prophetic preaching, like the Preaching
Woman whose heart is pierced, will lance our illusions and judge
our hearts.

Suppose preaching "comforts the afflicted and afflicts the comfortable," as the old adage says. In that case, the preacher's heart
must be careful as it discerns who are comfortable and who are
afflicted. Comfort is preached to the oppressed and affliction to
the powerful—a summary of prophetic preaching in the style,
the *línea*, of the Preaching Woman. Like the Tule tree, she witnesses the injustice of racism and roundly denounces it. One of
the biggest challenges for preachers in the United States is the call
to preach against racism, especially the hidden racism of the institutional church. The words of comfort for those who suffer racism,
and affliction for those who impose it, are discerned and fired in
the heart of the preacher's prayer. Most significantly, we discern
those places of institutional ecclesial racism, for they lurk in the
dankest corners of the church community. We are, after all, the
people of God, the Body of Christ, and the creation of the Holy
Spirit.[18] We are called to *be* who we are. The sole task of preaching
is to remind us of our identity. Racism has no place in the soul of
God's holy people. Institutional ecclesial racism is *the* sin of the

18. See Vatican II's *Lumen gentium* and Hans Küng's classic *The Church* (New York: Sheed & Ward, 1967).

church. It is found, among other places, in preached words not prayerfully discerned, hurtful words from positions of white male privilege, or the kinds of safe or neutral words that neither console victims of racism nor denounce perpetrators.

Dominant white church communities in the United States seldom think of the radical "we" of Christian community. Preachers are not exempt from this error. The "we" is too easily ignored in favor of the "us" and "them." As a longtime pastor in bilingual/bicultural communities, I would hear the "Monday" complaints from white people about the "messiness" of the parish facilities. One Mexican American pastor I know responded, "Isn't it wonderful our church is being used again," his words re-shaping alleged "messiness" into "community." Institutional ecclesial racism has no place in the "we" of the people of God and must be firmly denounced. Racism is discerned in words that are "nice" but not kind and respectful. One particularly "nice" white parishioner constantly complained about the "Hispanic" community and "what they are doing to 'our' parish." A sweet smile always accompanied the complaining. The necessary confrontation that finally happened was painful for both of us. Preachers are trained in the seminary to be "nice," but such niceness routinely betrays passive aggression that is, at the core, racist. It must be excised from our communities, and the surgery is painful. Father José Marins, the theologian to base ecclesial communities, observed that our parishes are like persons on an operating table. We know that radical surgery will save the patient's life, but we give transfusions (our preaching!) that bring about death. Rather than "niceness," preachers must offer kindness and respect for the human dignity of the oppressed, which ultimately honors all people, including the racist, because it calls us back to "we." Denouncing "niceness" may be difficult, but pastors and preachers cannot overlook the consolation we owe to the oppressed or the denunciation to the oppressor. Our truest "we" cannot tolerate racism and hate disguised as "niceness."

Preaching denounces racism. It places itself in solidarity with the victims of racism. It neither caters to nor mollifies oppressors.

Rather, preaching always seeks, in the spirit of the prophets, the justice of God's reign: "Thus says the Lord: For three transgressions of Israel, and for four, I will not revoke the punishment; because they sell the righteous for silver, and the needy for a pair of sandals—they who trample the head of the poor into the dust of the earth, and push the afflicted out of the way" (Amos 2:6–7). In seeking justice, the church community, like the Preaching Woman, beautiful and strong like the Tule tree, *is* what she proclaims. Like the Living One born of the Virgin, we proclaim the Good News to the poor. The One who was dead and now lives forever (Rev 1:18) sends the Spirit of Love to give life in abundance to dry bones (Ezek 37:1–14). We hear the Living Word of the Risen One, crucified on Golgotha, nailed to the tree of death on Tepeyac. That Word, proclaimed by the *pueblo* and born of Santa María Tonantzin Guadalupe, strengthens us so that our limbs are strong like the everlasting Tule tree of death *and* life, silent witness to the genocide of racism, crying out for justice, dignity, and life.

13 Dismantling the Ecclesial Legacy of Colonial Attitudes

A. Anita Vincent

I look around the church, and I see pews filled with worshippers, almost all older white Americans. The sea of white faces is nearly homogenous but for the occasional appearance of a Brown or Black face, almost like a blemish in this "white garment" that is the predominant face of the Catholic Church in most parts of America. I simultaneously feel forsaken and at home—the "other" in that congregation (and the context that created it) and yet a beloved child of God, called to be in that place for that time. This conflicted feeling is a familiar one. Immigrants' presence in Catholic congregations is mainly unacknowledged, which means vital opportunities for conversations and relationship building are lost. Such conversations often begin with the homily that the community hears during Mass. This chapter confronts the church's entrenched institutional ecclesial racism, both conditioned and intended, and proposes a dialogue of respect that begins with the liturgical homily.

Attending to a Particular Story

As a person of color, a woman, and an immigrant, I have a rich, multilayered, complex, and sometimes unexpected and fresh worldview. As a teacher and catechist, I bring my worldview to the text of Scripture. I do not claim it to be exclusive or perfect because I know that the infinite variety of God's word is far too profound and generative to be limited in its manifestations. Still, I find my experiences and identity hidden, maligned, or ignored—not only in the look of the average parish but also in the use of the biblical text, in the commentaries that preachers use to prepare their homilies, and in the preachers themselves. My scriptural and existential hermeneutic, rooted in my identity as a person of color, a woman, and an immigrant, is complex even before adding the other roles that each of those identities encompasses: I am a mother, wife, daughter, sister, teacher, catechist, cantor, and minister. I am a director of religious education, a student, and a theologian. I am Indian and American. Each of these identities comes with a detailed history—a particular *story*—that entails a specific ontological lens. At any given moment, any of these identities could function in any permutation. Despite the weight of all these ontological realities, however, the fact remains that I am primarily invisible. I live as an immigrant woman of color within a church that tends to pay homage to white men with privilege and power—and the many resources that stem from that privilege and power.

At best, the tension between my life in the church and my lived experience has created ambiguity. Growing up Catholic in India, where a Hindu majority was ambivalent in its view of Christianity, I had always felt like an anomaly. I imagined that living in a self-proclaimed Christian country, where most of the population embraced Christianity (even if split into thousands of factions), would lessen that feeling. Little did I realize that I would be just as much, if not more, of an anomaly in America as I was in India. My faith impeded my being home in the country of my origin. My skin color and immigrant status were impediments to my being home in the country I adopted as my own. I was a stranger there, and I am a stranger here.

In India, my faith caused difficulties in my social life, but that faith was well nourished and nurtured within the Catholic Church in India. Much of the beauty and the rich depth of Indian culture was adapted to Catholic life, providing me with a unique insight into the biblical tradition and the message of the gospel, quite distinct from the hermeneutic of the typical American Christian theologian. The typical preacher, catechist, or parish minister often has no clue that the Bible can be seen through a lens other than that of accepted interpretations from Eurocentric sources. This lack of awareness by priests, deacons, and catechists of the presence of persons whose experience of the Bible and worship is distinct from the dominant culture is more common than not. As an immigrant, I am different from the predominantly white members of my parish (whether in Illinois, Indiana, New Jersey, or Pennsylvania). As a Catholic, I am different from my friends (and the friends of my parents) in India. Few people see, much less understand, the pain that this evokes, especially when I am made invisible and inaudible by the lack of acknowledgment, especially in the church that is my spiritual home. Few people understand the cost of our otherness to the community of faith and the community at large.

Unlearning: De-colonizing a Missionary Story

The poet-theologian Pádraig Ó Tuama describes his exploration of the Book of Ruth as an endeavor "to honor," not "to own" Scripture.[1] He also speaks to language's paradoxical power and limits to harm or heal, the capacity to listen to those we disagree with, and a "robust capacity to tell the truth."[2] That capacity emerges from the willingness to unlearn and relearn our social conditioning, especially concerning "the other" within our worship spaces. We are called to create and sustain a multicultural church as the Body of Christ. However, in doing that, we must also guarantee safe spaces for "the other" and recognize their immense social and psychological pain amid the privileged white community. Unlearning stories and interpretations that serve the comfort of

---

1. Pádraig Ó Tuama and Glenn Jordan, *Borders and Belonging: The Book of Ruth: Stories for Our Times* (London: Canterbury Press, 2021), xii.

2. Pádraig Ó Tuama, interview, "The Fantastic Argument of Being Alive," *On Being with Krista Tippet* (aired March 2, 2017).

the dominant culture starts with generously listening to the stories of those who have been oppressed and exploited, historically and currently. Relearning comes from being willing and courageous enough to lift up the unheard voices within a worship community that prefers to remain in its comfort zone.

Many Americans, for example, do not know that Christianity has existed and thrived in India since the apostolic age. The Syro-Malabar Church community holds to the tradition that the gospel of Jesus Christ was brought to them by St. Thomas the Apostle, and they follow the ancient Antiochene Rite. Christianity had been well established in India by the sixth century, particularly in the region of Kerala, where the vibrant community of the Syrian Orthodox Church still exists today.

European colonialism and imperialism, however, have con-stituted Indian history, at least since the Portuguese nobleman Vasco da Gama landed in Calicut in 1498. At that time, European explorers were prevailed upon to bring Christian missionaries with them to "save the souls" of the pagans.[3] While the Good News was not new to the people of Kerala, where Vasco da Gama landed, the form was new and different for both the Roman Catholic and Syro-Malabar communities. The Europeans firmly believed that Roman Catholicism was the superior form of Christianity, an idea categorically rejected by the Syro-Malabar community.

My own family traces its Catholicism to the arrival of the Jesuit missionary Francis Xavier, who catechized and baptized local peo-ple on the Coromandel Coast from 1542 until about 1545. How-ever, the Catholic missionaries who came after St. Francis quickly used India's caste system to their advantage, promising each caste a reward if they agreed to be baptized and become Catholic. The number of converts mattered to the economic prosperity of each missionary's particular European monarchy (Spanish, Portuguese, or Italian) and fed directly into the prosperity of the Holy See as the *de facto* head of the Holy Roman Empire.

---

3. See two papal bulls issued by Pope Nicholas V: *Dum Diversas* (1452) and *Romanus Pontifex* (1454), www.vatican.va.

The British followed the Portuguese and the Spanish to India, not so much to save souls as to trade with local populations in the interest of capitalist imperialism, turning India into another colony of the empire. British traders regarded the native merchants as racially, morally, intellectually, and existentially inferior, people who would be better off if they were taught Western civilization, culture, and religion. The colonialists set themselves up as masters and then wielded maximal, sovereign, and brutal power over the peoples of the subcontinent.

As with other European kingdoms that colonized various parts of the world and participated in the slave trade into the Americas, the British justified their (mis)treatment and subjugation of the natives with convenient interpretations of the Bible. But over time, the Indians who learned English read the Bible and quickly realized the discrepancy between the maxims and commandments of Jesus in the Gospels and the power structures of the purported Christians who ruled over them. Indians took their faith seriously, whether that faith was Hinduism, Jainism, Buddhism, Islam, or the historical Christian communities, and believed in conforming their lives to their faith. Seeing the hypocrisy of their British masters made them question the intentions and the integrity of the "white man"—a designation that soon came to include all Europeans. Soon, this disdain and abhorrence were aimed at all Christians. The historic Christian communities in India were not spared, even though they had been followers of Christ long before the colonizers arrived. The Indian populace did not distinguish between the well-meaning if ill-implemented Christianity of the missionaries and the "Christianity" of the British oppressors. Christianity, seen as the invaders' religion, was despised, and the majority Hindu population discriminated against Christians for their faith and caste. Missionaries were seen with a mix of acceptance and suspicion because missionary priests and nuns served in education and health care. The relationship between Indians of all religious affiliations and Christianity was, and remains, complex and multifaceted. Even today, Christianity is a persecuted religion in India.

Listening: Hearing the Tradition

This sad legacy is everywhere in the church. Nevertheless, Pope Francis exhorts us to an all-embracing faith that upholds the inherent dignity of every human person:

> There are those who appear to feel encouraged or at least permitted by their faith to support varieties of narrow and violent nationalism, xenophobia and contempt, and even the mistreatment of those who are different. Faith, and the humanism it inspires, must maintain a critical sense in the face of these tendencies, and prompt an immediate response whenever they rear their head. For this reason, *it is important that catechesis and preaching speak more directly and clearly about the social meaning of existence, the fraternal dimension of spirituality, our conviction of the inalienable dignity of each person*, and our reasons for loving and accepting all our brothers and sisters.[4]

Fratelli tutti scrutinizes and contextualizes the injustice and inhumane actions of human persons against other human persons within the greatest commandment of the Judeo-Christian tradition: "You shall love the Lord your God with all your heart, and with all your soul, and with all your strength, and with all your mind; and your neighbor as yourself" (Luke 10:27).[5] But the all-too-common notion that some people are superior to others fosters and perpetuates injustice. This notion of superiority contradicts the foundational conviction that every human person, created in God's image and likeness, has inherent dignity and is equal to all other human persons in God's eyes. It also leads to an ethos of racial supremacy, nationalism, xenophobia, and violence to preserve the privilege of the superior race.

---

4. Pope Francis, encyclical letter *Fratelli tutti, On Fraternity and Social Friendship* (October 3, 2020), no. 86 (emphasis mine), www.vatican.va.

5. Pope Francis, *Fratelli tutti*, no. 56.

Catholic social teaching clarifies that immigrants and refugees must be welcomed by the countries to which they come in the hope of stability, security, and opportunity. Respecting the dignity and equality of all persons, we give "unusual kindness" (Acts 28:2) to vulnerable and voiceless immigrants. We desire to follow Christ, who "came not to be served but to serve" (Matt 20:28). Magisterial teachings on social justice do not allow us to ignore aspects that force us to step out of our comfort zone. All of Catholic social teaching demands that we have a holistic reverence for life rather than fragmenting it according to convenience or preference. We pray for respect for life, from conception to natural death, emphasizing "conception" and "death," with the span of life between those points generally overlooked. However, God breathes life into that entire span and does not discriminate between the rich and the poor, white, Black and Brown, or male and female (Gal 3:28; 1 Cor 12:13), or even between followers of Christ and those who are not (Matt 5:45–48; *Nostra aetate* no. 5).

As a person born into the Roman Empire without citizenship, Jesus experienced the alienation of a stranger, even though he was in his own land. Like all those who conquered and colonized lands inhabited by Indigenous peoples, the Romans refused to acknowledge the dignity of the people they oppressed, denigrated, and sought to assimilate into their own language, culture, and religion. As the Greeks had done before them, the Romans brutally oppressed the people of their Judean colony. When Jesus was born, the Jewish people had long awaited the promised Messiah, whom they expected would liberate them from foreign occupation and oppression. Jesus understood the experience of oppression at the hands of a foreign power. Jesus understood the experience of being cast as the "other" because he was feared and misunderstood. Jesus understood the experience of being a stranger in his own land.

Jesus began his public ministry by announcing God's preferential option for the poor, vulnerable, and foreign (cf. Luke 4:18–19). Throughout his ministry, Jesus saw and heard the outsiders who were expected to remain invisible—the lepers, widows, children, and the sick. In interacting with these members of society, Jesus gave them the dignity inherent in every human person. If we are to preach God's love and redemption through the gospel of Jesus Christ, we, too, must learn to see, interpret, and then preach the word of God through the lens that Jesus himself used as he sought to give voice to the voiceless.

Relearning: From Scripture to Preaching

The voiceless identity is one that I inhabit. As a catechist and teacher, I am keenly aware of the meaning-making space between the speaker and the listener and that effective communication takes place within the terrain of the listener. I aim to communicate welcome, acceptance, and non-judgmental inclusion, sometimes creating a counter-narrative to the dominant narrative. However, there has been a glaring lack of prophetic imagination and announcement of the gospels' lifting up of the unseen ones in the homilies I have heard through the years. When I hear a Scripture passage proclaimed at Mass, I search for the one who is like me, unseen and voiceless, yet throbbing with life underneath the text of Scripture. I wonder whether Leah would have refused to marry Jacob if she had been consulted. Or whether Mary protested when she had to flee to Egypt with an infant. Or what Simon of Cyrene thought about carrying the cross for Jesus. Did anyone ask?

I have heard that lackluster homilies often come from a genuine fear: potential repercussions that arise when robust speech calls dominant culture and ecclesial institutions to the way of the gospel. My response is simple: Jesus's solidarity with the marginalized and his opposition to the institutional *status quo* came with a cost—his life. As followers of Jesus, are we ready to lay down our lives in the service of God's commandment? Are we willing to be the prophet who amplifies this voice of God heard in the widow, the orphan, the child, the criminal, the outsider—and bear the consequence?

These are challenging and discomforting questions. But we can interpret Scripture with creative theological imagination through the lens of the marginalized or voiceless. To help, I offer one such interpretation plus three additional passages for you to ponder. I invite you to sit with these words and allow the Spirit of God to speak to you, leading you to the memory of a particular life experience that augments the perspective of the unseen and unheard so that your preaching and teaching may be robust, truthful, and transformative.

An Example of Relearning:
Moses in Midian (Exodus 2:11–22)

Moses is desolate as he sits by a well in Midian. Forced to migrate, he is entirely out of his element, unprepared by his royal upbringing to live in the desert. Neither an Egyptian nor accepted by the Hebrews as one of them, Moses remains a foreigner in Midian— the quintessential uprooted migrant. His sense of displacement is evident in the name he gives his son: Gershom, "a stranger there." Moses is a refugee from the beginning of his story to the day he dies. He is adopted, pampered, threatened, and afraid. He becomes displaced, finds love, and finds a new place with his new family. Then he is uprooted once more, never again having a home. While he is recognized as the one through whom God liberates the Israelites from slavery, his predicament as a refugee and migrant is rarely mentioned. In this, he is like the migrants of color in this country whose stories of desolation, loneliness, and suffering are erased, replaced by more palatable stories of success. Migrants live a chronically uncertain reality. They endure the inevitable relinquishment of control over their own lives. They flee from danger and scarcity, hoping for safety and prosperity in a place that boasts of unlimited opportunities. However, they find themselves caged and oppressed, trying to understand a system designed to impede their progress. Their stories must be heard and lifted up.

The Torah instructs the Israelites to remember their sojourn as foreigners in Egypt. It commands them not to mistreat the stranger (Exod 22:21). Christian leaders have conveniently ignored the biblical mandate to welcome and care for the "stranger." They continue to allow (even advocate) restrictive laws with racist justifications. Pharaoh's daughter and her attendants could have drowned the infant Moses because he did not belong there. Jethro's daughters could have driven Moses away from the well because he was a stranger. Jethro himself could have reported him to the Egyptians and put Moses's life in danger. But they all reached into their consciences for a glimpse of the wholeness of God's presence in every person. They refused to let ethnicity, nationality, or race determine inclusion or exclusion. Jethro's daughters lifted a stranger and his voice to where these could be heard. As a member of the royal household, Moses had a voice in Egypt; in becoming Jethro's son-in-law, he had a voice in Midian.

Do we silence the voice of the "other" in giving voice to God's law, or does God's law mandate us to speak out for the "other"? Do we believe in a stingy, petty, restrictive, small God? Or do we believe in the God who is generous, unconditional, expansive, and bigger than anything we can conceive? If we can leave here with the determination to seek, acknowledge, and embrace the incarnation of God's love in the one who seems strange to us, perhaps we will experience our covenant with God and humanity in new and pleasant surprises.

Three Sample Passages for Your Relearning

1. The Aqedah (Genesis 22:1–19)
Abraham obeys God's directive to offer Isaac in sacrifice on Moriah. How does Sarah feel? Does she protest? And what does Isaac feel? Does he protest being tied and prepared for the sacrifice? How does Abraham wrestle with the conflict between love of God and love of son/human beings? Does the command to love God above all ever abrogate or minimize the love of neighbor? The Aqedah is often analogized with the passion, death, and resurrection of Jesus—how do such violence and fracture of relationships become whole again? How are we called to learn from and repair such profound relational harm?

2. The Parable of the Insistent Friend (Luke 11:5–13)

Jesus speaks this parable in the context of perseverance in prayer. When the man gives his friend the loaf of bread, does anyone consider his wife? Perhaps she saved those loaves for the children's breakfast. Maybe that is all the family had for the next day (or two). Which of the three men mentioned could be identified with God, and which could be the supplicant?

3. Simon of Cyrene (Mark 15:21; Matthew 27:32; Luke 23:26)

Simon is from northern Africa, possibly Jewish. In Black theology, Simon is Black. Is that why the Roman soldiers "compel" him, of all the people in the crowd, to carry Jesus's cross? Mark names Simon's sons—where are they when Simon is with Jesus? How does Simon's carrying of Jesus's cross symbolize or foreshadow the torture and suffering of persons of color? Simon demonstrates the dignity and the power of the oppressed as he shoulders the burden silently. Or does he protest? What transforms Simon—Jesus's loving gaze, the act of carrying the cross, or both?

Respectful Dismantling for a Transformed (and Transformational) Legacy

The Bible is filled with characters, including Jesus, who journey through their faith while laboring to bring existing cultural and political systems as close as possible to God's vision of a covenantal people. We continue in this labor. Today, the debate around immigrants and refugees is sharp and bitter. Many preachers, teachers, and ministers find this tension paralyzing. But as the pre-eminent Black Catholic scholar Cyprian Davis says, "History . . . has taught us that no one can remain silent in periods of great social turmoil and still retain any moral authority. It has also taught that there is no such thing as a political issue without moral consequences."[6] The United States bishops instruct the leaders and the faithful of

---

6. Cyprian Davis, *The History of Black Catholics in the United States* (New York: Crossroad Publishing Company, 1990), 117.

the church that we must welcome the stranger. They also emphasize that we must become aware of how "racist attitudes can linger in subtle ways, even when people get to know one another . . . unless we vigorously educate ourselves about our neighbors, learn to appreciate their heritages, encounter their own images of us."[7] An attitude of radical welcome may be challenging for pastors and ministers, but when we respectfully help immigrants join our communities, we are mutually enriched.

In the various congregations I have been a part of, I have observed many practices that "other" the immigrants in the community, often making them invisible. The experience is alienating but not unique because institutional ecclesial racism "others" all who are not white. But preachers and teachers can embolden the spiritual energy of a homily (or lesson plan, or retreat reflection) with courteous, inclusive language that attends to the suffering of the "other" among their hearers. You can offer words that create *belonging* for the stranger. You can lift up the wholeness of our existence and reestablish that belonging to the Cosmic Christ so that you can counter the alienations fostered by the church and society. You can challenge racism so that in restoring dignity to individuals and communities, you are also restoring dignity to the wholeness of their culture. You can become the matchmaker between the word of God and the diverse congregation.

How can the "stranger" teach you and shape your preaching? How can you exercise theological imagination to see the Scriptures through the eyes of the immigrant experience so that your words are relevant and truthful, inspiring the listener to transform the world? How can you find the "gaps where compassion can thrive in the midst of technical debates about law and tradition"?[8] How can you hold truth-telling in creative tension with wonder and joy, and combine that with justice and regeneration? How can you

---

7. United States Conference of Catholic Bishops, *Welcoming the Stranger among Us: Unity in Diversity* (November 15, 2000), www.usccb. org.

8. Ó Tuama, *Borders and Belonging*, 4.

present a vision and the hope of parousia, to speak words that allow us to live as if we are there? How can you help people envision and build the future they want to live in, where there is a place for everyone at the table? How can you form questions that will allow for an exploration of how we can be faith communities *now* and live in a better future than we ever dared to believe?

As you acknowledge, defend, and fortify the faith born out of struggle and challenge your congregation to respect other cultures and actively work to dismantle the evil of racism in church and society, your preaching may be met with anger, dismay, and pushback. These reactions may come from white bodies offended at your suggestions or people of color in your congregation who feel that their stories and experiences have been co-opted or misappropriated. Do not be disheartened or discouraged when this happens. *Expect* it to happen. Even *desire* it! Because such criticism allows you to engage in the dialectic of proximity and attentiveness to the Brown bodies that inhabit your preaching and communities. These conversations allow for the unspoken to be spoken.

Agreement is not the mandate in these initial conversations. The goal is not to bring everyone to uniformity of thought but to sow the seeds of the kin-dom of God. Learning and healing require persistence and time, especially in a world of daunting change. But the vision of a better future ahead and a transformed legacy now is a powerful one. We don't single-handedly make the *basileia* of God present. Instead, we each do our part, however small, and those tiny seeds grow with the power of God to bear much fruit. As God says, "So shall my word be that goes out from my mouth; it shall not return to me empty, but it shall accomplish that which I purpose, and succeed in the thing for which I sent it" (Isa 55:11).

14 Generational Trauma and Original Sin

Beth Blackburn

A young Black man is shot and killed in his car after being pulled over by a white police officer. His wife, pregnant and seated beside him, is not shot, but she is both witness and survivor. Both she and the female child in her womb are traumatized. Neither will ever be the same. The not-yet-born victim already carries all the eggs she will ever have, so her own children, already potential in her body, are also traumatized. The cost of trauma is multigenerational. Must it also be eternal? If preachers are to speak truthfully about racism, we must come to theological terms with trauma, scientifically understood.

What Is Trauma?

In Greek, the word *trauma* refers to a wound or injury inflicted upon a body by an act of violence. Trauma inflicts physical and emotional wounds, and these deadly wounds are just the start of a cycle of influence.[1]

Picture trauma for a moment by considering a real or imagined experience threatening your life. You might recognize the threat before it occurs, as with a group of bullies approaching you on the playground or a car heading directly at you on the highway. The danger might be happening in the present moment, like in a

---

1. See Cathy Caruth, *Unclaimed Experience: Trauma, Narrative, and History* (Baltimore, MD: Johns Hopkins University Press, 1996).

convenience store robbery. Or you may recall being assaulted as a child. Even if your thoughts about the moment are unclear, or you cannot speak of them, the threat registers itself in your mind and body. For people who live on constant high alert, trauma often is chronic. The line of separation between the person who experiences trauma as a victim and the one who experiences it as a witness can become blurred; each victim and each witness, unable to manage or escape the situation, can lose their sense of God-given identity and efficacy. A traumatic event causes a loss of self and a paralyzing lack of agency in the threat of the harm suffered.[2] Trauma thus changes the nature of the human being at the most basic level.

Sin and Science

Trauma's harm may seem obvious, but its intimate relationship to original sin might not seem evident initially. At the beginning of our salvation story, God created the heavens and the earth and everything within them, calling them all good. But at some point, our first ancestors, created by God, chose in their interactions to work against the will of their Creator. They charted their own path of the knowledge of good and evil, losing their innocence in a freely chosen and sinful corruption that takes on a life of its own.

The theological idea of the "corruption of nature" compares directly to recent genetic research on the effects of trauma on the human body. Like original sin, trauma erodes and deforms us at the cellular level, physically and emotionally, and moves down through generations, affecting the actions and reactions of those who may be completely unaware of that long-past initial traumatic moment, event, or history.

Consider one specific group of persons in our society who continue to suffer the negative impacts of this unwanted and unearned inheritance: descendants of the Black women, men, and children

---

2. Serene Jones, *Trauma and Grace: Theology in a Ruptured World* (Louisville, KY: Westminster John Knox Press, 2019), 13–15.

who were victims of the slave trade. Depriving human beings of their God-given freedoms and treating them as items to be owned means that *every* person labeled "slave" was traumatized—as have been, indirectly, all their descendants. From both the genetic and the theological standpoint, the atrocities committed against enslaved people continue to live on, unhealed, in our societies.

The Interconnectedness of Bodies

Each girl child is born with every egg her body will ever release. When a woman is pregnant with a female child, the eggs of that infant are present by the fifth month of the mother's pregnancy. The stored eggs of the mother and the unborn daughter share the same biological and chemical environment, with oxygen and nutrients passing from mother to infant through the placenta and umbilical cord. A pregnant woman, her female infant, and the infant's eggs all experience any trauma the mother experiences. Exposing the mother to a traumatic event directly and immediately impacts three generations.

While a woman is born with every egg wholly formed, a man's sperm continue to multiply from puberty onward. Each regeneration has the potential to be scarred by trauma. The imprint of trauma from the father or mother or both may be genetically passed on to future generations.[3]

This new science speaks directly to my ministry as a lay Episcopal catechist. I want to deepen my theological understanding of the sin of racism and its devastating consequences. I wonder about the events and people who have formed me and each of us. How has my ancestral heritage impacted my children's thoughts, beliefs, and intuitions about how to stay safe in this world? Have I passed down pain and my corruptly formed "gut reactions"? Despite my privileged social location as a white female, am I unwittingly

---

3. Tracy Bale, "Epigenetic and Transgenerational Reprogramming of Brain Development," *Nature Reviews Neuroscience* 16 (2015): 332, www.ncbi.nlm.nih.gov.

perpetuating the damage of my previous generations? What then about those who lived as enslaved people and their generations, those who never felt even a moment of relaxation, those who lived with the real possibility that their children could be sold and taken away forever? Think of the long list of daily fears, intimidations, dehumanizing interactions, and injuries. At some visceral level, crimes against one are committed against all—and past trauma calls out to them and their descendants, persons alive today, to be wary, lash out, or run. This fear is palpable in Rev. Dietra Wise-Baker's opening chapter of this book. Fear runs deep, wide, and long.

As we consider the connections and implications of generational trauma and original sin, how might we, as faith leaders, deal with the malformation of what God intended to be good? How can we respond to the world without being held in sin's shadow? Pain and our reaction to pain have entered the world. No matter how many generations ago the original trauma occurred, we remain forever tied to it. Our response to the ongoing pain in this world sometimes manifests itself visibly. Often our reaction is buried more deeply in an unknown visceral change within our bodies that impacts how we react to life's events. We may not understand these responses or be able to articulate them, but we are nonetheless pulled down and stifled by trauma. For some of us, the damage may be traceable to a specific event, like the Holocaust, famine, or war. For others, the damage may be cumulative across generations of suffering or fear, past and present.

Epigenetics: The Inner Voice that Directs

Fortunately, science is beginning to uncover the changes that trauma causes in our bodies, as well as in the bodies of those who came before and who will come after us. Epigenetics, the study of how life events and our responses to those events affect how our genes express themselves, is one such science. This field examines how cells can change how they function, even when the DNA sequence remains unaltered. The differences between genetics and epigenetics are complex, but a text written for scientists and public health professionals offers a helpful distinction between them: "Genetic information provides the blue print [sic] for the manufacture of all the proteins necessary to create a living organism, whereas the epigenetic information provides additional instructions on how, where, and when the genetic information will be used."[4] In a sense, genetic material offers the plan, and epigenetic material offers instructions on how to implement the plan.

Why is this important? Epigenetics "regulate[s] how and why certain genes are turned on and turned off," much like switches.[5] These switches, called epigenetic tags, control functions like our gut instincts, informing us when we are in danger and cueing us on how to react to that danger. Consider, for example, scientists' developing understanding of the stress hormone cortisol. As you probably know, stress is the rudder that drives our reactions during difficult times in life—our "fight/flight/freeze" situations. When a mother is exposed to high levels of stress, the cortisol level in the amniotic fluid surrounding her baby increases, creating an imbalance. Researchers have discovered that these highly stressed mothers are more likely to have babies who are premature or of lower birth rate, with links to other adverse, long-lasting neonatal outcomes and health consequences, including allergies, asthma, immune disorders, cardiovascular disease, and mood disorders (for example, depression or anxiety).[6]

Rachel Yehuda, one of the world's leading experts in posttraumatic stress disorder (PTSD), has found that high levels of

---

4. Mukesh Verma, "The Human Epigenome and Cancer," in *Human Genome Epidemiology: Building the Evidence for Using Genetic Information to Improve Health and Prevent Disease,* ed. Muin Khoury et al. (Oxford: Oxford University Press, 2010), 551.

5. National Institutes of Health, "Epigenomics and Epigenetics Research," May 19, 2022, www.epi.grants.cancer.gov.

6. Maria Emilia Solano et al., "Highway to Health; or How Prenatal Factors Determine Disease Risks in the Later Life of the Offspring," *Journal of Reproductive Immunology* 90, no. 1 (June 2011): 3–8, www.doi.org/10.1016/j.jri.2011.01.023.

cortisol in the amniotic fluid surrounding a baby in utero result in low cortisol levels in the infant after birth. Yehuda and a scientific team reviewed relevant studies and found that these low levels persisted in Holocaust survivors—and in their children.[7] Yehuda uncovered similar findings in a study of pregnant women who survived the 9/11 terrorist attacks. In their second or third trimester, pregnant women who developed PTSD delivered children who also had low cortisol levels.[8] Epigenetic mechanisms are at the core of these study findings, in which adverse effects persist beyond the life of the person who experienced the trauma. Researchers in yet another study uncovered seventeen genes that expressed themselves differently in those who developed PTSD compared to those who did not, including eight that "may reflect stable risk factors for or 'scars' of PTSD."[9] These studies and others like them reveal mental and emotional health changes that can be identified biologically.

As part of our biology, epigenetic mechanisms serve a purpose. All humans are born into varying circumstances: times of peace or war, moments of great abundance, and seasons of sad divisions. Reactions to these circumstances are part of our Creator-given design. To survive, we need to prepare for this variable world even before entering it. The epigenetic changes from the traumas our parents experienced help prime us to survive in similar situations. These changes are good news if we are born into the same circumstances that our parents experienced; however, it makes sense that

7. Rachel Yehuda and Jonathan Seckl, "Minireview: Stress-Related Psychiatric Disorders with Low Cortisol Levels: A Metabolic Hypothesis," *Endocrinology* 152, no. 12 (December 1, 2011): 4496–503, www.press.doi.org/10.1210.en.2011-1218.

8. Rachel Yehuda et al., "Gene Expression Patterns Associated with Posttraumatic Stress Disorder Following Exposure to the World Trade Center Attacks," *Biological Psychiatry* 66, no. 7 (October 1, 2009): 708–11, https://doi.org/10.1016/j.biopsych.2009.02.034.

9. Casey Sarapas et al., "Genetic Markers for PTSD Risk and Resilience among Survivors of the World Trade Center Attacks," *Disease Markers* 30, nos. 2–3 (2011): 101, www.pubmed.ncbi.nlm.nih.gov.

these inherited adaptations can rapidly become detrimental when the situation(s) that caused them to develop no longer exist. The child of a parent who experienced life in a war zone may inherit the impulse to recoil at loud noises. This response would be helpful in a bomb threat or a school shooting, but a heightened startle response would also keep a person in a perpetual, highly reactive state, even when no danger is present.

A child—or an adult—living in constant wariness resulting from a parental experience may have no idea of the source of their perpetual reactivity or even recognize its presence. I am speaking of a single generation, from parental stressor to child, effect. But epigenetic science is today beginning to make an even more startling claim: that the impact of trauma is not only intergenerational—that is, from mother to child—but also transgenerational, through at least the third and fourth generations—grandchildren and great-grandchildren and so on. A team of researchers led by Benjamin R. Carone points out that "mechanisms exist that could allow organisms to 'inform' their progeny about prevailing environmental conditions. Under certain historical circumstances—for example, repeated exposure over evolutionary time to a moderately toxic environment that persists for tens of generations—such non-Mendelian information transfer could be adaptive."[10] This adaptation is survival oriented. Passed on to future generations, it quickly becomes damaging when those original conditions change. One person's chronic, highly reactive state may actually be passed down through multiple generations.

Rachel Yehuda and Amy Lehrner, in a research review published in *World Psychiatry,* note the presence of ongoing research "about the impact of historical events such as colonization, slavery, and displacement trauma in many cultures, including First Nation

---

10. Benjamin R. Carone et al., "Paternally Induced Transgenerational Environmental Reprogramming of Metabolic Gene Expression in Mammals," *Cell* 143, no. 7 (2010): 1084, www.pubmed.ncbi.nlm.nih.gov.

and native American communities, African Americans, Australian aboriginals and New Zealand Maori, as well as in societies exposed to genocide, ethnic cleansing, or war."[11] The increasing scientific acceptance of intergenerational effects from trauma, along with early results, creates a "mandate," they argue, for longitudinal studies to help us understand the workings of transgenerational transfer of trauma and stress.[12]

Imagine the ongoing epigenetic damage inflicted on Black bodies, for example, by generations of enslavement and racism. The epigenetic tags of slavery's dehumanizing legacy may well linger on in the bodies of the children, women, and men who still suffer the historic and contemporary effects of personal and communal racism. The science is new, but the resonant theology that we human beings are subject to the effects of original sin is not.

An Undeniable Responsibility to Act

Trauma injures its victims physically and mentally. But what does it do to those who inflict the wounds? The corruption of human nature runs on a two-way street. When I harm another, something changes within me. This effect is actual for all of us. When one person causes harm to another, one causes harm to oneself.

Given human history's cycles of harm and injury, have we humans reached a point of no return? I sit at my desk only a day after the school shooting in Uvalde, Texas, and a week after the shooting at Tops Market in Buffalo, New York. Many people are talking about the prevalence of evil in the world, not understanding how people can hate so much as to take another person's life. Our faith, however, poses a different conversation. Rather than existing "out there" in the world, this evil has taken up residence in

---

11. Rachel Yehuda and Amy Lehrner, "Intergenerational Transmission of Trauma Effects: Putative Role of Epigenetic Mechanisms," *World Psychiatry* 17, no. 3 (2018): 244, www.pubmed.ncbi.nlm.nih.gov.

12. Yehuda and Lehrner, "Intergenerational Transmission," 244.

each of us. Sin enters the world and corrupts the nature of human-kind. Such deeply embedded corruption bursts forth! Will God give up on us, as in the Genesis story of Noah and the flood? Are we no better than Sodom and Gomorrah, where God could not find ten good people? Can we hope for a healing path for ourselves and our corrupt society?

God calls us as people of faith to follow in Jesus's footsteps. Unless we follow Jesus in his way of justice and healing, we take the name of God in vain. God calls us to respond responsibly to trauma and sin in our midst. God charges us to correct the people we have become and to heal those we encounter. Even if the task is difficult or dangerous, we Christians must take up this cross, or we are not the people we claim to be.

The Bible tells us that at the end of time, all secrets will be made known, and every heart will be opened (see, for example, 2 Pet 3:10; Luke 8:17; Matt 10:26). Each of us may well have to deal with some personal hell before we can go forward into the kingdom. Think about it. We will know the hearts of the ones we have hurt and see every bit of their pain and isolation. We will understand everything they experienced because their experiences will become ours. We are one body in Christ. It is impossible to have pain in one part of the body and not feel it in another. We will experience their agony. If we do not do the work of healing here, the suffering will only continue to grow.

How to Heal and Develop Relationships

We seek understanding and strive for better relationships. But when trauma impacts our ability to read people and situations correctly, we contribute instead to the harm.[13] How do we develop healthy relationships if our entire genetic history leads us to expect that other people intend us harm?

---

13. Bessel A. van der Kolk, *The Body Keeps the Score: Brain, Mind, and Body in the Healing of Trauma* (New York: Viking Penquin, 2015), 61.

Listening with the Ears of the Heart

One pathway out of trauma is to create safe spaces to speak about our pain. Since trauma affects a person's ability to speak of what happened, this step toward healing is difficult. Listening is crucial if we wish to aid in another's healing process. When a person can name his or her trauma, and each one's voice is heard, spoken aloud, this act of mutual attention, both individually and communally, is the first foundation of healing. To attend well as listeners, we must understand our own biases and set them aside, as well as our desire to speak our own opinions. Why does my sister or brother need to express what has happened? What does this group of people understand of this world that I do not? Stepping out of ourselves, we can understand the deep need for the other to be seen, heard, and known.

Developing Relationship through Forgiveness

When one person sins against another, forgiveness is not complete until the trust lost in the relationship is back in place and the relationship can go forward. The person harmed struggles to go forward without holding onto pain or bitterness. The person who has perpetrated harm struggles to understand how trust has been betrayed and lost. The work of forgiveness is a long, tedious, and painful process. Throwing out an "I'm sorry" without entering into the other's pain is like trying to put out a fire with gasoline; it simply increases the pain. In the same way, a quick "I'll pray for you" as we turn away and do nothing only increases another's pain. As generational science and theology teach us, human beings are experts at piling misery upon misery.

Repairing Racial Trust

How will the stories of those whose bodies have been traumatized by slavery be told and heard? Who will listen? We must grow enough in empathy to listen closely and feel the depth and breadth of one another's pain and fear as if they were our own. Sorrow and remorse about our collective history will become a pathway of the heart. Without remorse, the past happens again. Remorse, not shame, is the path to relationship. Past inequity and injustice cannot be undone, but if we listen and repent with mind and heart, we can hope to understand, love, and heal our world and the people we strive to encounter. Life can only be lived forward. The unforgiven cannot undo the harm any more than the traumatized can remove the damage. Will we courageously join together as one body, or will we be forever scattered?

Preaching as a Response to
Our Shared Pain as the One Body

[B]y no means clearing the guilty, visiting the iniquity of the parents upon the children to the third and the fourth generation.
—Numbers 14:18b

Can we dare to believe that our long-suffering God is pained by the harm we do to each other? When someone harms those we love, we feel the pain. When we harm each other, God suffers because each of us is a beloved child of the Divine. Harm is passed down through generations, and we are one body. We are affected by one another's transgressions.

The church is in the business of forgiveness and redemption; it is also a source of knowledge and must aid in spreading understanding—of opening minds and hearts. Can we teach empathy from the pulpit? We will not know unless we try. Certainly, we can teach our hearers to deepen their understanding of others' experiences and stories. The burgeoning science of genetics offers a view of that path and affirms our calling to help heal this broken world. The people who lived lives of slavery are crying out across the generations. Their offspring who walk the earth today still suffer, reacting to the old and new pain of the ongoing sin of racism that still plagues our culture.

As preachers, we must speak openly about racism and sin—so much so that it becomes common understanding. The desire is not to redirect hatred but rather to grow in knowledge and virtue so that hatred finds nowhere to germinate and grow. If hate is simply redirected because of our preaching, we have failed. In one of Paul's most famous passages in the New Testament, he makes a powerful statement that without love, we are nothing (1 Corinthians 13). Black and Brown people of all generations—those who were refused entry, had their children locked in cages, were treated as inferior, were hung from ropes, or were pushed into mass graves—carry scars, visible here and now. These scars demand care and healing.

Let's be honest. The feeling that white bodies are superior to dark bodies has not gone away. In a world more interconnected than at any time in history, we continue to find ways to divide or exclude. In a world of misunderstanding, the white bodies of the world must make way for healing. This task involves more than placing "Black Lives Matter" placards on our front lawns. Neither will money, spent without relationship, ease our consciences or allow us to wash our hands of the trauma of racism. We need first to commit our hearts and minds because we are talking about true relationship. Trauma is a wall that continues to exist between "them" and "us." We will not be able to remove that wall with silence. The preacher's task is to lead forward, name the pain, and point the way to become one body in Christ. And not only preachers: every Christian must participate in the work. As Paul says, "The Lord commanded that those who proclaim the gospel should get their living by the gospel" (1 Cor 9:14). All Christians can and must proclaim the good news of redemption—through empathy, words, and actions. By the grace of God and with diligent work, we can go forward in a renewed effort to be one body in Christ.

15 African American Songs of Resistance and Hope

Manuel Williams

During the years of African American enslavement, my family for generations lived and died in the Black Belt of Alabama—a place so named in part because of the number of counties in this region where enslaved African Americans and their descendants constitute a majority of the population. The region's topography played a crucial part in creating this majority. The Black Belt is a fertile plain, twenty-five to thirty miles wide and stretching over three hundred miles across central Alabama and northeastern Mississippi. This area of dark, rich soils became one of the South's most important agricultural areas before the Civil War, filled with numerous plantations and associated commerce rooted in the enslavement of Africans. The Black Belt is also the area where some essential elements of the music and spirituality of African American people formed. From the blues of the Mississippi Delta to the moans, work chants, shouts, spirituals, and hymns of Alabama and Georgia, music helped enslaved persons and their descendants survive the terrors of slavery, Jim Crow, lynching, and segregation. Today, mass incarceration, a mutation of slavery allied with voter suppression, is an intense effort to reverse the gains of more than a century of struggle for full citizenship in this country. Songs of resistance and hope still provide solace and inspiration.

I am a child of the modern civil rights movement. Having grown up in an ecumenical African American family, I was able to witness firsthand the range of how this musicality was employed, not only in worship but also as a powerful personal and communal tool in the struggle against segregation and the racism that under-girds it. The rich diversity of African American music and preaching was an essential element of worship—and foundational for the social action and protests that directly responded to that worship. Sometimes the preacher quoted hymns or spirituals or gospel songs; sometimes he or she intoned them and "set up" the soloist or choir or other musicians; sometimes the preacher "moved" the message of the homily or sermon by singing and making the song his or hers, oft times with Spirit-led improvisation or ad-libbing, all of it leading the congregation to renewed strength and vigor to contend with and survive the daily ravages of white supremacy.

In the lives and faith of my four great-grandmothers, I have come to discern how African American songs helped them survive and how these songs might help the preacher and believer of this day to survive our enduring struggle to dismantle systemic racism and continue to build the beloved community. The liberating gospel of Jesus Christ has helped African Americans to survive these past four hundred years. It is perhaps the second-most powerful tool, after the U.S. Constitution, in maintaining that survival and allowing us and other believers to create a nation and a church replete with freedom and justice.

As a young child and well into my early adulthood and formation for ministry, I enjoyed the company of these incredible women, all of whom lived to advanced old age. As a newly ordained presbyter, I preached and presided at the funeral of my family's last surviving matriarch. I have come to appreciate how critically important their songs and the songs of their ancestors were in maintaining their spiritual, psychological, emotional, and (I dare say) physical well-being in a hostile and abusive larger world. All four were profoundly and uniquely devout. Communal worship and the preached word were essential in their lives, enabling them to create legacies of service and advancement that are still evident in the lives and professions of their descendants. These legacies include contributions toward a more humane and just world that my grandmothers might never have imagined but that would undoubtedly make them proud.

I never met any of my great-grandfathers. I know them only through my great-grandmothers' stories. In testimony to the brutality of the world they lived in, all four men died many years before their spouses, the final one in the same hospital and the same week I was born. Whether farming, laboring, working on the railroads, or being incarcerated for not knowing their place, the pervasive racism they faced shortened their lives. The women they loved survived, however, and at some mean level, prospered against incredible odds: Black, poor, female, and faith-filled, they survived! Their stories are stories for our time and our task in this book.

Black, Poor, Female, and Faith-filled

Little Mama

Minerva Echols, a South Carolinian of Gullah heritage, was my father's paternal grandmother. The Gullah people are descendants of West and Central African tribal groups who retained many vestiges of language and culture that other descendants of enslaved Africans lost. Gullah people are found primarily along the coasts of South Carolina, North Carolina, Georgia, and Florida. Minerva was baptized in St. Peter Catholic Church in Charleston, South Carolina. Somehow her family came to Alabama—I suspect that her parents or grandparents were enslaved persons sold to slave auctioneers in Montgomery, Alabama, a major distribution center for enslaved Africans. Of all my great-grandmothers, I had the least contact with her, but I remember how exotic and mystical she seemed to me. There were altars in her home, a rosary perpetually in her hands, and the smell of incense and other burnt offerings permeating the air. She often hummed in words and melodies that I did not understand then but that I know now must have been vestiges of the African language and music her ancestors kept— language and music that survived the Middle Passage and endured in the coastal areas of South Carolina. She was a tiny woman whom I had never heard spoken of, or to, by any name other than "Little Mama."

Mary

My father's maternal grandmother was Mary Siggers, a domestic worker all her life. Mary was a gentle spirit and a devout Baptist. I remember her catching the Spirit and "shouting" on several occasions when we worshiped with her and my grandmother at Shiloh Missionary Baptist Church. When the pastor had preached a powerful word and had begun to sing or "whoop" the sermon, she and any number of primarily older women would enter a state of high emotion, deliverance, and release, all manifested in words, utterances, tears, and bodily movements that could be equally frightening and fascinating to my young Catholic eyes and mind. Despite her Baptist faith and its disdain for alcoholic beverages, on some Friday evenings, after dealing with her white employers all week, a bottle of Wild Irish Rose wine gave her some measure of release and comfort that would later be augmented by a good "shout" on Sunday morning at Shiloh.

Mama Hannah

Hannah Rice Carpenter was my mother's paternal grandmother. "Mama Hannah," as she was universally known, was a Primitive Baptist. Her faith community was known as "foot washing Baptists" because that ritual was performed regularly in their worship. She was a tall, stern, and very dark-skinned woman. She had somehow managed almost to complete her high school education, and in her extraordinarily rural and agrarian west Alabama county, that qualified her to be a teacher. She knew the Scriptures well and would consistently quote them for encouragement and admonishment: "Son, let the Lord fight your battles for you!," she would tell me after some skirmish I'd had with another child. As often on her lips as the words of the sacred texts were the melodies and hymns of her people. Her sense of community and kinship was expansive, no doubt fueled by the large family she and her siblings mothered and fathered. I often heard that she and my great-grandfather, "Papa Phil," moved from Greene County, Alabama, to Pickens County, Alabama, because too many of the young people in the county were first cousins, and there was no one for them to court and marry. I rarely met or encountered another adult or child who, according to Mama Hannah, was not a cousin or blood relative in some fashion. As an adult, I later learned that the move from Greene County to Pickens County was also motivated by the news that Papa Phil, a railroad man, had another family in far-off Saint Louis, so he did not remain long in Pickens County!

Miss Sis

My mother's maternal grandmother was Millie Parker Minor McGee, the granddaughter of Native Americans and enslaved African Americans and the daughter of emancipated African Americans. My relationship with her was the most extensive and formative for me. Millie's second husband, George McGee, was the great-grandfather who died within days of my birth. I spent many summers and school weekends "sitting at her feet," as the elders' mentoring and forming of the young were called in my community. Millie McGee was a subsistence farmer with my great-grandfather and a cook of great skill and acclaim. She was employed for a while as a cook for a U.S. government prisoner-of-war camp, which housed captured German troops during World War II and had been purposefully located in our rural, remote county. Relatives and the community knew her as "Sis" or "Miss Sis" because it was said that she was a sister to anyone in need. Her charity and compassion were legendary in the hamlet between Carrollton and Aliceville in Pickens County. She outlived two husbands (Mr. Minor and my great-grandfather, "Pappa"), all her siblings, and several of her children and grandchildren, yet she remained steadfast, unmovable, and always abiding in her faith in God and God's son, Jesus Christ. At the center of her faith was her membership at Mt. Calvary Baptist Church, where she was a missionary, mother of the church, and prayer warrior.

When I was in grade school, spending some summers and occasional weekends with Sis, she was already well into her late seventies and eighties but strong in body, energetic, and engaging, still cooking robust meals for breakfast as if she and I would be going into cotton fields or vegetable patches to work all morning until the noonday sun required respite and refueling. I watched in awe as the women of the missionary society gathered on some Sunday afternoons, all attired in white to pray and sing the spirituals and the songs of Zion. Sometimes I would recognize the words. Other times, the women would just moan and hum in plaintive melodies while one of them sang or uttered prayers of intercession with a fervor suggesting that the Throne of Grace and Mercy was right there on that porch. Months after my ordination, I preached her funeral service after she had lived 103 years. She had announced to my grandmother as she prepared for bed that it was time for her to go to the Lord, and sometime that night she did.

One of the lessons she taught me has stayed with me till this day, and some fifty-plus years later, I am still moved to tears at its retelling. One summer, a family, whose homestead was nearly a mile from Sis's house, sent one of the little boys from the family each day to ask to borrow some foodstuff. "Miss Sis, my Mama says can she borrow some flour?" "Sure, baby." My great-grandmother gathered the flour and gave it to the child with tenderness and warmth, saying, "Tell your Mama if she needs anything else to send you on back directly. Be careful walking home, baby." This exchange lasted for several more days: they needed cornmeal, sugar, eggs. On the fifth day, I answered the door on the back porch, and before Sis got there, I said to the boy, who appeared to be a little younger than I, "Your Mama don't ever go to the store?" Before the final word escaped my lips, Sis grabbed me from behind, moved me away from the door, bent down to look the boy in the eyes, and asked what she could send his mother that day. After she had packed up several blocks of her home-churned butter, she encouraged the child to get on home before the summer heat started to melt it. Then she turned to me and asked, "What did we have for breakfast this morning?" I cheerfully recalled that she'd made biscuits, rice, country ham, eggs, smothered chicken, and peach preserves. She then asked me, "Son, did you have enough?" "Yes, Ma'am, and there still some on the stove," as I pointed to the wood-burning stove she used with such skill and, to my eyes, magic. She then sat me down on the porch and told me that little boy didn't have the kind of breakfast we enjoyed and that he had a lot of brothers and sisters and no daddy at the house and that his Mama sent him every day because they needed what she gave them to keep from being hungry. As tears welled in my eyes, she told me I made that child feel bad and that when somebody needs something, you have to make them feel like they are doing you a favor by letting you help them: "That's what Jesus told us to do, baby. Be cheerful and not stingy. God loveth a cheerful giver, the Bible says!"

> **Lord I want to be a Christian. In my heart, in my heart. Lord I want to be a Christian in my heart.**[1]

Decades later, I came to realize that in that moment and so many others, Sis was teaching me about justice, about giving to every child of God what she or he is due, not out of self-serving charity but with an intense awareness that systems and structures and individual choices deprive millions of our sisters and brothers of what they need to live full and free lives becoming all their Creator intended them to be. Sis was saying that because we had more than enough, our sustenance and our abundance in a very real sense belonged to that family down the road and that as followers of Jesus, we not only had to share but to do so in a way that honored the dignity and worth of those with whom we share.

In thirty-five years of pastoral ministry and preaching the gospel, I have come to realize even more fervently that preaching the gospel of Jesus Christ must conform to his words in Luke: "The Spirit of the Lord is upon me, because he has anointed me to bring good news to the poor. He has sent me to proclaim release to the captives and recovery of sight to the blind, to let the oppressed go free, to proclaim the year of the Lord's favor" (Luke 4:18–19). If it does not foundationally speak this message, preaching is at best

---

1. Lyric from "Lord I Want to be a Christian," African American spiritual. Public domain.

ineffective. Or it is in the words of a sermon on this Lukan text by the late Rev. Dr. Prathia Wynn Hall, "Indeed, if what we do in the pulpit is not good news to the poor, deliverance to the captives, sight to the blind, healing for the broken, and freedom for the oppressed, it may be sweet, it may be eloquent, it may even be deep, but it ain't preaching."[2]

A preacher from my childhood who exemplified the admonishment of Dr. Hall was the Christian Methodist Episcopal circuit-riding preacher in west Alabama whom I knew as Reverend Poole. A dear friend of my grandmother, Hannah Rice Carpenter, Reverend Poole was among a small cadre of adults who frequently gifted me with books. Perhaps he saw in me a nascent preacher. I recall him saying something to the effect that a preacher must study the Bible hard, think it through, pray to the Holy Spirit, and let the Spirit run. These steps would aid in authentic and prophetic preaching.

I join my colleagues and friends in writing this chapter of this book because I believe, as they have so powerfully and eloquently written, that people of faith and citizens of this country desperately need to hear the gospel of peace and justice to bring them to mature faith and to deal with and begin to heal the trauma that white supremacy has inflicted upon Black bodies, all people of color and, yes, on white bodies, too. This essay and, indeed, the entire book is offered to those who preach in the spirit of the Reverend Poole. It is the sacred obligation of all preachers, of whatever vocation, especially in our American context, to seriously ponder what their Christian faith demands of them and their hearers in acknowledging and beginning to dismantle the systems, structures, attitudes, and behaviors of white supremacy. White supremacy keeps African Americans, Indigenous Americans, and all people of color knocking on metaphorical doors each day, asking and demanding not eggs or flour or cornmeal, but justice and access to everything that will afford us full participation in the political,

---

2. Prathia Hall, "Between the Wilderness and the Cliff," *The African American Pulpit* 8, no. 4 (Fall 2005): 44–48.

210 | *Ancestors and Stories*

economic, social, and cultural systems of this country—and this church. The written statement from the initial gathering of the Black Catholic Clergy Caucus following the 1968 assassination of Rev. Dr. Martin Luther King Jr. says, "The Catholic Church in the United States [is] primarily a white racist institution," and that statement remains essentially true today.[3] The attempt to reduce the entire gospel and social justice teaching of the church to the absolute primacy of fetal life over every other human life and other life issues while cloaking this unbiblical radicalism in feigned concern for the Black unborn reeks of abject racism. The reticence or refusal of the Catholic hierarchy and other clergy to preach with tenacity and boldness that "racism is a sin: a sin that divides the human family, blots out the image of God among specific members of that family, and violates the fundamental human dignity of those called to be children of the same Father"[4] is not merely regrettable—it is ultimately racist and sinful. If preachers fail to proclaim the essential gospel message and its condemnation of racism with the same boldness that they proclaim the hierarchy's uncritical prioritization of fetal life, then they are not prophets of the kingdom but rather are chaplains of the empire of the culture of death. Failure to preach the gospel has resulted in millions of our sisters and brothers in the faith either harboring racism in ignorance or advancing or promoting it with intention and never considering what the gospel of Jesus Christ has to say about it. How in God's name can adamancy against abortion grant absolution and scandalous approval to those who rabidly advance a political and social agenda replete with white supremacist tenets and objectives that are completely antithetical to a consistent gospel of

3. Black Catholic Clergy Caucus, "A Statement of the Black Catholic Clergy Caucus," in *Black Theology: A Documentary History, Volume I, 1966–1979*, ed. James H. Cone and Gayraud S. Wilmore (Maryknoll, NY: Orbis Books, 1993), 230, www.wherepeteris.com.

4. United States Catholic Conference, "Brothers and Sisters to Us: United States Bishops' Pastoral Statement on Racism in Our Day," (Washington, DC: United States Catholic Conference, November 14, 1979), 3.

life? These tenets are a total renunciation of Luke 4:18–19, Jesus's inaugural sermon! My great-grandmother Sis knew the truth of the spiritual, and I can still hear her singing.

Everybody talking 'bout heaven ain't going there![5]

In the aftermath of the massacre of ten African Americans in a supermarket in Buffalo, New York, on May 14, 2022, I began my Sunday homily the very next day by reminding the community of a powerful truth of our liturgical experience: The homily or sermon, always grounded in Scripture, should also always be prayed and preached in the context of what is happening in our world, our country, our church, our local faith communities, and even appropriately in the life of the preacher. And I shared my fear that in thousands of Catholic communities across this country, homilies would be given that day that did not even mention or refer in any way to the white supremacist murders in Buffalo. Failure to speak was a failure to honor the sacred texts of that day, for surely those texts had something applicable to that tragedy. But failure to speak also dishonored the lives of those slaughtered; it makes complicit a church, a nation, and any preacher who refuses to address or ignores the systemic white supremacy that fuels such deadly deeds.

I have compassion for preachers who are not people of color and whose livelihoods and repute depend, in whatever measure, on the goodwill and acceptance of those to whom they preach. Dr. Martin Luther King Jr., in his famous "Letter from Birmingham Jail," with eloquence only he commanded, compassionately but boldly challenged the Christian clergy leaders of Birmingham to not be derelict or obstinate in failing to preach a challenging word: "But the judgment of God is upon the church as never before. If today's church does not recapture the sacrificial spirit of the early church, it will lose its authenticity, forfeit the loyalty of millions, and be dismissed as an irrelevant social club with no meaning for

---

5. Song title, African American spiritual. Public domain.

the twentieth century."[6] Dr. King's words are no less apt for our day as religious leaders continue to shy away from challenging Christian believers to reject white supremacy.

I hope that the deft, artful, and creative use of African American songs of resistance and hope will provide a vehicle so that a dialogue begins and that some hard truths and challenges to live authentic discipleship can be heard. As Mama Hannah might say, my aim is to *put the hay where the horses can get it.* African American music, in all its marvelous variety, has formed and enriched so much of what we define as American culture: popular, sacred, and otherwise. As the musicologist Nolan Williams says, "Music and the arts are, in fact, expressions of beauty that lead us toward the most beautiful. They are tools that transcend gender, race and creed. Music is perhaps the chief universal language that inherently has the power to speak and to reach all people across all spectrums."[7]

This beauty and power of African American song allowed my great-grandmothers and their ancestors to find beauty and transcendence in a hostile world that deemed them inconsequential. Williams notes, "When John Newton overheard my enslaved fore-bearers singing in the hull of ships during the Middle Passage, he was inspired to write *Amazing Grace.* The melody for this tune was derived from the pentatonic 'chantings' of the slaves."[8] Years later, the descendants of those enslaved persons would "take" Newton's hymn text and that melody, which was genetically and spiritually rooted deep in their souls, and make "Amazing Grace" an anthem or a lament that invigorated or consoled, depending on how it was sung. One need only look at recorded versions of a white congregation singing this hymn and compare that rendition to how it is

6. Martin Luther King Jr., "Letter from Birmingham Jail," *The Martin Luther King, Jr., Research and Education Institute* (1963, 2004), https://kinginstitute.stanford.edu.

7. Nolan Williams Jr., "A Perspective on Spirituality and the Musical Arts in the African American Tradition," *The African American Pulpit* 18, no. 3 (Summer 2008): 29.

8. Williams, "Perspective on Spirituality," 31.

sung in an African American worship context to hear, see, and feel the difference.

How then can a preacher today access this rich corpus of African American song in preaching to invite authentic discipleship and thereby dismantle systemic racism? The voices of my teachers of preaching and liturgy speak to me, those still present and those who have joined the ancestors, and so I am cautious and deliberate in inviting preachers to use recorded music as an arrow in their quiver of antiracism preaching. But if the preacher does not have the musical acumen personally or the musical staff to do so, then effective and rare use of technology can enhance the preaching moment. Similarly, I am reluctant to use songs other than sacred ones in the liturgical preaching event. Still, there are, again, rare and compelling moments when the use of such music (preferably live, but recorded if necessary) can likewise augment the power and effectiveness of the preaching event. As a preacher with a modicum of singing skills, I once ended one of the Easter Johannine discourses on love by singing Stevie Wonder's "Love's in Need of Love Today." The lyrics perfectly enforced the good news and the challenge offered in the preceding homily. After their momentary surprise, the song's refrain became a congregational piece, as many in the assembly joined in singing.

My great-grandmothers prayed from the rich corpus of African American spirituals, hymns, laments, and gospel songs that kept them rooted and able to face each new day. As preachers called to proclaim a gospel of life and inclusion, called to enlist our hearers in dismantling white supremacy in hearts, minds, and systems, we can access that corpus (recited, sung, or played electronically) as a vehicle to engage assemblies. These songs can help inspire reflection, dialogue, and action, building the kingdom by preparing us to destroy white supremacy. We can also include carefully chosen selections from the available array of protest songs, folk songs, jazz, and hip hop in our liturgical preaching, and these same songs more freely in our presentations to other assemblies in this critical task of building the beloved community.

My teacher and mentor, Servant of God Sister Thea Bowman, FSPA, PhD, wrote in her introductory essay to the *Lead Me, Guide Me* hymnal, "Song is not an object to be admired so much as an instrument to teach, to comfort, inspire, persuade, convince, and motivate. Music is chosen precisely for its effects upon the worshipping community. . . . Black sacred song is designed to move."[9] Sister Thea's words about music certainly apply to its place in antiracism preaching. Every word that precedes my musings in these pages is designed to move the preacher and his or her assembly to bring glad tidings to the poor, to proclaim liberty to the captives and recovery of sight to the blind, to free the oppressed and to proclaim a year acceptable to the Lord.

My colleagues and I earnestly hope that in this book you have indeed, as the Reverend Poole said all those years ago, *studied these texts and the sacred texts hard* and that you have *thought them through,* which has led you to *be open to the Holy Spirit's guidance* about our critical antiracism preaching task, and, as you *let the Spirit run,* may the Spirit of the Pentecost church allow you to *let yourself go!*

> ### Ev'ry time I feel the Spirit moving in my heart, I will pray![10]

---

9. Thea Bowman, "The Gift of African American Sacred Song," in *Lead Me, Guide Me* (hymnal) (Chicago: GIA Publications, 1987).

10. Lyric from "Ev'ry Time I Feel the Spirit," African American spiritual. Public domain.

Contributors

Ms. BETH BLACKBURN is an Episcopal lay catechist in Hickory, North Carolina. Beth has a MAPS Catechesis of the Good Shepherd degree from Aquinas Institute of Theology.

REV. JAMES PIERCE CAVANAUGH, OP, holds a master of divinity degree from Aquinas Institute of Theology and is an ordained presbyter in the Dominican Central Province. He serves on the campus ministry team at Fenwick High School in Oak Park, Illinois.

REV. STEWART CLEM is associate professor of moral theology at Aquinas Institute of Theology. As a priest of the Episcopal Church (USA), he preaches at the Church of St. Michael and St. George in St. Louis.

REV. GREGORY HEILLE, OP, serves as professor of preaching and evangelization and directs the doctor of ministry in preaching program at Aquinas Institute of Theology. With Deborah Wilhelm, he codirects Aquinas Institute of Theology's Lilly-funded Delaplane Preaching Initiative.

REV. PETER D. HILL, CSsR, is a citizen of the Commonwealth of Dominica, serving as co-director of formation for the Redemptorists in San Antonio, Texas. Peter is a graduate of the Aquinas Institute doctor of ministry in preaching program.

Ms. LYNNE LANG is the founding executive director of Restoration Matters in St. Louis. She takes a virtue-based approach to repair harm and restore relationships impacted by gun violence and racism, leading a nationwide restorative leadership training initiative for Catholic schools, congregations, and community leaders.

DR. VALERIE D. LEWIS-MOSLEY, RN, is a Dominican lay associate and a retired director of religious education in the Archdiocese of Newark. She holds a DMin from Drew Theological School and is an adjunct professor at Caldwell University and the Xavier University of Louisiana Institute for Black Catholic studies.

DEACON MICHAEL A. MEYER is a senior deputy general counsel at United Health Group and a permanent deacon in the Diocese of Metuchen. Mike ministers at Saint Catherine of Siena Parish in Pittstown, New Jersey, and holds a doctor of ministry in preaching degree from Aquinas Institute of Theology.

MR. LOUIS J. MILONE is a doctor of ministry in preaching student at Aquinas Institute of Theology and director of faith formation at the Cathedral of St. Matthew the Apostle in Washington, DC.

REV. MAURICE J. NUTT, CSsR, is a Redemptorist missionary preacher living in New Orleans. An Aquinas Institute of Theology doctor of ministry in preaching graduate, Maurice has written *Thea Bowman: Faithful and Free* and *Down Deep in My Soul: An African American Catholic Theology of Preaching.*

Rev. Vincent J. Pastro is a presbyter of the Archdiocese of Seattle and an Aquinas Institute doctor of ministry in preaching graduate. Vince has retired from long-term ministry as pastor to a Mexican immigrant parish in Tacoma to co-author a book on Santa Maria Tonantzin Guadalupe.

Dr. A. Anita Vincent holds a MAPS Catechesis of the Good Shepherd degree from Aquinas Institute of Theology and a ThD degree from LaSalle University. She serves as director of religious education at St. Theresa of the Child Jesus Church in Bethlehem, Pennsylvania.

Dr. Deborah L. Wilhelm, OSB Cam Oblate, codirects the Aquinas Delaplane Preaching Initiative and is an adjunct professor of preaching and evangelization at Aquinas Institute. Deb is a teacher and author who holds a doctor of ministry in preaching degree from Aquinas Institute of Theology and resides in Fall Creek, Oregon.

Rev. Manuel Williams, CR, is a member of the Congregation of the Resurrection. Manuel holds a master of divinity degree from Aquinas Institute of Theology and is a current Doctor of Ministry in Preaching student. He serves as pastor of Resurrection Catholic Church and CEO of Resurrection Catholic Missions of the South, Montgomery, Alabama.

Rev. Dietra Wise Baker is ordained in the Christian Church (Disciples of Christ) and holds the Aquinas Institute of Theology doctor of ministry in preaching degree. She serves as assistant professor of contextual education and community engagement and organizer of the Gamaliel Race and Power Institute at Eden Theological Seminary in St. Louis.